America's Premier Gunmakers
WINCHESTER

America's Premier Gunmakers
WINCHESTER

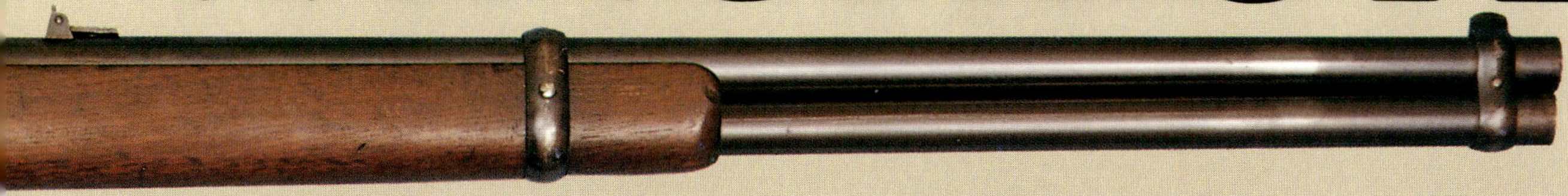

K D Kirkland

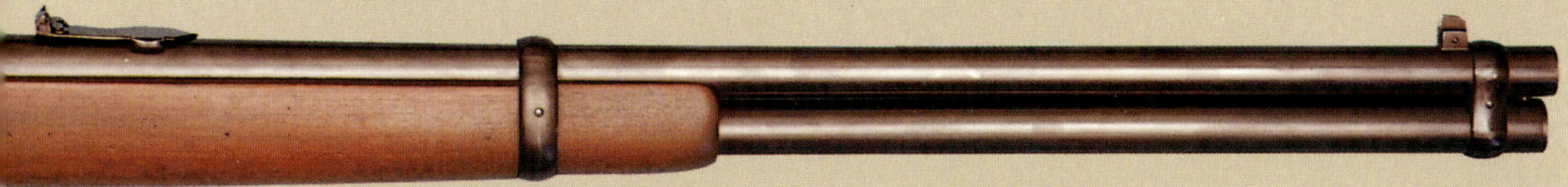

BISON GROUP

First published in 1989 by
Brompton Books Corp
15 Sherwood Place
Greenwich, CT 06830

ISBN 0 86124 514 8

Printed in Hong Kong

Designed by Ruth DeJauregui
Edited by Marie Cahill and Timothy Jacobs
Captioned by Marie Cahill

Acknowledgements

The author and publisher wish to thank Janice Murphy at US Repeating Arms, Bruce Kaye at Theodore Roosevelt National Park, Elizabeth Holmes at Buffalo Bill Historical Center, Oster Loh at Olin Corporation and last but not least Sylvia Kirkland for her assistance in preparing the manuscript.

Photo Credits

All photos courtesy of Buffalo Bill Historical Center, Cody, Wyoming except:

American Graphic Systems Archives 11 (bottom), 48 (all), 89
Archiv Gerstenberg 67
Browning 12, 12-13, 51, 59 (top), 62-63
Cinema Shop 65, 66, 80, 82-83, 89, 106 (bottom right)
Denver Public Library, Western History Division 88-89
Lloyd G Ingles, California Academy of Sciences 99 (center)
J&J Kidd 10-11, 15, 18-19, 30, 30-31, 34-35 (all), 38-39, 42-43, 58-59 (top), 66-67, 94, 94-95, 111
Library of Congress 70-71
Lowie Museum of Anthropology, University of California, Berkeley 81
Olin Industries, Incorporated 7, 11 (center), 13, 16, 17, 19, 37, 45 (center), 46, 47, 49 (all), 52 (top), 53, 56, 61, 62, 63, 64, 68, 69, 72, 73, 75, 76, 77 (bottom), 80 (right), 87 (bottom), 92, 93, 96 (bottom), 97, 100, 106 (top, bottom left), 108, 109
Theodore Roosevelt National Park Visitor Center, Medora, North Dakota 44 (all), 45 (top, bottom)
United States Air Force 41
United States Navy 85, 87 (top)
US Repeating Arms Company 4-5 (bottom), 28, 39 (bottom), 40-41 (second from bottom), 91 (all), 96 (top), 98-99, 98 (all), 99 (top, bottom), 100-101 (bottom) 102-103 (top, bottom), 103 (all), 104-105 (all), 107

Page 1: Oliver F Winchester, the founder and guiding force of the Winchester Repeating Arms Company.

Page 2-3, top to bottom: A sampling of Winchester classics—the Model 1866, the first gun to bear the name of the Winchester Repeating Arms Company; the Model 73, the gun that Buffalo Bill Cody called The Boss; the Model 1886, with its revolutionary lever action mechanism; and the Model 94, one of the most popular hunting rifles ever built.

These pages, above and below: The old and the new—The Model 52 Rimfire Rifle and the Model 70 Win-Cam Bolt Action Center Fire Rifle.

Table of Contents

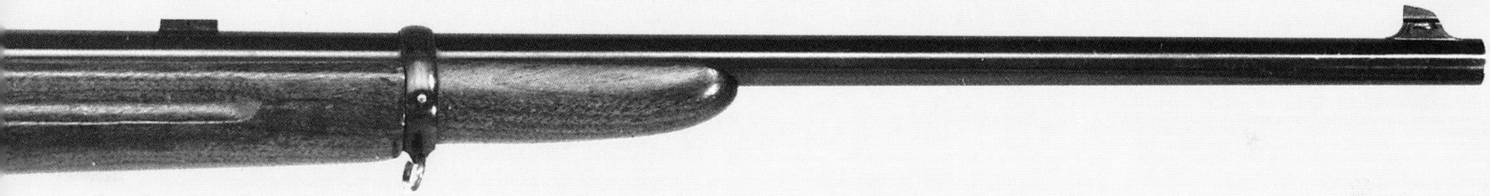

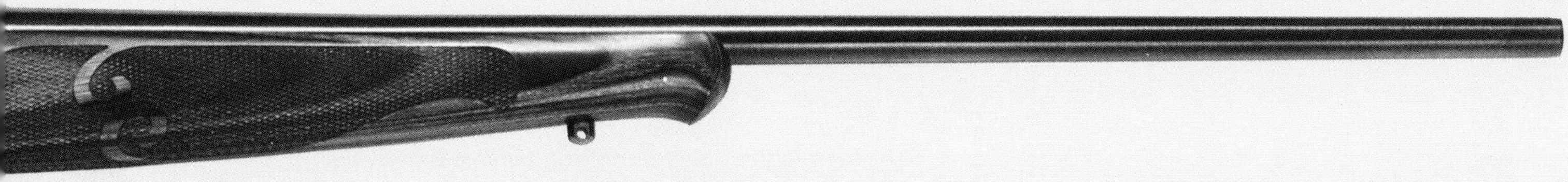

Oliver F

Oliver F Winchester was born in Boston in 1810. His impoverished youth was followed by an apprenticeship with a carpenter. By age 21, he became a master builder, but the world of business lured him to Baltimore where he operated a men's clothing store. In 1848, the now successful Winchester settled in New Haven, Connecticut and established the nation's first shirt factory. This venture made him wealthy and a leading citizen of 'The Elm City,' but he still searched for further opportunities.

Winchester first invested his talent and money in the gun business in 1855, when he became one of the original stockholders of the Volcanic Repeating Arms Company. This company had been formed in Norwich, Connecticut with the goal of developing and marketing a repeating rifle, an item that had long been a gleam in the eye of many inventors. The business failed in February of 1857, despite several cash advances by Winchester totaling over $25,000; however, he did manage to take over all the major claims against the company and bought out the other investors. In April of that year, the company was reorganized as the New Haven Arms Company with Winchester as President and Treasurer.

The company continued production of the Volcanic Arms models and ammunitions but soon hired Benjamin Henry, a wizard gunmaker, to turn the old, rather weak Volcanic lever action and its ammunition into a new, more viable, weapons system. In only three years, Henry's Rifle was ready to be sold. He had not only come close to perfecting the metallic rimfire cartridge, but had given the New Haven Arms Company ammunition that was considerably more potent than their old Volcanic Arms self-contained cartridge-bullets. The new Henry cartridge of .44 caliber propelled a 216 grain bullet at 1200 feet per second. Henry's work ranks as one of the most important developments in firearms history—his repeating rifle was the first truly practical magazine fed, breechloading, repeating firearm.

The Henry Rifle, however, was rejected by the US Army, who preferred the old-fashioned single shot rifle to anything that even hinted of innovation. It took the Civil War to prove once and for all the superiority of the New Haven Arms Company's Henry repeater. Though rejected as armament for federal troops, militias from Connecticut and other states armed themselves with the new lever actions. The demand for ammunition was so great that the US Army, which did eventually purchase 1200 of the rifles, had to buy five million rounds from the company for its volunteer regiments.

By the end of the Civil War, the company's net worth amounted to $354,000, and in February of 1867, its name was changed to the Winchester Repeating Arms Company. The deep recession following the Civil War nearly doomed the enterprise, but a timely order from the Mexican rebel Juarez, as well as various Turkish sultans, supplied sufficient business to ensure the company's continued existence.

Winchester Repeating Arms was housed in a brick building of four floors located at 9 Artizan Street in New Haven and employed 100 workers. The standard workweek at Winchester during this period was from seven o'clock in the morning to six o'clock in the evening (with an hour for lunch Monday through Friday), and Saturday from seven o'clock in the morning to five o'clock in the evening. Only those

Manufactured by the New Haven Arms Company under the direction of Oliver F Winchester, the Henry Repeating Rifle *(above)* was the first practical magazine fed, breechloading, repeating firearm. *At right:* The Volcanic Repeating Arms Company offices in New Haven, Connecticut.

Winchester's Company

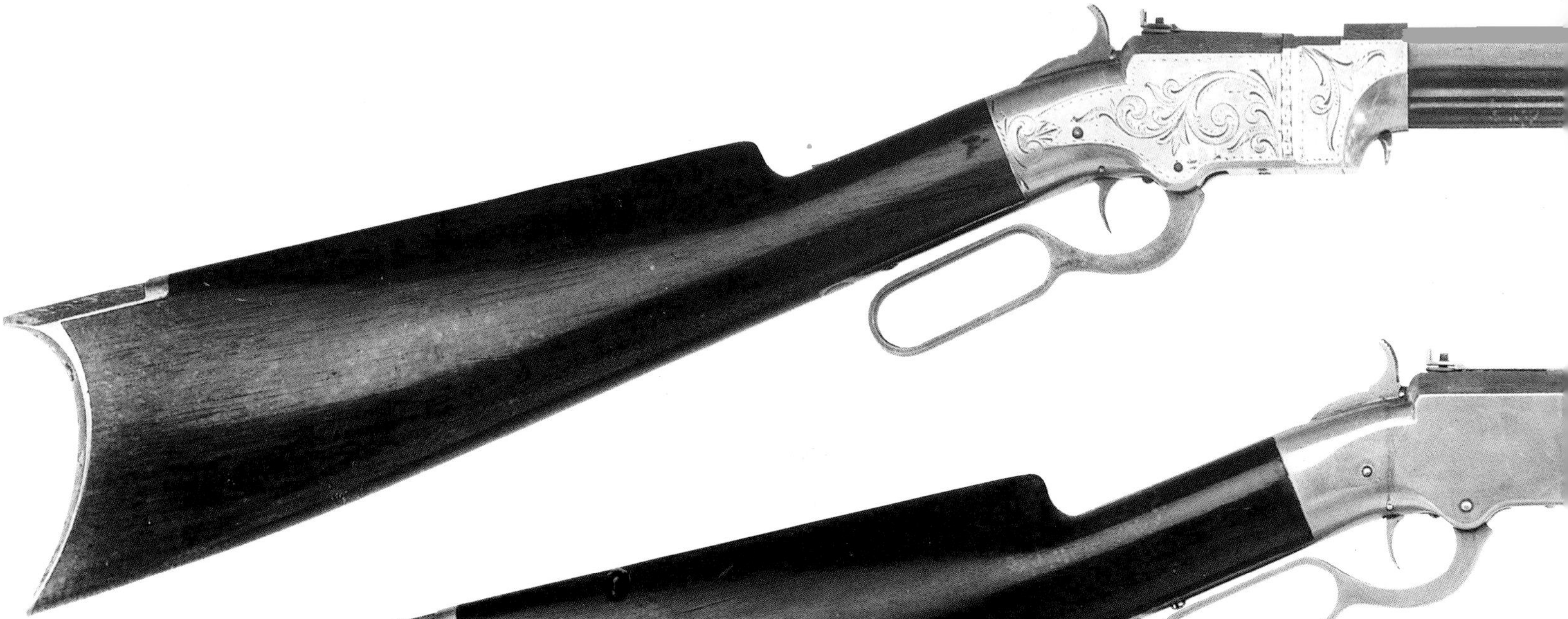

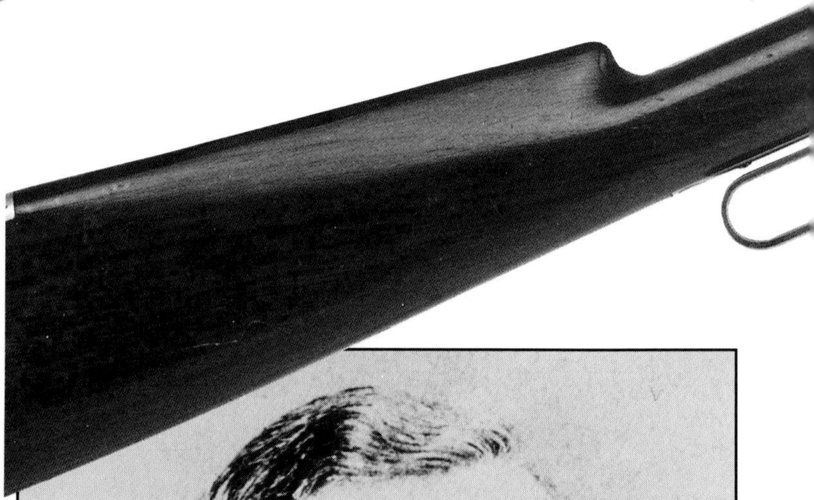

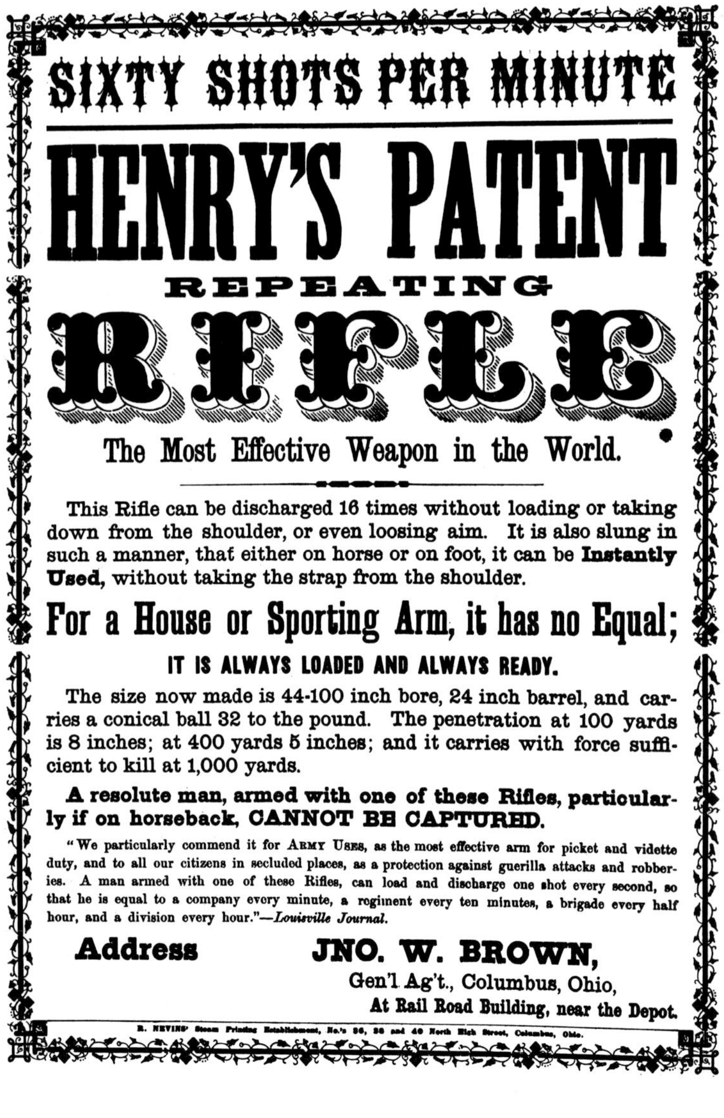

SIXTY SHOTS PER MINUTE

HENRY'S PATENT

REPEATING

RIFLE.

The Most Effective Weapon in the World.

This Rifle can be discharged 16 times without loading or taking down from the shoulder, or even loosing aim. It is also slung in such a manner, that either on horse or on foot, it can be **Instantly Used**, without taking the strap from the shoulder.

For a House or Sporting Arm, it has no Equal;

IT IS ALWAYS LOADED AND ALWAYS READY.

The size now made is 44-100 inch bore, 24 inch barrel, and carries a conical ball 32 to the pound. The penetration at 100 yards is 8 inches; at 400 yards 5 inches; and it carries with force sufficient to kill at 1,000 yards.

A resolute man, armed with one of these Rifles, particularly if on horseback, CANNOT BE CAPTURED.

"We particularly commend it for ARMY USES, as the most effective arm for picket and vidette duty, and to all our citizens in secluded places, as a protection against guerilla attacks and robberies. A man armed with one of these Rifles, can load and discharge one shot every second, so that he is equal to a company every minute, a regiment every ten minutes, a brigade every half hour, and a division every hour."—*Louisville Journal.*

Address **JNO. W. BROWN,**

Gen'l Ag't., Columbus, Ohio,

At Rail Road Building, near the Depot.

R. NEVINS' Steam Printing Establishment, No.'s 36, 38 and 40 North High Street, Columbus, Ohio.

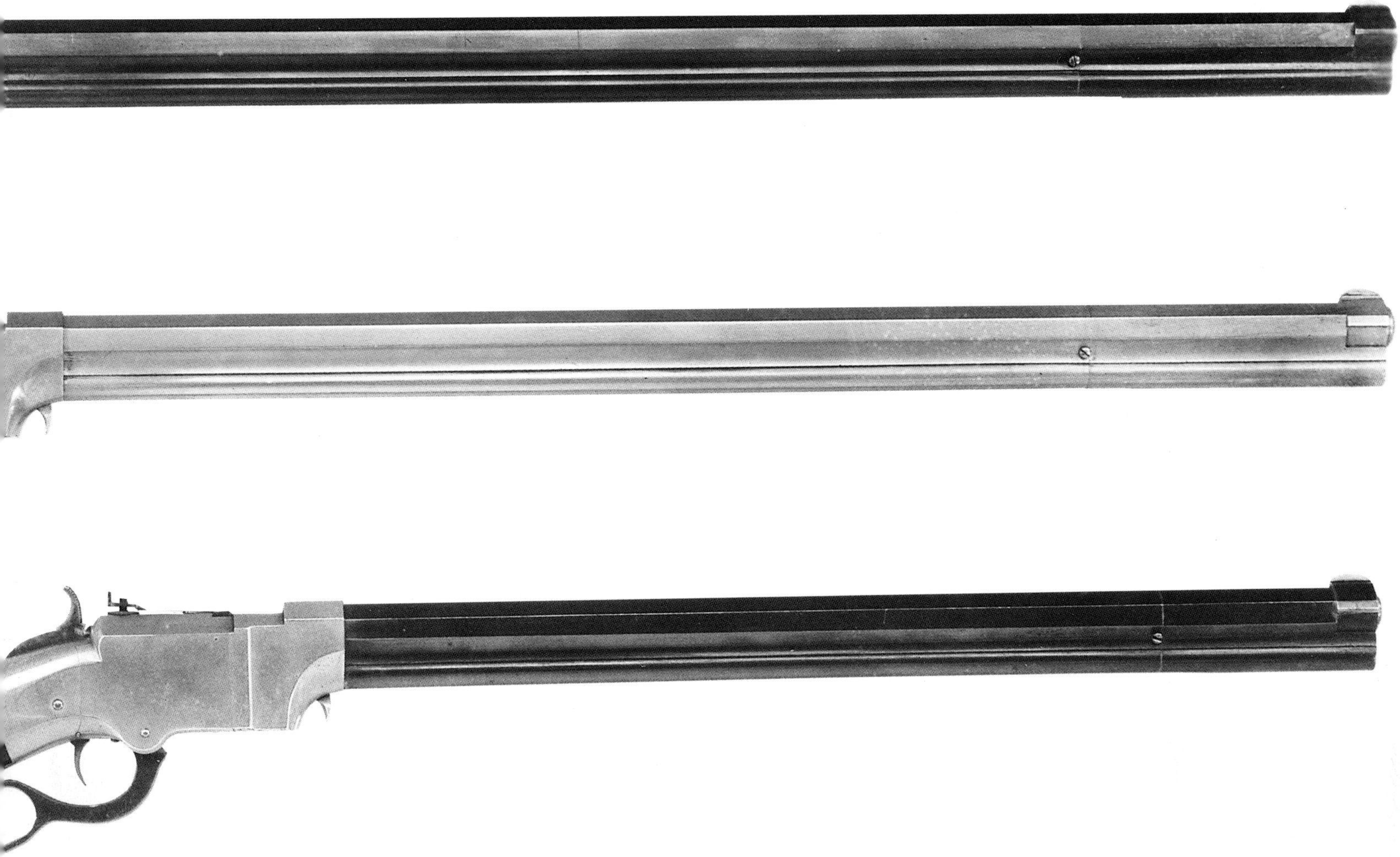

***At left:* Benjamin Henry, creator of the famed Henry Repeating Rifle, at about the time of the Civil War. *Far left:* An advertisement for the Henry Repeating Rifle. These classic firearms *(above, top to bottom)*—two rifles and a carbine—were manufactured by the Volcanic Repeating Arms Company, the forerunner of the New Haven Arms Company.**

employees who had perfect attendance with no tardiness received the full 60 hours pay, and not surprisingly most of the work force lived within easy walking distance of the 'Winchester Works.'

In 1872, a new plant was completed at the corner of Munson and Canal streets (Canal Street would later be renamed Winchester Avenue). These buildings were along the west side of the street, where the Olin 'B' Track parking lot is today located. Most of the original buildings have been torn down in recent years. Of the still-existing buildings, 5-F—built in 1883—and the Custom Shop buildings (6-B)—built in 1887—are the oldest. In 1866, the first gun to bear the name of Winchester—the Model 1866 or, as it was known then, the 'New Model Winchester'—appeared. The '66' was an improved Henry rifle with the addition of a loading port on the side of the receiver and a wood forearm. These two improvements made the difference between a good gun and a true classic.

In 1873 (the first time that the actual year of introduction was used as a Winchester model designation), the Model 1873 Rifle and the world's first center fire metallic cartridge, the .44-40 Winchester, were introduced. The Model 1873 was manufactured from 1873 until 1924, with total production of 720,000 pieces. The largest production year was 1891, when over 41,000 Model 73s were manufactured. Designated 'The Boss' by Buffalo Bill Cody, this was the gun, more than any other, that became legendary. Even more important to the company than the Model 73 itself was that Winchester had entered the general metallic-cased ammunition business. Prior to 1873, Winchester had produced ammunition to fit its own rifles and pistols only. Oliver Winchester's genius lay in being able to organize, manufacture and set up distributing systems that successfully produced and marketed his rifles. He had continually enlarged the company's armory facilities and brought in new and improved machinery. His introduction of new, mass production methods and his relentless emphasis on research had made his firm one of the earliest to profit from the benefits of modern industrial technology. While wages of workers had risen from $1.50 a day to $3.50, Winchester's production costs actually fell. Rifle barrels, for example, went from $800 per hundred to a cost of just under $80 for the same number. The industrial revolution was an era when industrialists, merchants and inventors of every description were hard at work pushing the United States into the forefront of world commerce. Oliver Winchester was a member of this elite group and like his contemporaries he was also not one to shrink from his civic duties, serving as a councilman for the city of New Haven during the Civil War, becoming Lieutenant Governor of the state of Connecticut and in 1878 being instrumental in the formation of the Board of Associated Charities, a forerunner of today's United Fund. On 10 December 1880, Oliver F Winchester died and his son's brother-in-law, William W Converse, was elected to succeed him as President of the firm.

ED SCHIEFFELIN
In 1877 prospector Ed Schieffelin dared to search for silver in the San Pedro Valley - a land frequented by hostile Apaches. He had been warned by troopers at the newly established Camp Huachuca, some 20 miles distant, that all he would find would be his own tombstone. That warning inspired the name of his first claim. Two years later, after the influx of miners to the silver rich hills, the miner's camp became a city known as Tombstone. Schieffelin, having been a prospector since age 17, soon grew restless to explore new country and when offered $ 300,000 for his claims in 1880, he quickly accepted. He left the now prosperous city he had founded, a rich man.
Although wealthy enough to live comfortably for the rest of his life, Schieffelin continued to prospect the West, including Alaska, until his death in Oregon in 1897.

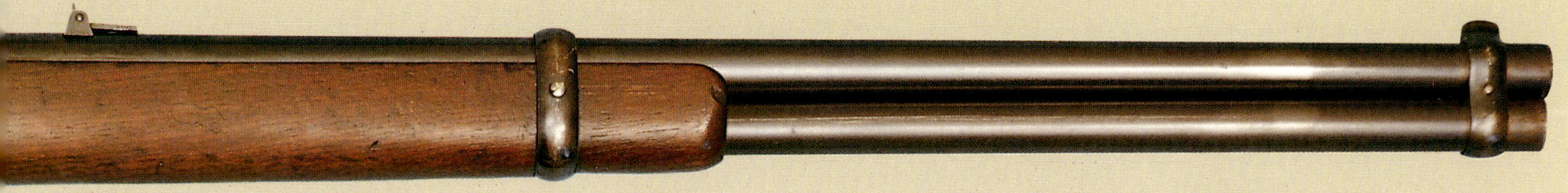

At right: **The trade card for the New Haven Arms Company, the manufacturer of the Henry Repeating Rifle. *Below left:* An exhibit at the Tombstone Courthouse State Historic Park honoring Ed Schiefflin (below), the prospector who discovered the Lucky Cuss Mine that started the rush to Tombstone, Arizona. Schiefflin always carried a Henry Repeating Rifle in his travels. *At top:* The Winchester Model 66 was an improved version of the Henry Repeating Rifle. The addition of a loading port on the side of the receiver and a wood forearm made a good gun a true classic.**

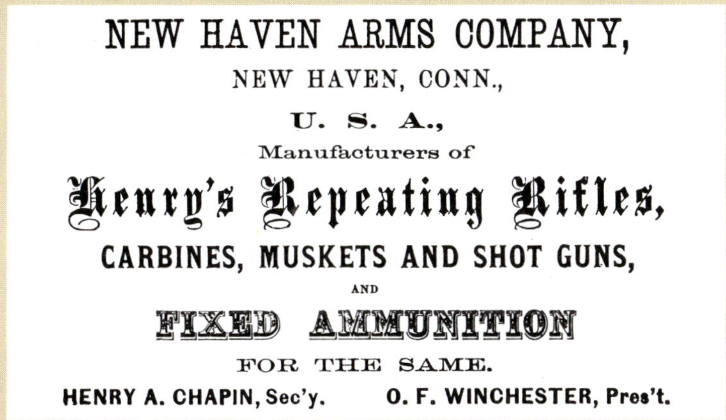
NEW HAVEN ARMS COMPANY,
NEW HAVEN, CONN.,
U. S. A.,
Manufacturers of
Henry's Repeating Rifles,
CARBINES, MUSKETS AND SHOT GUNS,
AND
FIXED AMMUNITION
FOR THE SAME.
HENRY A. CHAPIN, Sec'y. O. F. WINCHESTER, Pres't.

Winchester and Browning

In 1885, through the hard work and bargaining skills of Thomas G Bennett, who had recently become President of Winchester, a long and profitable agreement between the company and John Moses Browning began. One of Bennett's trips to Browning's headquarters in Ogden, Utah netted the designs for the 1885 Single Shot Rifle and the 1886 Lever Action Rifle for only $8000. These rifles were the first Winchesters adapted to the very long range shooting prevalent in the western United States.

In the ensuing years, Browning sold Winchester over 40 gun designs outright, of which seven rifles and three shotguns were actually manufactured and became the mainstays of the Winchester product line. By the turn of the century, Browning had perfected automatic firearm designs, including his truly groundbreaking automatic (actually, semiautomatic) shotgun.

It was over the issue of Thomas G Bennett's extraordinarily cautious approach to the automatic shotgun design that Winchester lost its special relationship with John Moses Browning. Further difficulty arose from the fact that Browning's designs had previously been sold to Winchester on a fee simple basis that did not include the payment of royalties. With the advent of this new design, Browning expressed a desire to receive royalties for it and other designs to follow. While this was no doubt an exacerbating factor in the deterioration of the Winchester-Browning relationship, it can be seen by the following narrative that it was not the primary difficulty by any stretch of the imagination. Browning's break with Winchester was well publicized, and in later years Browning recalled the circumstances as follows:

'It was not a very dignified parting, I admit, but I was younger then. Bennett was the most conservative of men, and admittedly the automatic was something of an inno-

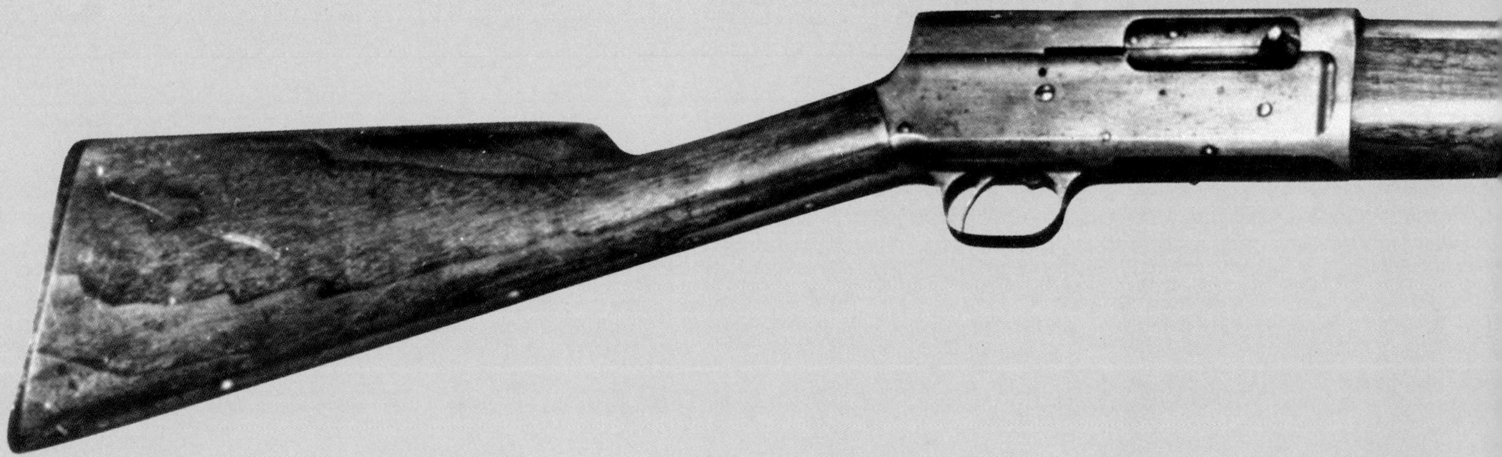

vation. To put it simply, he was afraid of it, and so were the few men in his confidence. They were afraid that it would take ten years to develop such a gun to the point where it would be a profitable manufacturing article. It doesn't take many weak spots to eat up all the profit.

'Don't think of him as a coward. He enlisted at 16 and fought through the Civil War, coming out a captain. Cowards don't do things like that. But he didn't replace the old 73 and 76 models until competition forced him to it. The 86 pulled him out of that hole. Winchester had a fine record. It was their boast at one time that the company had not borrowed a cent for 40 years. The factory was a temple, and Bennett was the high priest.

'He never had an official of the company present at any of our confabs. His conservativeness worked pretty well. He is a big man, and he looked so solid in his chair that I had the feeling I could come back year after year, find him there, make a deal without any wasted words, and get back to work. It was a comfortable feeling...

'The automatic shotgun put Bennett in a tough position. I'll bet he'd have shelled out a hundred thousand dollars just to have had it banished forever from the earth, leaving him with his levers and pumps. If he made the gun and it proved a failure, as he and his advisors seemed to have half suspected, it would leave a blot on the Winchester name. Even if he made it and it proved a big success, it would seriously hurt one of the best-paying arms in his line—the 97 shotgun. If a competitor got it, and it caught the popular fancy, he'd be left a long jump behind in an important branch of the business. That's why he marked time for two years, and why, once I'd forced a showdown, I got so mad.'

Far left: **John M Browning designed numerous firearms for Winchester. Browning and Thomas G Bennett, president of Winchester, *(right)* ended the relationship following a dispute over the design of Browning's revolutionary automatic shotgun *(below).***

Winchester Smokeless

The decade of the 1880s was a period of great growth in the ammunition business, increasing fivefold while the business climate in general remained stable. Winchester became one of the largest ammunition manufacturers in the world during this period. In 1888 Winchester, in partnership with the Union Metallic Cartridge Company and Marcellus Hartley, bought out the Remington Arms Company of Ilion, New York, but this arrangement was short lived and was officially dissolved in 1896, when all of Winchester's interest was sold to Mr Hartley; the Sherman Anti-Trust Law was chiefly to blame. Still, by 1890 Winchester was the pre-eminent arms and ammunition manufacturer in the United States.

That was an era in which new developments in firearms designs were beginning to grow out of new developments in the type of gunpowder used in cartridges. The old 'black' powder had served for hundreds of years, but was prone to cause any rifle, pistol or shotgun to belch huge clouds of sulfurous smoke with each shot. It could be said that a new era in firearms design arrived when the old black powder formula was incrementally improved upon—by way of a phenomenal chain of developments that resulted in the invention of modern, relatively clean-burning and more efficient 'smokeless' powder.

Black powder had been known for centuries in China before it was introduced into the Western world and put to use in warfare. It is a matter of conjecture who was the first European to discover that a combination of charcoal, sulphur and saltpeter would burn violently enough to propel a projectile. In any event, since its first use in firearms around the middle of the fourteenth century, black powder continued to be made of these ingredients. The charcoal produces gas volume, sulphur the temperature, and saltpeter the oxygen to facilitate fast burning. At first, little care was taken for the quality of the gunpowder—if it worked, it worked, that was all.

Over the years, the importance of using pure ingredients was recognized, and a moderate control over the relative power of each charge was achieved by varying the grain size. Still, the tried and true combination of 75 parts saltpeter, 10 parts sulphur and 15 parts charcoal remained the basic formula for gunpowder.

The lethality of the first weapons using black powder were less important against an enemy than the unnerving effect of the flame and smoke they produced. Gradually, firearms were improved and their superiority was eventually established over the battle-axe, the sword, the spear, the longbow and the crossbow—and the art of war was revolutionized.

Then came the nineteenth century, during which the increase in the efficiency of firearms—especially the rifle—had been rapid.

By 1890, however, technical developments both in guns and ammunition had just about reached the limits imposed by the use of black powder. Little more could be done to improve the equilibrium of weight, barrel length and rifling twist of firearms using this type of propellant. To obtain greater velocities and flatter trajectories with the same calibers and weights of bullets, the powder loads and cartridge cases had been lengthened to the extent that such powerful black powder cartridges as the Sharps .40-90 and the Winchester .40-110-260 Express measured nearly four inches long.

These dimensions made their use in repeating arms very problematic, and even the single shot weapons capable of handling them were about as large and heavy as could be made and still be used as a shoulder arm.

The principal limitations of black powder as a propellant are its incomplete combustion which lessens its efficiency (and hence, its potential power-to-volume ratio) and fouls the barrel of a firearm, the heavy smoke it gives off when fired which not only stinks but also reveals the position of the shooter to an enemy or game, and the fast rate at which it burns after ignition—which would prove to provide a far less powerful 'push' than the comparatively extended burn of smokeless powder.

At right: **This Winchester Model 1893 Pump Action Repeating Shotgun was used to quell an attempted train robbery near Tombstone. Lawman Jeff Milton survived the gunfight, but the outlaw was mortally wounded.**

and the Age of Powder

The road to the arms maker's goal of higher velocity, flatter trajectory, and better accuracy and range of shooting could only be unblocked by the development of a propellant superior to black powder. Two discoveries that were made during the 1840s were important to the development of such a superior gunpowder. In 1845, the inventor Schoenbein of Basel, Switzerland first produced nitrocellulose, or 'guncotton,' by nitrating cellulose. A year later an Italian chemist, Asconio Sobero, discovered nitroglycerin, formed by the action of nitric and sulphuric acids on glycerin. Nitrocellulose and nitroglycerin are powerful explosives. They contain carbon and hydrogen in combination with available oxygen to support combustion; both are unstable and capable of rearranging themselves with extreme rapidity into more stable compounds in the form of gases and with a concomitant great increase in volume.

In their original form, neither nitrocellulose nor nitroglycerin are usable for small arms, due to their instability. However, in 1885 a French Government chemist named Vieille discovered that nitrocellulose, when dissolved in ether or alcohol, produces a stable colloid which can be dried and used as a substitute for black powder. It proved impossible, however, to adapt nitroglycerin by a similar process, but within a few years Alfred Nobel and Sir Frederick Able combined nitrocellulose with nitroglycerin to produce a similar product. In both processes, the resulting pasty colloid was easy to handle and could be dried into grains, flakes or cylinders of various sizes. When detonated in the granular form, these mixtures produced very little smoke—hence, the granulated colloids came to be known as 'smokeless powder.'

Powder made by the Vieille process became known as single-base or bulk smokeless. The methods of its manufacture were sufficiently advanced by the late 1880s for powder companies to begin supplying the market in bulk. The powder made by the use of nitroglycerin was called double-base or dense smokeless. More powerful, and originally somewhat more difficult to control, this latter powder was made available during the early 1890s.

In addition to the characteristic the name suggests, smokeless powder burns cleaner than black powder and is by weight and volume many more times as powerful. Even more important is the control which can be exercised over the rate at which it burns. This is done by manufacturing the powder in different shapes and sizes, and by coating the grains with graphite. Slowing down the rate of combustion makes it possible to overcome the inertia of the projectile and start it on its way before the full pressure of the gas is developed. This 'slow' buildup of pressure gives greater velocity to the projectile through an extended push.

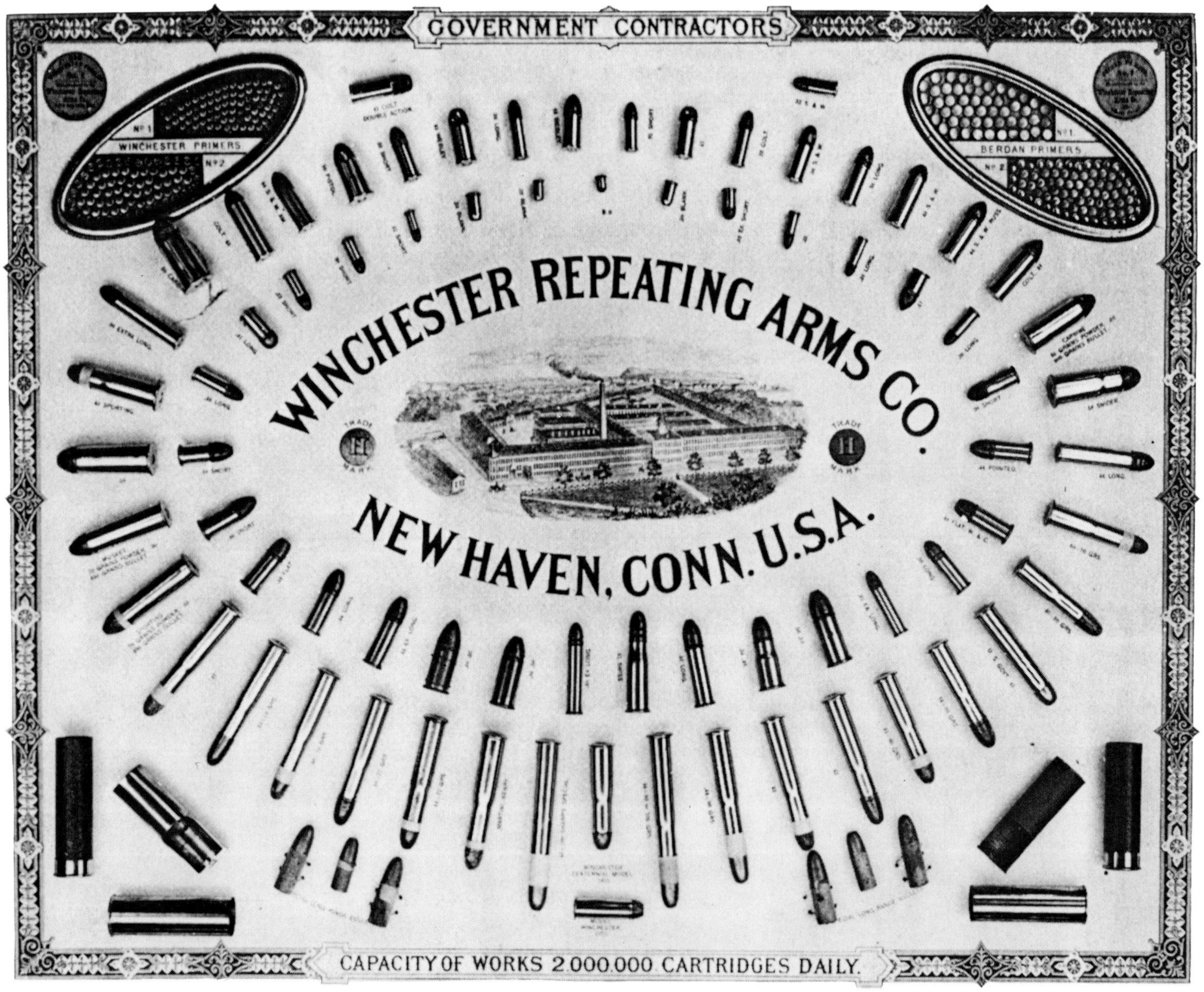

Increased velocity gives flatter trajectories to bullets and improves the accuracy of shooting. The greater power of smokeless powder makes possible both the use of relatively compact cartridges, and increase in potential velocities. In turn, higher velocities make possible the use of lighter bullets which, due to their speed at the moment of impact with a target, have an effect as satisfactory as the large, heavy pieces of lead that were hurled by the heavier-caliber black powder firearms.

While the superior qualities of smokeless powder insured its adoption, the introduction of smokeless powder added to the complexity of design and manufacture of both guns and ammunition. A whole host of chemical, metallurgical, and ballistical problems had to be solved before satisfactory results could be obtained. Among the more immediate consequences was the birth of the modern rifle and the subsequent evolution of guns with greater accuracy. Also, the use of smokeless powder hastened the substitution of scientific methods and laboratory techniques for rule-of-thumb and empirical procedures in the manufacture of guns and ammunition.

One of the major problems affecting all ammunition companies using the early smokeless powder came from the much-increased variety of powder mixtures. Black powder had long been standardized and limited to a few brands. But, in the case of smokeless powder, the different methods used in its manufacture and the wide variety of forms manufactured—each with a different burning speed—combined with the constant experimentation in improving all of the above, smokeless powder became available in dozens of varieties, each with its own particular characteristics.

It was several years before the performance of these various powders could be properly analyzed, and then standardized in ammunition use. To add to the problem, the powder companies at first had great difficulty controlling the quality of smokeless powder. Variations in different batches of the same brands made it even more difficult for ammunition producers to maintain a uniform performance in their own product.

At left: **A display of Winchester cartridges, circa 1879.** ***Below:*** **Various early Winchester cartridges, including the cartridge** ***(center)*** **produced by the Volcanic Arms Company.**

The greater potency of the new propellant made for a more delicate balance between the kind of powder used, the weight of the bullet and the design of the case; it was somewhat tricky to arrive at optimal performance. Of course, the dangers from overloading were increased, especially after 'double-base' or dense smokeless powder became available.

As one authority pointed out: 'If we load an abnormal amount of smokeless powder into a cartridge, or use a heavier or tighter, or harder bullet, or crowd a lot of powder into a small powder chamber, the pressure curve rises very rapidly. For example, if a maximum safe charge in a certain cartridge gives 50,000 pounds pressure, one grain of additional weight may give 60,000 pounds and cause the brass cartridge case to expand so much that it sticks tightly in the chamber and is difficult to extract, and 3 grains of powder above the maximum charge may give about 75,000 pounds and blow out the primer, and allow gas to get back into the gun's mechanism, and 5 grains above the normal maximum charge may disrupt the case entirely, and the powerful gas escaping to the rear may completely demolish the breech action of the weapon.'

Often the solution of one problem led to another. This is illustrated in connection with bullet design and construction. As we have said, the greater pressure and higher velocity generated by smokeless powder permitted the use of smaller-caliber bullets with the same, or a better, impact on the target than larger calibers using black powder. Decreasing the caliber, however, reduced the diameter of bullets relative to their length. In order to keep them from 'keyholing' or tumbling end-over-end in flight, it became necessary to increase their rate of spin, which was done by increasing the twist of the rifling in the gun barrels. This brought a further complication: when the lead or lead alloy bullets were forced at the greater speed through the rifling, they tended to disintegrate or become deformed.

By 'jacketing,' bullets within a thin layer of gilding metal or cupro-nickel, ammunition companies were able to overcome this tendency of the soft-lead bullets to disintegrate. Furthermore, the hard surface gave the projectile a better hold on the rifling of the gun barrel, increasing its spin and accuracy in flight and resulting in greater penetration of the target.

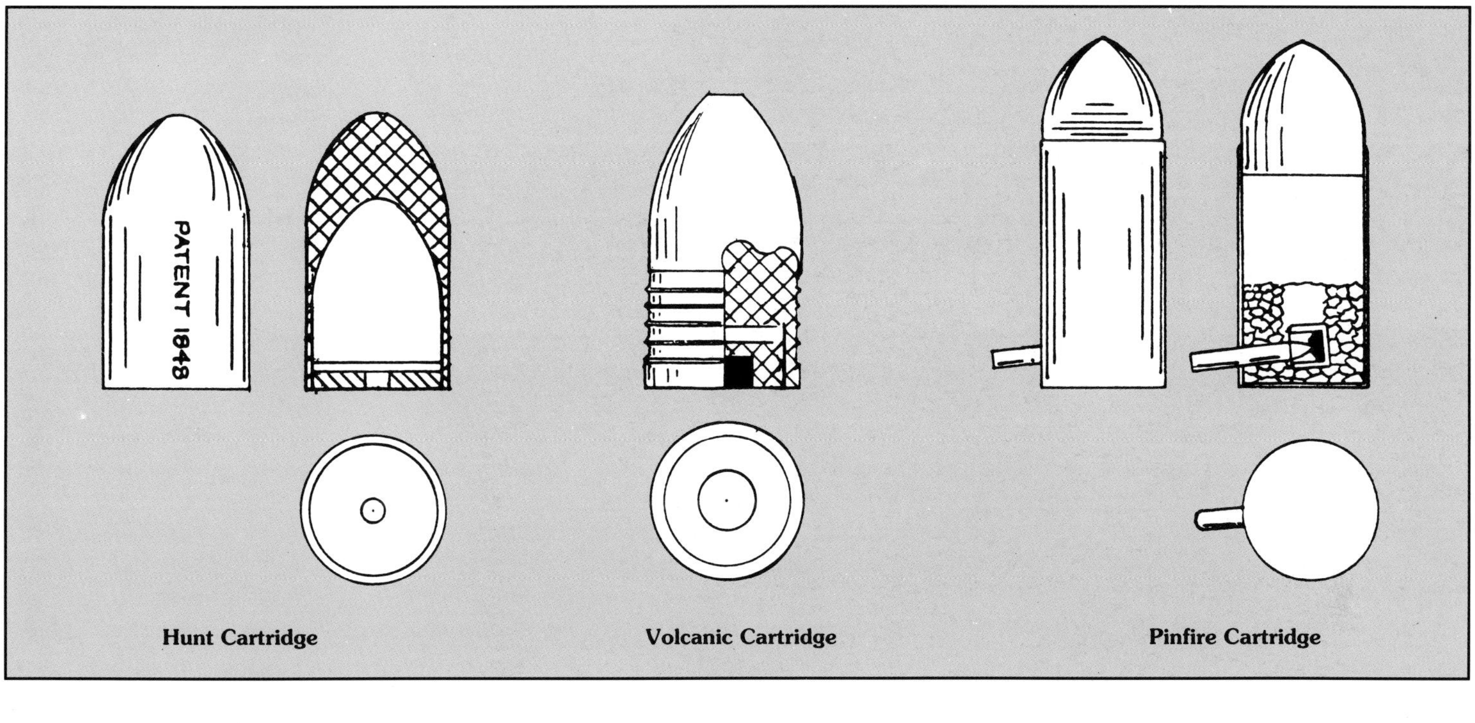

It was then discovered that completely jacketed bullets could penetrate a target without necessarily inflicting any serious damage, which was not a desirable trait for game-hunting cartridges. Finally, a solution was arrived at wherein the noses of jacketed bullets were left uncovered, and this allowed for mushrooming upon impact.

The difference in the penetration of a softnose and a fully jacketed bullet is illustrated by tests made of the WCF (Winchester Center Fire) .30 caliber smokeless powder cartridge. From a distance of 15 feet, the soft-nose bullet went through 12 dry pine boards, each seven-eighths of an inch thick. The fully jacketed bullet penetrated through 35 boards from the same distance.

The adoption of smokeless ammunition was a slow process. Not for some 10 years after the new propellant was first introduced were smokeless loads sufficiently perfected to meet the approval of any large number of shooters.

Winchester began experimenting with smokeless powder as early as 1888. Indicative of the difficulties encountered is the fact that the first announcement of smokeless loads did not come until five years later, the catalog for 1893 carrying the statement that the Company would load, on order, its paper Rival shot shells with smokeless (also known as 'nitro') powder.

The following year the Company announced that it was carrying one product line of loaded smokeless paper shot shells in stock. This was the Winchester Leader, the Rival being changed to black powder. This policy was continued until 1905, when a second smokeless load was added. At the same time the number of hand-loaders' shells (which were empty, but came already primed) to be used with smokeless powder was increased from two to four product lines during the same period.

While the use of smokeless powder in shot shells presented some problems, it proved much more difficult to use the new propellant in metallic cartridges. Winchester management devoted most of its attention to the solution of this latter problem during the succeeding years.

The first smokeless metallic cartridge produced by the Company, the .30 US Army, for use in the Winchester Single Shot and the newly-adopted United States service rifle, the Krag-Jorgensen, was announced in the Company catalog for April 1894.

With the statement that 'new smokeless cartridges will be added as fast as experimental work permits,' the list of smokeless loads was increased to 17 the following year. Actually, in all but four of these cartridges, smokeless powder was substituted for black powder without any attempt to attain higher velocities.

This was explained in the following head note to the list: 'The smokeless cartridges enumerated below may be divided into two classes. In the one class are those cartridges in which black powder has been replaced with smokeless powder. In these, to meet the requirements of the guns for which black powder cartridges were intended, no attempt has been made to get additional velocity. The name of the black powder cartridge has been retained, and the word 'Smokeless' added. The smokeless cartridge in point of excellence differs from the black powder cartridge only in smokelessness and cleanliness. Velocity and penetration remain the same. In the other class, cartridges may be numbered the .236 Navy, .25-35 Winchester, .30 US Army, and .30 Winchester Smokeless. These are purely smokeless cartridges.

'The velocities obtained cannot be gotten with black powder, nor have we been successfully able to use lead or alloys without metal patches (jackets). These are cartridges belonging entirely to the smokeless powder class, and cannot be used with black powder. Their excellence is in high velocity and consequent flat trajectory. The full metal patch gives great penetration. The soft nose bullet will expand to give effects upon animal tissues very much greater than the small caliber would otherwise enable.'

The production of even this rather modest list of smokeless loads had, by 1895, taxed the ingenuity and facilities of the management, and TG Bennett had already taken steps to put the work on a more scientific basis by establishing a laboratory. This laboratory had its beginning in about 1886 when Thomas Addis, the Company's foreign sales agent, purchased a Schultz chronoscope in Europe. This was a device which measured bullet velocities, and evidence of the Company's deepening commitment to the 'scientific approach' came a short time later, when Addis acquired, also in Europe, a Boulenge chronoscope, which was a superior instrument used for the same purpose.

Addis (at such times as he was in New Haven) and TG Bennett did considerable testing with the chronoscopes. These experiments appear to have continued on an intermittent basis, largely when the two men could spare time from other duties, and did bear some fruit after a bit of

trial and error: in February 1889, the Company catalog included its first ballistics table, which was expanded in later editions.

With the advent of smokeless powder, laboratory testing had taken on a new significance. After it was clear that the new powder had come to stay, TG Bennett moved to put the laboratory on a more formal basis and, in 1894, he employed Edward Uhl, a recent graduate of the Yale Sheffield Scientific School, to take charge.

This laboratory represented a major step in the direction of scientific control over developmental work and manufacturing processes. This is well illustrated in the case of priming mixtures. Prior to the introduction of the laboratory, the development and production of priming mixtures were entrusted to the primer shop foreman, who had long experience in the work. New mixtures were tried out empirically, and the foreman had a 'little black book' into which he entered the various formulas. This information was available only to the foreman who kept it a closely guarded secret. It is said that the Company did not dare fire the primer shop foreman, for without his little black book, the primer shop would shut down. Adding to the complexity this system imposed, there was always also the possibility that he would go over to a competitor for more money.

At top: **A Winchester Model 1886 .45-90 Caliber WCF Rifle, and an advertisement *(above)* for new high power cartridges for the Model 1886. Cartridges of this sort created a revolution in firearms design.**

The demands for smokeless powder primers made this system inadequate. The new propellant required a different kind of primer 'burn' than did black powder. Hundreds of mixtures were tried, and the configuration of the primer was changed many times before satisfactory results could be obtained. However, with the application of chemical analysis it was not only possible to compound more accurate and satisfactory mixtures, but in the laboratory, the existing formulas lost their mystery and the little black book lost its significance.

Essentially the same condition applied in the case of metal working. The tempering methods used to anneal brass, harden steel and so forth had been evolved over many years of empirical observation. The men in charge of these operations were master craftsmen who had a 'feel' for their work. With the advent of smokeless powder, greater pressures were put upon gun chambers and cartridge cases, and greater heat was generated. The Company, already deep into their fascination with science, gave up on traditional metallurgy and plunged into the laboratory with that aspect of their operations as well.

The importance of metallurgy is illustrated by the following example from 1898, after the laboratory was in operation. Working on a Government order for .30 caliber smokeless ammunition to be used in the Spanish-American War, the Company had lot after lot of ammunition rejected by the Government inspector because of defects. These took the form of 'cut-offs,' or separation of cartridge cases about a half-inch from cartridge bases; splits in the necks of cartridge cases; and weaknesses in casings that allowed expansion in the firing chamber to the point that some cartridges could not be ejected after being fired.

Henry Brewer, a metallurgist par excellence, was brought in to help solve the difficulty. According to him, the cartridges lacked the proper crystal structures in various parts of their designs, and only after careful analysis had the proper crystal structure for each part of the cartridge been arrived at.

As the manufacture of smokeless powder ammunition was pushed ahead, the operations of the laboratory expanded. By 1901, the work had become extensive enough to warrant the establishment of a chemical division and Joseph Wild, a graduate of the Yale Sheffield Scientific School, was put in charge. In 1904 he was succeeded by William Buell, a graduate of the same school, with several years experience in the laboratories of the Pennsylvania Railroad. Buell was an exceptionally able chemical engineer and under his direction the work of the laboratory assumed increasing significance over succeeding years.

Winchester kept the promise it made in 1895 to add new smokeless cartridges as fast as they could be developed. By 1905, the list had grown to 100 and in 1914 the total came to 175. Many of these were available in both full jacketed and softnose bullets, so the actual number of individual loads was probably at least 20 percent greater than indicated.

A considerable number of these new cartridges were still black powder types with smokeless powder substituted, but—as with some of those mentioned earlier in this chapter—with no attempt to achieve higher velocities. These were designed to be used in firearms manufactured before smokeless powder was introduced. Due to the greater pressures developed with smokeless powder, it was dangerous to use high pressure smokeless loads in these black powder firearms.

A second group, including a line of Winchester high velocity cartridges, was described as giving higher velocity and increased muzzle energy, with only a moderate increase in initial pressure. Many of these cartridges could be used safely in the Company's Model 86 and Model 92 rifles, originally designed for black powder ammunition, but users were cautioned against using high velocity cartridges in the Model 73.

The third class of smokeless cartridges were high power loads such as the 6mm Navy, the .30 US Army, the British

Below: **Various examples of black powder cartridges. Smokeless cartridges of the same size as these cartridges were more powerful because the powder was more volatile, and thus more potent per volume.**

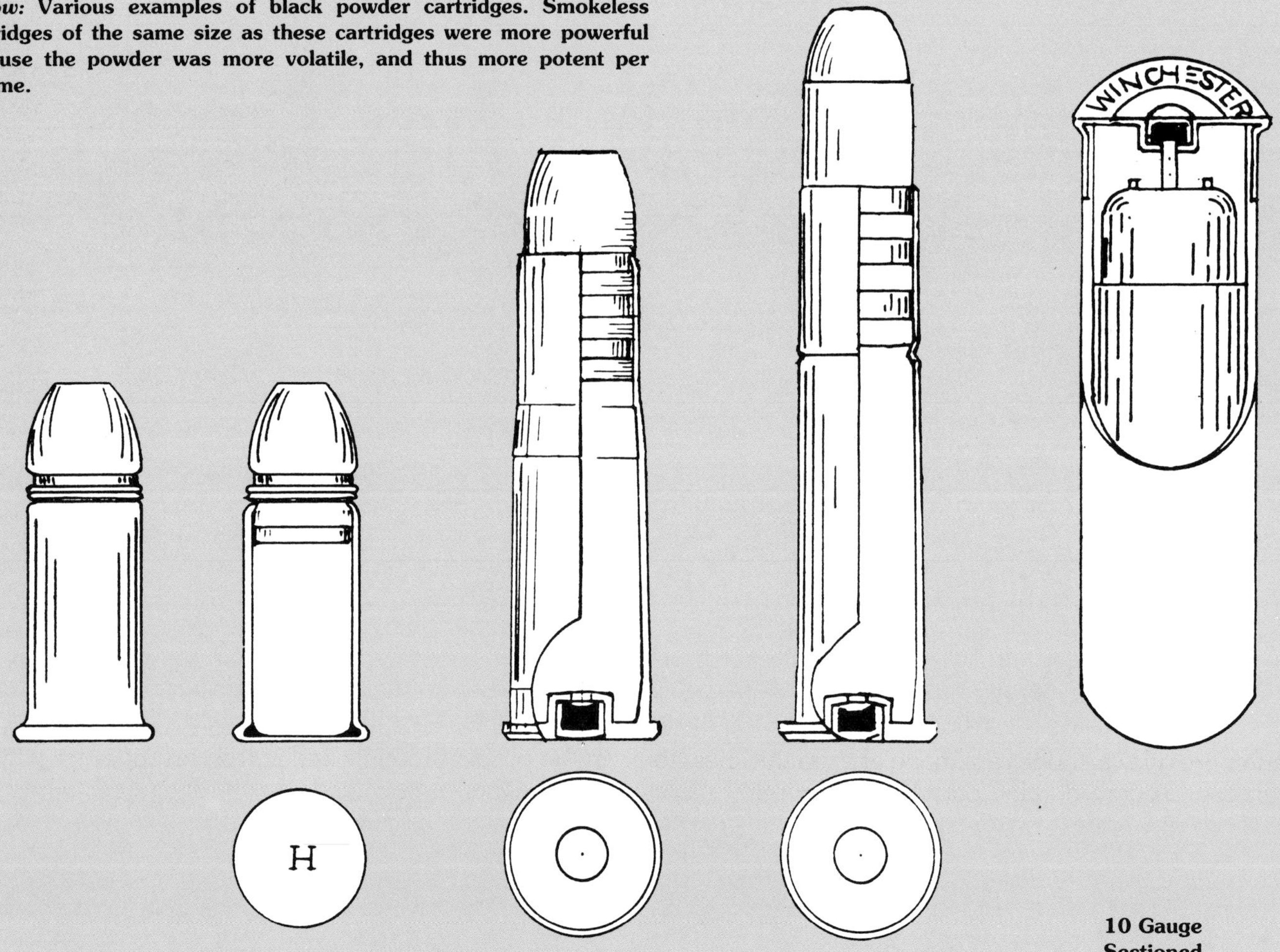

Henry .44 Flat Rimfire **.45-75 Center Fire** **.45-70-500 Center Fire** **10 Gauge Sectioned Shot Shell**

.303, and such Winchester calibers as .30-30, .33, .35 and .405, and could be used safely only in guns designed especially to handle high pressures. Not all of the smokeless loads offered in 1914 had been originally developed by Winchester. In line with its policy of producing a full line of ammunition for all types of firearms, the Company expanded its manufacture to include practically all the new cartridges brought out by the US Government and the other arms and ammunition companies.

While adding smokeless loads to its ammunition line, Winchester did not reduce the manufacture of black powder metallic cartridges and components. Including loaded and empty primed cartridge cases, bullets, blanks and other components, the catalog for 1914 listed approximately the same 375 black powder items that had appeared in 1890.

Beginning in 1911, the Company offered to load rimfire and center fire black powder pistol cartridges with 'Lesmok' at no extra cost. Lesmok was a semi-smokeless powder developed by Du Pont. This powder added a slight degree of muzzle velocity, and hence, accuracy to small caliber ammunition. While it gave off more smoke and caused more bore fouling than smokeless, the fouling was of such a nature that it did not cake and harden in the barrel, and firing did not have to be interrupted for cleaning.

While sales of factory-loaded ammunition had grown enormously over the preceding quarter century, a large number of shooters during the early 1890s still preferred to load or reload their own metallic cartridges. The reasons for this preference are well stated in the following quote from AC Gould's book, *Modern American Rifles,* published in 1892.

'Every person who shoots a rifle will be likely to sometime prepare ammunition. One rarely finds an expert rifleman who uses factory cartridges, especially if he shoots at targets, or where extreme accuracy is desired. Factory made cartridges are expensive and, however excellent when leaving the factories, may rapidly deteriorate by being stored in an unfavorable place. Tyros usually shoot factory cartridges; the old and skillful marksman rarely does. But, besides the questions of economy and more reliability in properly reloaded cartridges, is the necessity of reloading when one is located away from the large cities, where it is impossible to procure the products of the factories.

'If residing in a section where gun dealers are numerous, the great variety of cartridges make a very large stock necessary (if the dealer would keep a full line) and as many of the cartridges would be seldom called for, the stock would become old and deteriorate. Therefore, only the most called-for rimfire and center fire cartridges are found in the average gun store. Thus it seems necessary for a rifleman—if he desires to economize, to have reliable ammunition and to be able to supply himself with such at will—to possess a knowledge of how to reload rifle cartridges.'

Winchester had long supplied the demands of the hand loaders, and continued to advertise the fact that 'shells of all our center fire rifle cartridges are made of extra thickness for this purpose.' A considerable part of the Company's sales was made up of ammunition components, including primed and unprimed empty cartridge cases, wads, bullets and extra primers.

In 1890, the Company listed in its catalog two types of reloading tools, in addition to bullet molds and charge cups for measuring powder. Also included were directions for reloading and recommendations of the best types of powders. Between 1890 and 1915, there was no change in policy and the Company continued to cater to the hand loaders using black powder.

The hand loading of smokeless powder was a different proposition, and beginning in 1898 the Company made every effort to discourage the practice. While this attitude may have been colored by a desire to increase the sale of factory-made ammunition, the main reason was based upon the increasing number of accidents suffered by shooters using hand loaded smokeless cartridges.

As a large number of these accidents involved Winchester firearms, the management was especially interested in taking steps to eliminate them. In the catalog for 1898 the Company, under the heading, 'Reloading Smokeless Powder Cartridges Impractical,' explained its attitude as follows.

'We are constantly in receipt of letters of inquiry regarding the reloading of smokeless powder rifle ammunition, and we therefore make the following general statement.

'It has been the common experience of persons using reloaded smokeless powder cartridges to have a large number of shells so reloaded rupture in the gun. Extensive experiments carried on by the Winchester Repeating Arms Company—and by the Ordnance Department of the United States Army—with shells, guns and smokeless powders of nearly every known manufacture, have alike failed to find a remedy for this difficulty.

'Experiments show that after the first firing with smokeless powder, the metal of the shell undergoes a slow but decided change, the exact nature of which the best experts have as yet failed to determine. No immediate deterioration attends the shooting of smokeless powder: for, by reloading and shooting immediately, the shells may be shot many times with no sign of rupture.

'If, however, the fired shells are not allowed to stand for two or three days, no matter whether they are cleaned or uncleaned; wet or dry; or loaded or unloaded, the result is always the same—namely, the metal becomes brittle, and rupture of the shells at the next discharge is probable.

'For this reason, the Winchester Repeating Arms Company cautions its patrons against the reloading of smokeless powder rifle ammunition, and wishes to do its utmost to discourage this practice.'

It turned out that the cartridge casings had an adverse reaction to the residue left by the primers then being used; with some thought and effort, this danger was overcome. However, the use of the very potent double-base smokeless powder had become more prevalent. This gave birth to a new danger—namely, overloading. This gave rise to the following warning concerning hand loading in the Winchester catalog of 1900.

'The many smokeless powders on the market differ so greatly in their various qualities and characteristics, that their use may be attended with very great danger through improper loading. Many smokeless powders—excellent powders in themselves and perfectly safe and satisfactory if used in the proper amounts and in the cartridges for which they are designed—may become very dangerous when used in other cartridges, or in the wrong amounts.

'Smokeless powder varies greatly in bulk, density, rapidity of combustion chamber pressure and charge required, and for this reason it is very unsafe to load smokeless powder, unless the means of determining the chamber pressures are at hand. Thirty grains of one powder might be a perfectly safe and satisfactory load, while 30 grains of another pow-

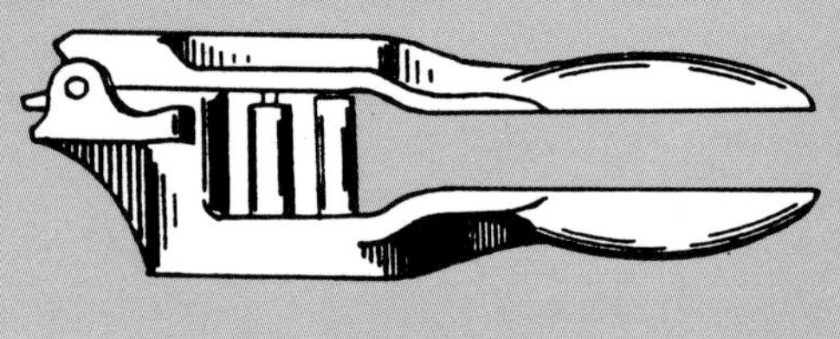

Reloading Tool
First Type—1874-1875

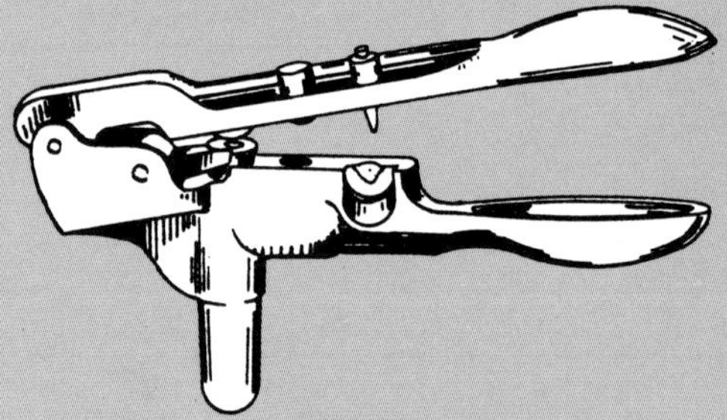

Reloading Tool
Second Type
First Listed 1875

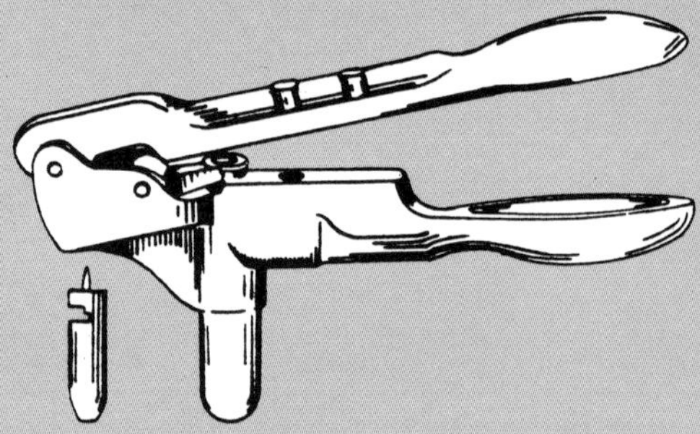

Reloading Tool
Third Type
First Listed 1879

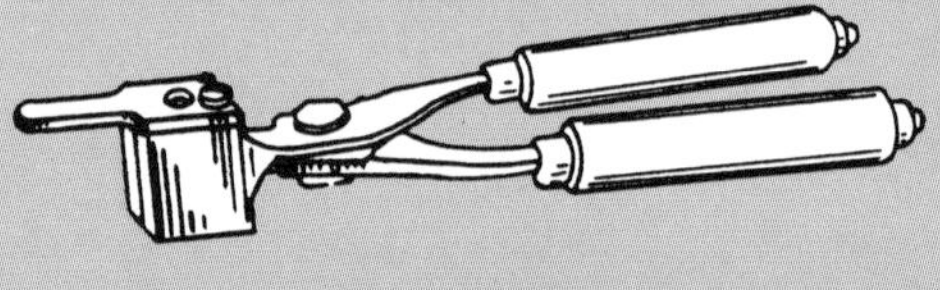

Bullet Mold
Winchester .44-40 Cartridge

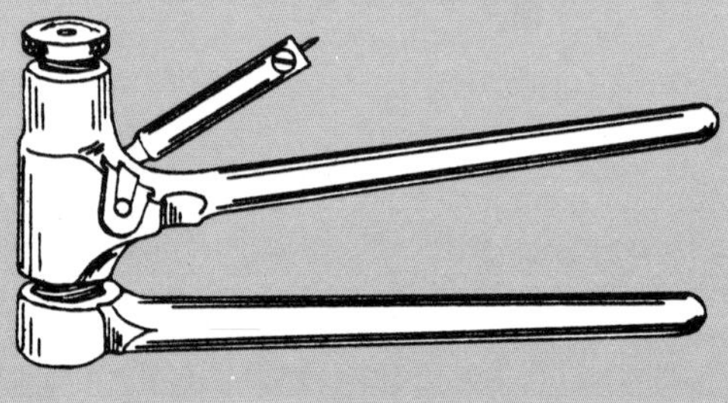

Reloading Tool
Model 1891

der in the same cartridge might burst the strongest nickel steel barrel.

'Many things tend to increase the chamber pressure to an extent little to be expected by the novice. An increase of but a few grains in powder charge will sometimes produce the most astonishing results, and what was previously a perfectly safe load may thus be rendered a very dangerous one indeed.'

Winchester was joined in this campaign by the other ammunition manufacturers and by the powder companies. How effective these warnings were in minimizing the hand loading of metallic cartridges is impossible to determine, but the following is an interesting observation by Townsend Whelen, writing in 1918. 'An acquaintance with thousands of riflemen throughout our country enables me to assert that very few of them load their own ammunition.'

There is no question that these warnings helped to alert shooters to the necessity of being aware, more than ever before, of the potency of some of the new grades of gunpowder.

While the advantages of smokeless over black powder were not as striking in shot shells as in rifle ammunition, the relative cleanness and ballistic economy of smokeless were sufficient to bring about its popularity in shotgun ammunition. The smooth bores and larger diameters of shotgun barrels, as compared to the rifling twists and relatively small diameters of rifle barrels, made for a relatively simpler adaption of designs from black powder to smokeless powder ammunition; even so, the difficulties encountered were formidable enough.

As was the case with metallic cartridges, the varieties of smokeless powder types (including the stronger, double-base types) necessitated continual changes in the composition of priming mixtures, and the balance between powder charges and the weight of the shot. Among other things, the greater heat generated by smokeless powder tended to melt shot made of pure lead. Therefore, chilled shot—made by adding antimony as a hardening agent—had to be used. Also, the higher explosive pressures necessitated the use of wads that were more elastic. Beyond that, a number of changes were made in the design of the head and brass portions of the heavy paper shot shells in order to increase their strength.

Because of the higher pressures developed by smokeless loads, all the ammunition companies had trouble with their paper shot shells 'cutting off,' or separating at the junction of the paper body with the brass head of the shell.

On 9 June 1896, John Gardner, superintendent of Winchester's cartridge shop, was granted US Patent 25611 on a method of construction designed to overcome this difficulty. The essential feature of his patent was the use of circumferential grooves around the 'collar' of the brass head of the shell. These grooves not only held the paper part of the cartridge more firmly in place, but also acted as a shock absorber by flattening against the walls of the chamber when the shell was discharged.

The advantages of this type of construction were so obvious that it was quickly adopted by other ammunition companies. Winchester brought suit against these concerns and forced them to abandon its use. However, Gardner's patent covered only the use of grooves around the entire circumference of the brass heads. Winchester's competitors found that they could get the same effects by indenting their name in the same position, and in this way were able to get the same effect without infringing on his patent.

Gardner's patent solved but one of the many problems connected with adapting shotgun ammunition to smokeless powder. Many of the same laboratory techniques applied in the case of smokeless metallic ammunition had to be applied to cure the ailments of smokeless shot shells. Winchester did not reduce its offerings of black powder shot shells because, as was the case with metallic ammunition, smokeless powder did not eliminate the demand for black powder loads.

Many shotguns were still in use which were not strong enough to handle the more powerful smokeless ammunition. Also, the smokeless loads cost more. In 1914, for example, the list price of loaded 'Nublack' 12-gauge black powder shells was $25 per thousand, while the corresponding smokeless loads in the Repeater and Leader brands were quoted at, respectively, $37.50 and $48 per thousand.

In respect to the hand loading of smokeless powder shot shells, Winchester—beyond cautioning against overloading—issued no warnings. On the contrary, beginning in 1895 and continuing thereafter, the Company included tables in its catalog giving the comparative strength of the various kinds of smokeless powder and their equivalents in black powders for the benefit of handloaders.

Also touted in the catalog were the advantages of the Company's empty shot shells that were designed for smokeless hand loads, and also, special wads and primers were added to the line of hand load ammunition components.

Nevertheless, the advent of smokeless powder did have an effect on shot shell hand loading, and contributed to a subsequent decline in the practice. Henry Brewer explained this phenomenon in the following quote.

'Black powder loading was a pretty simple affair, but when smokeless powder came on the market, shot shell loading became very different and much greater knowledge, skill, and experience was required. There were a good many accidents resulting from overloading by inexperienced handloaders. As a result, quite a business was built up in various localities where game shooting was prevalent, by local handloaders who bought the empty shells, powder, wads and shot, and loaded the shells to meet the requirements and whims of their particular customers.

'These handloaders were usually themselves sportsmen and knew the requirements of the local sportsmen, and they also knew from personal experience good loads from poor loads. The local sportsmen came to rely on their advice as to loads and many of them built up a big reputation for their product and had correspondingly large sales.

'This was especially true in the Chesapeake Bay region, noted for its duck and goose hunting. As a matter of fact, these handloaders were doing a better job than the factory loaders, for they were in closer touch with the shooters and were themselves shooters and sportsmen, and were constantly testing the results of their loads in the field.

'From the foregoing, it is apparent that the initial effect of smokeless powder was not to reduce handloading, but to put it more into the hands of specialists. It was only after the ammunition companies noted the popularity of these special loads and decided to expand their own offerings that handloading of smokeless shot shells as well as black powder loads began to decline.'

Until around 1895, neither Winchester nor the Union Metallic Cartridge Company seems to have made any particular effort to push their sales of factory loaded shells. Winchester did not even list loaded shells in its catalog until 1894, and during the early 1890s, there is evidence that both

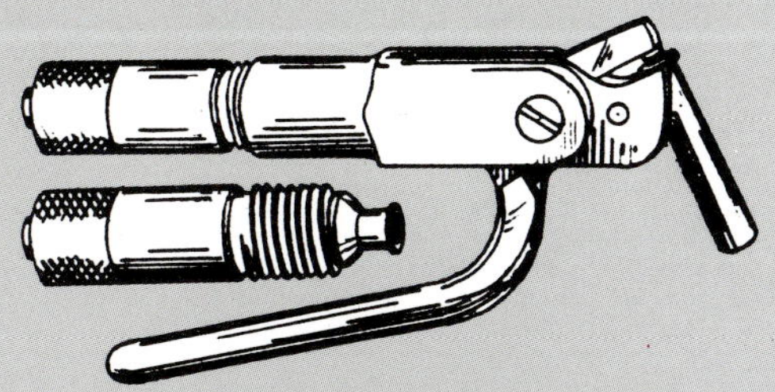

Reloading Tool
Model 1894

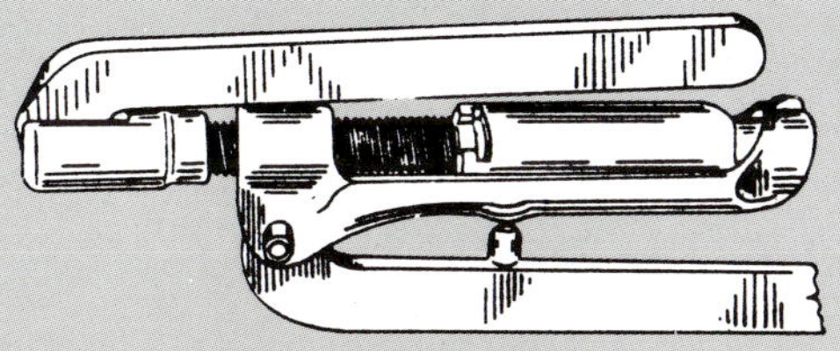

New Model
Reloading Tool

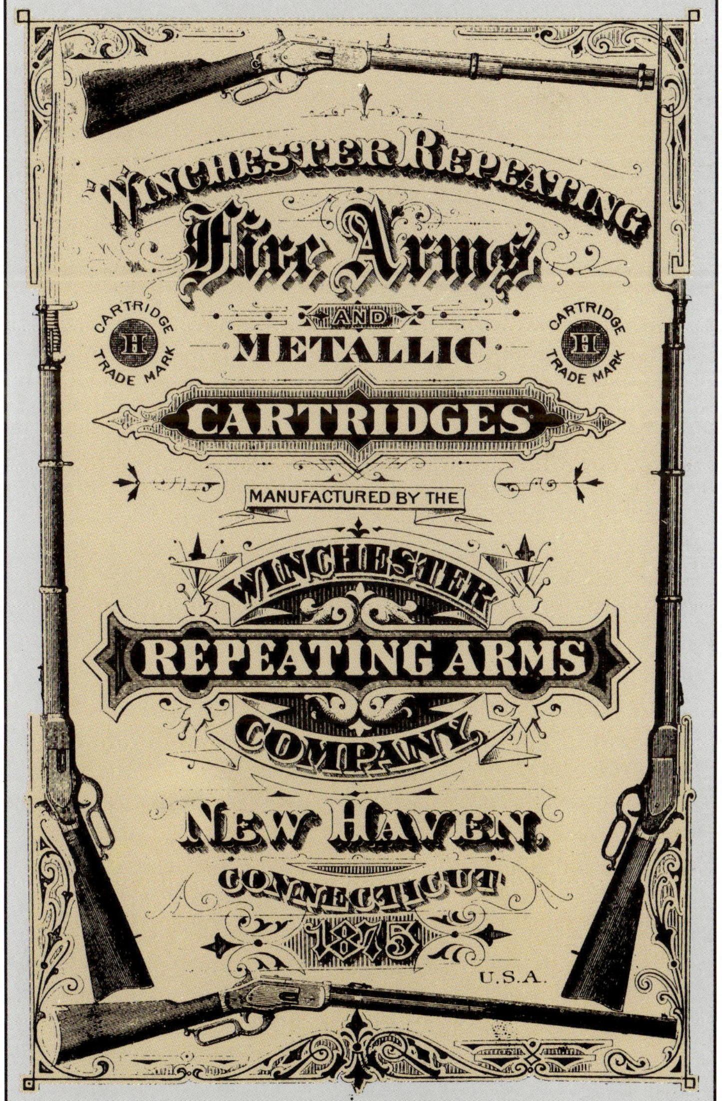

Far left and at top: **Winchester sold a number of reloading tools and bullet molds. The advent of smokeless powder contributed to the decline of hand loading.** ***Above:*** **An advertisement for the Winchester Repeating Arms Company.**

companies were willing to sign an agreement not to load shot shells as long as they and the US Cartridge Company could continue to control the supply of components.

Several considerations apparently led to this lack of enthusiasm. The sale of components was highly profitable, and the early loading machines were relatively inefficient. The cost of factory loaded shells was too high to compete vigorously with hand loading economy, and there was no reason to think that the demand for loaded shells would be very great.

Between 1890 and 1895, the general situation changed. The rise of competing firms not only threatened the Winchester, UMC and USCC control over the manufacture of components, but specialized loading companies were beginning to build up large markets. Machinery had been improved sufficiently to make the margin between costs and selling prices more competitive.

Finally, the sales of factory loaded shells had shown a remarkable increase. Winchester's annual production of loaded shells, for example, grew from 23.2 million in 1890 to 67.5 million in 1895. It may be assumed that the production of loaded shells by UMC and the US Cartridge Company increased in approximately the same proportion.

Noting the success of the special hand loaders, Winchester management decided, in 1896, to expand its offerings of individual shot shell loads, and Bert Claridge was hired to take charge of shot shell loading. This was an excellent choice. Claridge had been in charge of the shot shell loading department of a large sporting goods house in Baltimore. He was an expert shooter, famous among the hunters and sportsmen of the Chesapeake Bay region for the quality of his hand loaded shot shells, and he knew from personal experience what powder-and-shot combination gave the best results under given conditions.

Under Claridge's direction, Winchester's list of shot shell loads began to multiply. He not only increased the number of standard loads, but paid particular attention to 'special orders,' which in many cases developed considerable sales volume. It was Henry Brewer's judgment that 'No other one feature of our loaded shell job played such an important part in building our sales as did Bert Claridge. Under his guidance, we led all the loading companies in smokeless shells, in spite of the fact UMC had always led in black powder Loads. Smokeless loads sold on quality to the more particular shooters, and it was Claridge who put our smokeless loads ahead of all others as to quality.'

This move by Winchester to cater more to the individual demands of shooters was followed by the other ammunition companies, and marked a decline in popularity of hand loading. From the early days of black powder, someone had always been interested in getting special performance from their firearm—a function that hand loading had always pointedly had, and which was now supplied, except for the very particular shooters, by many factory loads.

The demand for factory loaded shot shells continued to expand. Winchester's annual output of loaded shells grew from 67.5 million in 1895 to 243.4 million in 1907.

The use of smokeless powder, plus catering to the demands of individual shooters, multiplied the variety of loads in shot shells. In 1885, just prior to its first sale of loaded shells, Winchester carried only four brands of paper shot shells and two brass shells. In 1914, the catalog listed two types of brass shells, four empty paper shot shells, and six brands of loaded paper shot shells.

This small number of brands completely obscures an almost fantastic increase in individual loads that were being manufactured by the latter date. It was an expansion that was closely related to the relationships among the powder companies, the loading companies, and the users of shot shells. Prior to the advent of factory loaded shells, powder companies had concentrated their sales efforts on the hand loaders. Dealer and jobber connections were carefully built up, and powder companies employed expert shooters as 'missionary salesmen,' whose function was to build up a preference for particular brands of powder.

When the manufacturers started loading shells at the factory, they not unnaturally stressed the qualities of their ammunition and did not feature the powder brands. This move threatened to upset or destroy the whole pattern of consumer-dealer-jobber relationships built up by the powder companies. Not wishing to fight the powder companies in their efforts to expand the sales of factory loads, the ammunition companies began quite early to furnish shot shells loaded with the brand of powder specified by the buyers. This, in itself, added to the multiplicity of different loads; but, because shooters also had preference for different combinations of powder and shot sizes, the companies also extended this option to purchasers.

Even before smokeless powder became widely adopted, the variety of individual shot shell loads had mushroomed. In 1895, just a year after it had first listed loaded shells in its catalog, Winchester was prepared to furnish to its customers, at no extra cost, a choice among 23 combinations of shot-and-powder loads, 16 sizes of shot, and at least 12 brands of powder.

The result was between four and five thousand individual loads. After the introduction of smokeless powder, the list grew steadily—largely because of the increase in powder brands. It has been estimated that, by 1907, Winchester's total allowable loads came to 14,383.

The increased variety of shot shell loads added greatly to the manufacturing problem in this part of the business. The shooting season began in the fall and continued through the winter. Orders began to come in during the late spring and early summer—but until these orders were received and the particular loads were known, production could not begin. The result was intense activity during the summer months, followed by a comparative lull in activity in the off-season.

Assembling the finished product for shipment was a complex task. Each case had to be carefully labeled. Not infrequently, an individual order would call for several varieties of powder. The Company also had to be careful not to have excessive stock on hand at the end of the season—partly because particular loads might not be popular the following season, and partly because shot shells loaded with smokeless powder were subject to extreme deterioration unless very carefully stored.

Beginning around 1901, ammunition companies moved to spread their production over a longer period by making special agreements with jobbers. Under this arrangement, if a jobber would order shells by the carload on or before March 15, he would be allowed to pay for the shipment the following September and still receive a discount. These arrangements were carefully worked out under the supervision of the Ammunition Manufacturers' Association.

Sometime around 1907, the Company began to restrict the extreme variety of their factory loads by listing definite shot sizes for each of the smokeless loads which would be

furnished at standard prices. Orders for shot sizes not on the standard list were accepted only at an increased price. About the same time, the Company began to restrict its powder loads to specific brands.

While these moves helped somewhat to reduce the variety of loads, no determined attempt was made to actually cut the list of loads until after World War I. In 1921, the various ammunition companies moved to eliminate some 5200 loads from their shot shell lists. These 5200 loads that were eliminated comprised but 10 percent of all their business.

Above: **A typical ammunition factory during the Civil War era. Notice the number of female workers and the box of .43 caliber cartridges, a popular cartridge of the time.**

TEXAS
RANGER

With the cooperation of the Department of Commerce, the manufacturers moved to simplify shot shell loads still further. In 1924 a committee, consisting of George R Watrous of the Winchester Repeating Arms Company and HJ Strugnell of the Remington Arms Company, was appointed by the ammunition manufacturers to study the possibility of a further reduction in number of loads. On 1 January 1925, the manufacturers further reduced load combinations to 1747 in all. Further elimination brought the list down to 137, total, by 1947. As you may well suspect, this marked a resurgence in hand loading, as there are always those who are willing to economise—and to take their chances on their own expertise.

Mention has already been made of the importance of improved machinery in loading shot shells. There is some evidence of a considerable improvement in these machines and in the general methods of manufacture during the 1890–1914 period. Available information is lacking for any discussion of these beyond noting a general trend toward increasing labor productivity. It is of interest that, of some 77 patents taken out by Winchester during this period, 51 covered metallic ammunition and shot shell design, 11 applied to primers and 15 to machinery used in the manufacture of both metallic ammunition and shot shells.

Not all the ideas contained in these patents were utilized, of course, but at the same time a number of improvements were introduced which were either not patentable or which the Company felt could be kept secret without being patented. The importance attached to certain of these "secret" manufacturing processes is illustrated by the following experience of Henry Brewer.

While no date is specified, it must have been around 1900 when he was called into the office by TG Bennett, and was told that the Union Metallic Cartridge Company was being sued by a workman who had been injured in their loading room. They had asked Bennett to send someone familiar with loading machines to examine their machines, so he could testify as a loading expert that they were designed and operated with a reasonable degree of safety.

Brewer states, 'Mr Bennett directed that I go to UMC and do whatever I could to help them in the matter. I was greatly elated, because this gave me an opportunity of seeing the UMC loading room—so far as I know, no Winchester representative had ever been in their loading room. It seemed to me a great opportunity to see how they did things—and possibly pick up some good ideas.

***At left:* The Winchester Colt Commemorative set, honoring two guns that tamed the Wild West. The receiver of this Winchester Model 94 features a portrait of Oliver F Winchester etched in gold.**

'I therefore said to Mr Bennett, "There is no objection, I suppose, to my keeping my eyes open and seeing what I can see?" Mr Bennett replied, "Now Brewer, you are going there at their request, do what they ask you to do, but don't go prying into things that are none of our business." Mr Arthur Hooper, Vice President, who was sitting at the adjoining desk spoke up, "Why, Tom, there is no objection, is there, to the young man keeping his eyes open?" So I went determined to learn all that I could that might be of help to Winchester.'

Brewer made the most of his opportunity, and when he returned to New Haven, he informed TG Bennett that Union Metallic Cartridge Company had Winchester 'licked a mile in the matter of the cost of loading.' This, he explained, was because the UMC loading machines were operated by one operator each, whereas the Winchester loading machines required four operators. The UMC machines had automatic devices for feeding wads and shells, whereas the Winchester machine required one girl to feed shells and two girls to feed wads, and a boy to tend the machine.

The speed of the Winchester machine was limited to the speed of the girl feeder, and our daily output was generally a little less than 25,000 shells per day, whereas the UMC loading machines were turning out over 30,000 comparable loads per day with only one operator.

Brewer went on to say, 'I suggested to Mr Bennett that we immediately design automatic wad feeds and automatic shell feeds for our loading room, so that we could reduce the number of operators and increase the output to equal that of UMC loaders, and I told him that I thought if we could accomplish this, we could save $50,000 per year.

'Mr Bennett turned to Mr Hooper and said to him, "Hooper, what would you give to be a young man again? Listen to this young man, saving $50,000 a year," and they both had a good-hearted laugh over it. However, Mr Bennett, with his usual confidence in the men under him, approved the plan, authorized our designing automatic feeds—and, after several years of experimental work and very costly building of the automatic feeds, all of our shot shell machines were so equipped.

'This development of automatic feeds again brought attention to automatic shell feeds, and we continued to develop automatic feeds for our various machines, notably in the Paper Shot Shell Department, and in time we developed automatic paper shot shell feeds, which were used in our shot shell headers, our shot shell primers and our other machines.

'When we were saving an amount which I estimated at $200,000 a year, I had great pleasure in going to Mr

Bennett and calling his attention to the fact that he had laughed at me when I said we could save $50,000 a year, and that I now estimated we were saving in excess of $200,000 a year as a result of my two-hour visit to the UMC loading room.'

One problem connected with shot shell manufacture involved the purchase and storage of shot. Prior to 1912, Winchester purchased its shot from outside concerns. Shot was shipped in cloth bags weighing 25 pounds each. These had to be carefully stored and handled to prevent the bags from bursting. Adding to the complexity of shot-handling operations in those days was that, during the course of production, the Company had to handle a large variety of shot sizes.

Because the demand for particular sizes varied from season to season, it was not possible to purchase the required amounts until orders began to come in, without running the danger of building shot inventories beyond current needs. Also—if, for any reason, the required shot failed to arrive by the time it was needed, production schedules were seriously disrupted.

In spite of these difficulties, the Company took no steps to produce its own shot until 1911. In that year, the National Lead Company—which had been Winchester's own source of shot—purchased the US Cartridge Company, and thereby became a direct competitor with Winchester in the ammunition field.

Winchester management was unwilling to have its principal source of shot in the hands of a competitor, and immediately started to build its own shot tower in New Haven. The structure was completed in 1912, at a total cost of $190,000. The tower was nine stories high, and the equipment used was of the latest design and was almost completely automatic.

Conveyors carried the lead to the top floor, where it was melted, poured into sieves to give the required sizes and dropped into a water tank 154 feet below. Sorting, polishing, sizing and inspection were all done mechanically, without the shot being handled by workman. A duplicate set of machinery guarded against a breakdown, and an average of about 50 tons of shot could be produced in a day's operations.

Located close to the shot shell loading rooms, the use of the shot tower greatly simplified Winchester's manufacturing problems. Shot was ordered to be made at the tower in the sizes and amounts needed by the loading room, and was, upon production, transferred directly without the necessity of storage and extra handling. Inventories now kept track of easily-handled lead 'pigs.'

By 1914, Winchester management could look upon its ammunition development with considerable satisfaction. The problems brought about by the introduction of smokeless powder and the expansion of factory loading had been met and brought under control, an impressive list of new cartridges and shot-shell loads had been added to the line, and the addition of the shot tower had further integrated Winchester's ammunition manufacturing processes.

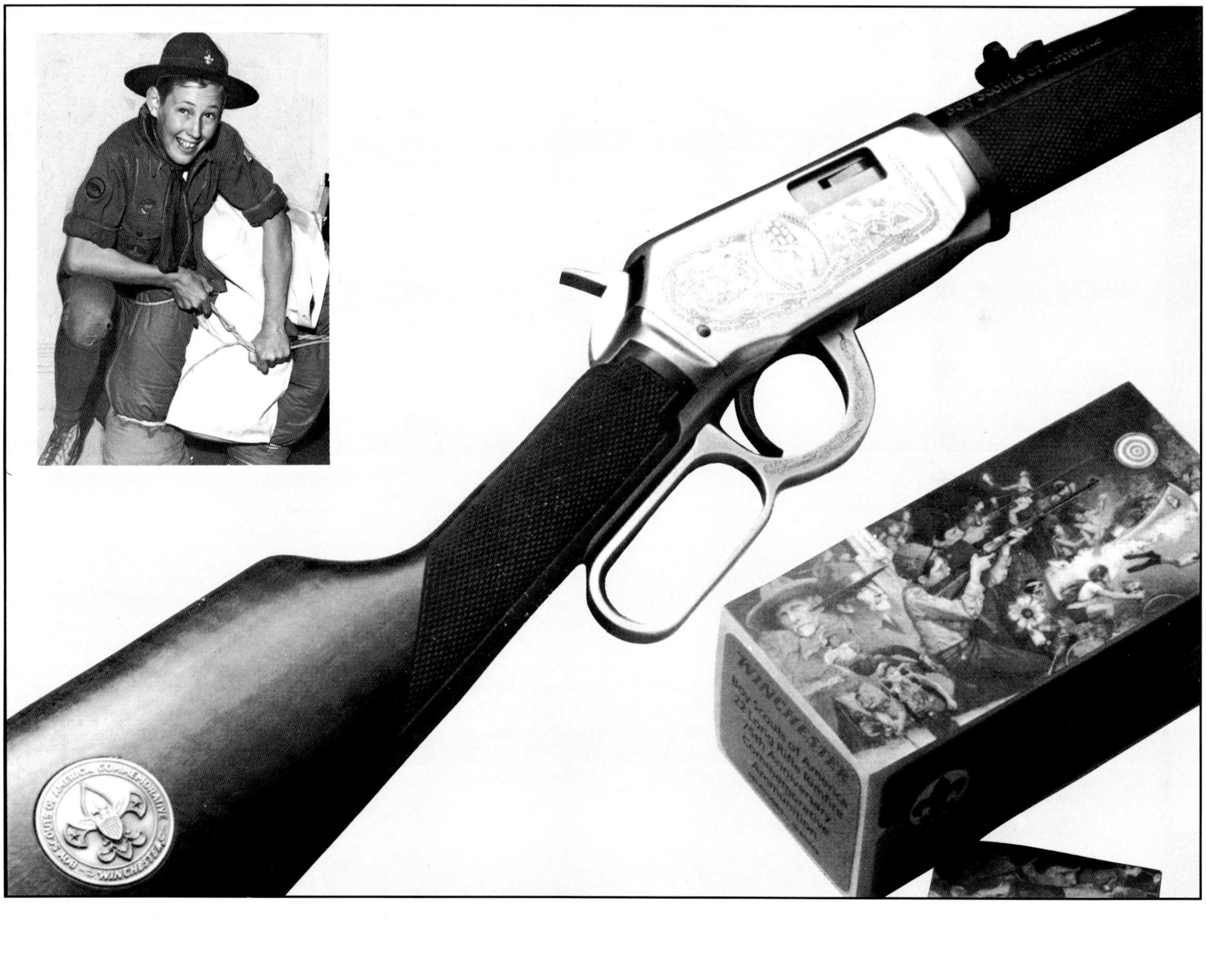

Below: **The Model 9422 Commemorative Rifle—complete with its own .22 caliber ammunition—honors the Boy Scouts of America.** ***At right:*** **The Winchester Shot Tower, which was completed in 1912.**

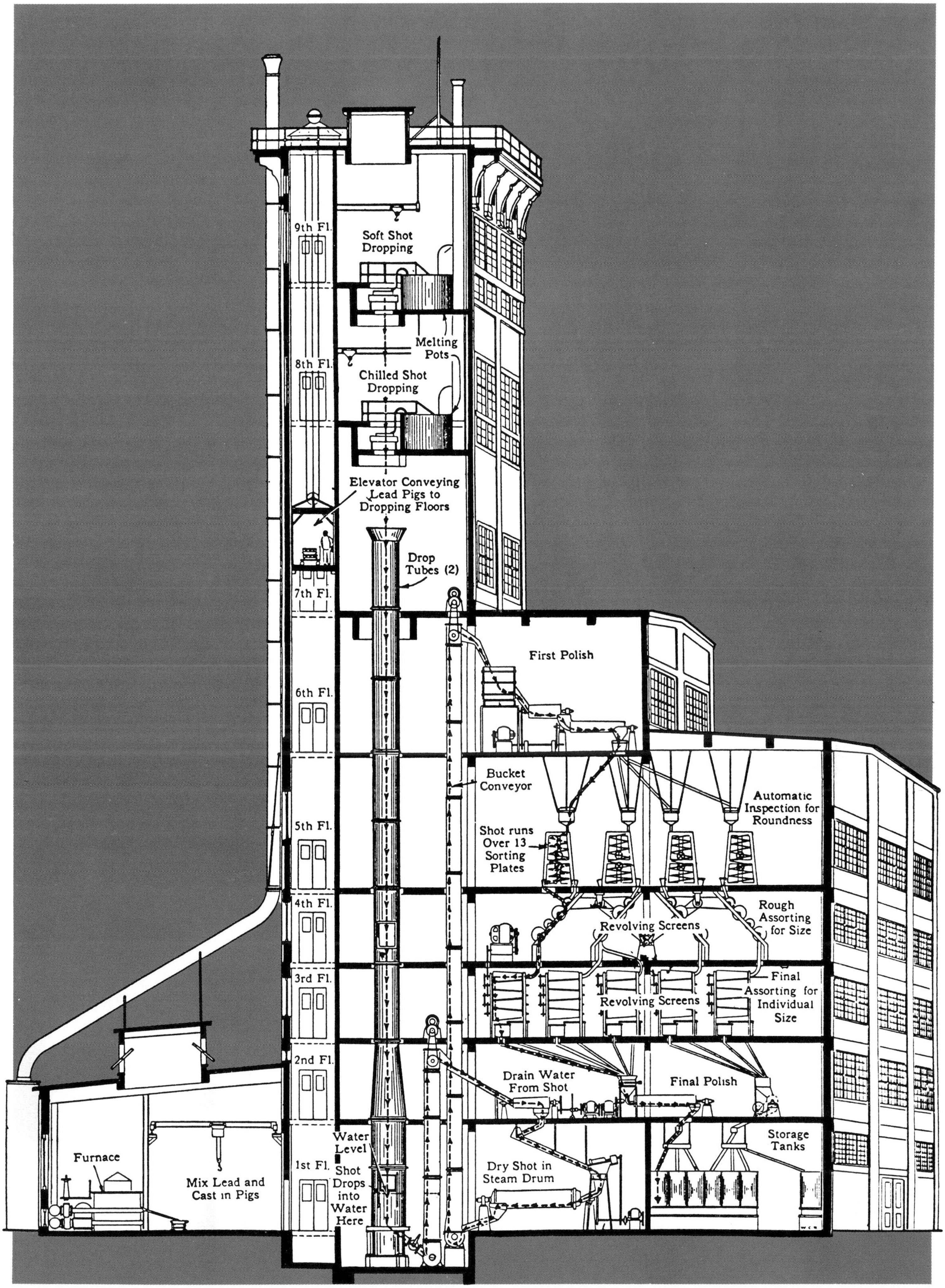
9th Fl.
Soft Shot Dropping
Melting Pots
8th Fl.
Chilled Shot Dropping
Elevator Conveying Lead Pigs to Dropping Floors
Drop Tubes (2)
7th Fl.
First Polish
6th Fl.
Bucket Conveyor
Automatic Inspection for Roundness
5th Fl.
Shot runs Over 13 Sorting Plates
4th Fl.
Rough Assorting for Size
Revolving Screens
3rd Fl.
Final Assorting for Individual Size
Revolving Screens
2nd Fl.
Drain Water From Shot
Final Polish
Water Level
Storage Tanks
1st Fl.
Shot Drops into Water Here
Dry Shot in Steam Drum
Furnace
Mix Lead and Cast in Pigs

The Company Twentieth

By the start of the twentieth century, Winchester's reputation as a manufacturer of quality firearms was well established. *Below:* The Winchester Model 1887, the first successful repeating shotgun. This particular shotgun was used by railway express car guards. *Above:* The Winchester Model 1897, one of the most popular shotguns ever made.

Enters the Century

The 20-year period surrounding the turn of the century was marked by level prices, reflecting a generally stable business atmosphere. This stability was exemplified by Winchester's price list, which had only the most minor changes—most of these additions or deletions to the catalogue—over a period of 24 years. The company prospered, and many new products entered the line, including the Winchester Pump Action; the Model 1890 Rimfire; the Model 92 Center Fire Lever Action; the Model 94, the first Winchester designed for smokeless powder; the Model 97 Pump Shotgun; the Model 1898 Breech Loading Saluting Cannon; the Model 03, the first really successful American semiautomatic and the Model 12.

In 1916, John Edward Otterson was elected as the first Vice President and General Superintendent of Winchester, becoming the first company head who was not a member of the Winchester family. With war impending in Europe, a vast expansion of the old Winchester plant was undertaken to fulfill the war contracts. Winchester became the supplier of Enfields to the British army, eventually delivering over a half million rifles and bayonets to the Western front. When America entered the war in 1917, the company switched to manufacturing arms for the US Army. More than 50,000 Browning Automatic Rifles and several hundred million rounds of ammunition were sold.

During World War I, the short barreled version of the Winchester Model 97 shotgun (widely known as a 'riot gun') was used by the American troops as a trench gun. Groups of American soldiers that were especially skilled at trap shooting were armed with these guns and stationed where they could fire at any hand grenades thrown and thus deflect them from falling into the American trenches.

The Americans generally fired .34 caliber buck shot in their shotguns, each load consisting of six shot pellets. They also employed these guns against German soldiers, and the ensuing German casualties prompted the German government to contact Secretary of State Lansing on 14 September 1918 and protest the use of the shotguns by the American Army, calling attention to the fact that according to the laws of war every prisoner found to have in his possession such guns or ammunition would immediately forfeit his life.

The passage in the Hague Decrees alluded to in the German protest refers to the use of arms calculated to cause 'unnecessary' suffering. The American reply noted that the shotguns did not fall under the Hague ban and that if the Germans carried out their death threat 'in a single instance' the United States Government knew what to do in the way of reprisals and gave notice of its intention to carry them out.

The Americans continued their grisly work, and by November 1918 two more models (the Winchester Hammerless and the Remington) were scheduled to be brought into production when Germany suddenly surrendered. The author's own grandfather was one of these shotgun-toting Dough Boys and remembers him recounting stories of this period.

Employment at Winchester rose to more than 15,000 during the war, the highest it would ever be, but several things went wrong during this period. Prices had been stable for almost 25 years and had lulled the company into signing long term fixed price contracts just as wages and costs of goods were making dramatic upward trends. The expansion of the plant had been carried on haphazardly and new buildings had been erected among the old ones. Instead of increasing efficiency, the expansion had decreased efficiency

Above: **The Model 1903 Rifle, chambered for the company's new smokeless .22 caliber automatic rimfire cartridge.** ***At right:*** **The Model 90. This rimfire, pump action rifle was widely used for small game and target shooting.** ***Below:*** **The Winchester plant in 1914—and in 1919 (below right), after the expansion.**

by making it impossible to consolidate operations into the new buildings because they were so spread out.

At the end of the war, contracts were cancelled—this idled large portions of the plant principally because sales of sporting arms lagged. But the biggest worry in 1919 was the amount of income tax the company would have to pay for its war years profits. Estimations of the amount of tax actually owed ranged from 18 to 80 percent, and this caused so much concern in management that, in order to be prepared to pay the tax and still leave enough money for 'new projects,' Winchester borrowed $3 million from Kidder Peabody.

This last sum was in addition to a loan of $16 million the company had borrowed to finance the recent expansion, of which only $8 million had been paid off. Even when the income tax problem was resolved with the payment of $3.14 million to the government, the arms and ammunition business was deemed too small to pay off the remaining indebtedness—which now stood at about $17 million dollars total. Therefore, an agreement between the stockholders, Kidder Peabody, Otterson and Louis K Liggett to reorganize the company and expand into new areas was signed.

Mr Liggett was the founder and President of the United Drug Company and had made millions of dollars organizing the first nationwide chain of drug stores and supplying them with his own brands of merchandise under the trade name of Rexall. Kidder Peabody thought very highly of him and considered the Winchester resurrection possible only if he were directly involved in the planning and operation of the new experiment.

In early 1920, the Winchester Company was organized with JE Otterson as President and was divided into two divisions—The Winchester Repeating Arms Company, manufacturer of the firearms and ammunition, and the Winchester Company, which was to establish a chain of Winchester dealer agents and open Winchester retail stores that would sell all of the new Winchester line of home hardware.

This new hardware product line, usually manufactured at the arms plant, included knives, cutlery, fishing equipment, hand tools, skis, wrenches, batteries, flashlights, carpenter tools, ice skates, roller skates, paint, varnish, brushes, baseball bats, athletic equipment, kitchen appliances, washing machines, and the Ice-O-Later gas refrigerator. This major

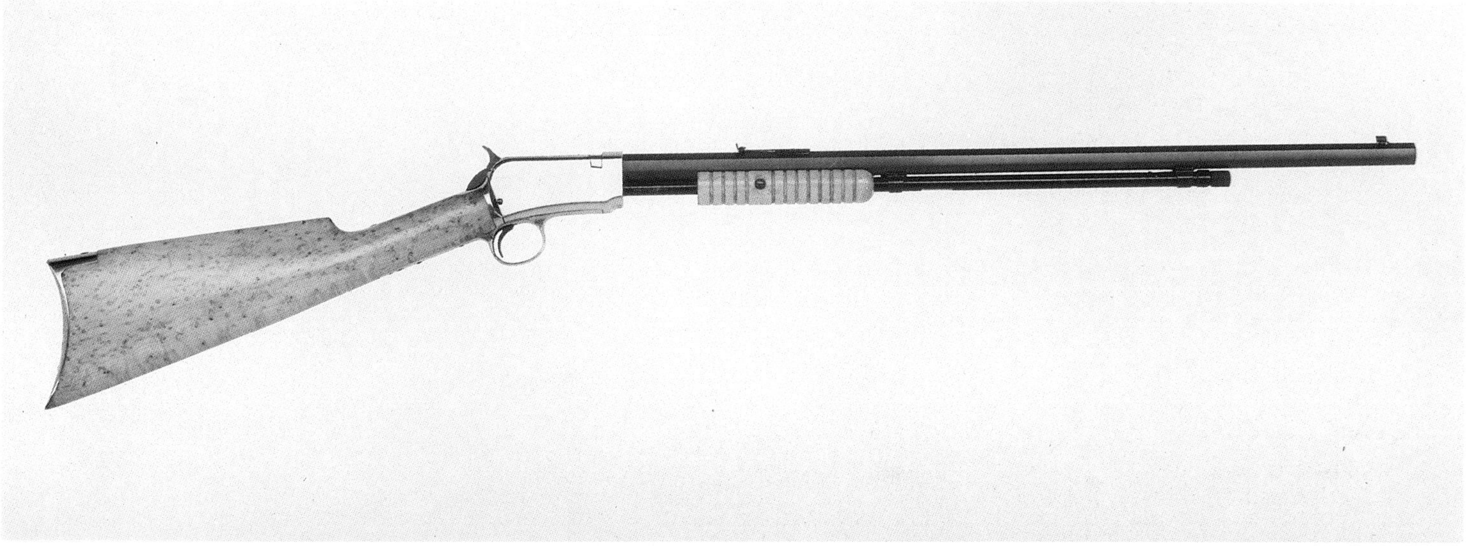

The most famous of the Winchester line—the Model 94. Although similar in external appearance to the Model 92, this gun differed from previous models in that it was the first sporting repeating rifle adapted for the smokeless cartridge. The Model 94 was especially popular in the West, where it quickly became standard equipment for settlers, hunters and ranchers. *Above, from top to bottom:* The Model 94 .32 Special Rifle, the Model 94 .357 Caliber Big Bore, the Model 94 .30-30 Caliber and the Model 94 Trapper Special .30-30 Caliber.

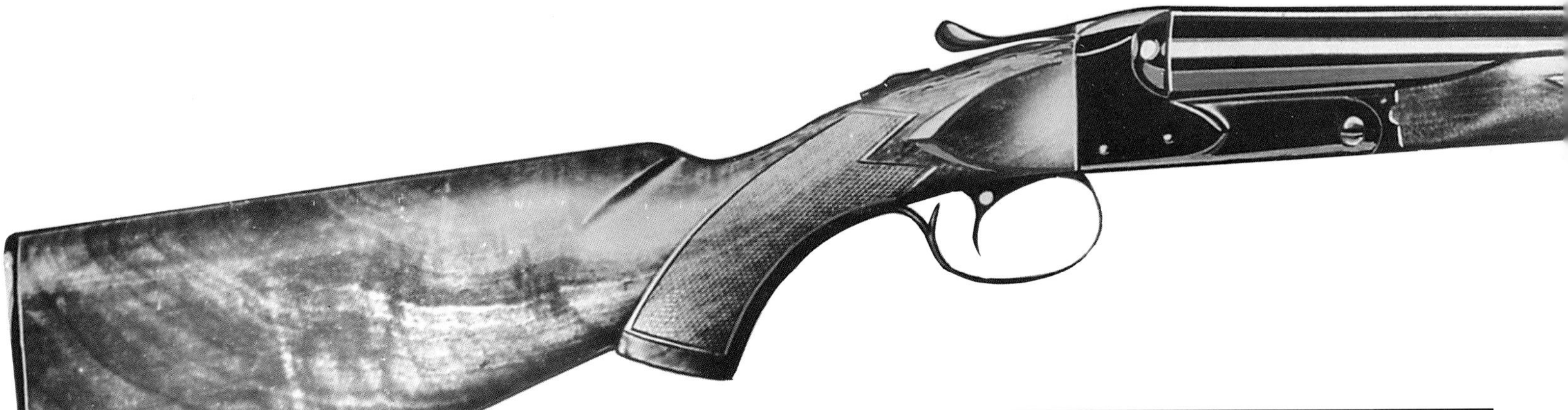

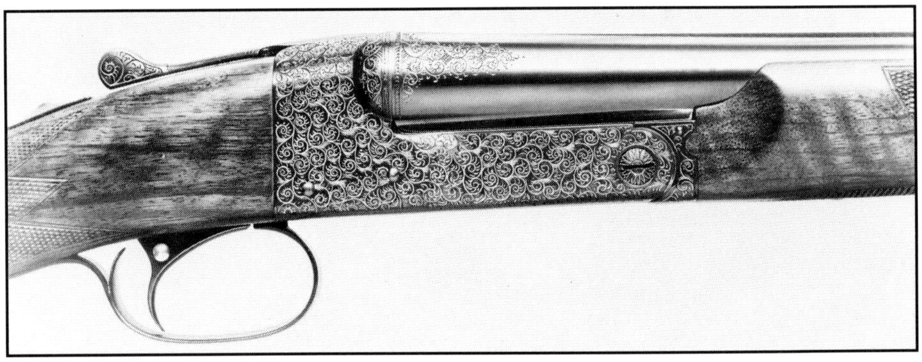

expansion into areas that were unfamiliar to the management and technical staffs appears to have been doomed from the very start. In order to buy expertise, hardware manufacturing companies were purchased, but this strategy generally failed because the only companies that were willing to sell out were usually weak and noncompetitive or possessing only obsolete product lines.

As Winchester's acquisitions and expansions roared into the 1920s, their debt service became staggering. Sales of all hardware product lines began to lag and costs continued to run uncontrolled, making all, or nearly all, of the lines more expensive than their respective competitions. Substantial pressure to give special concessions to in-house sales further aggravated the cash flow situation of the company. All available resources were being used to keep the hardware business afloat and keep the numerous creditor wolves from the door.

During this period, arms and ammunition profits continued to perform well; however, a lack of investment in design and production facilities or equipment was beginning to show in declining sales and increasing costs. Despite the lack of attention from management, the engineering departments were continuing to design and produce some fine new arms. The Model 52 rimfire rifle in 1920 and the Model 54 in 1924 were the first successful bolt action rifles produced by Winchester.

At top: The Model 21 Field Gun. _Above:_ The intricately engraved receiver of the Model 21 Grand American. _At bottom:_ The Model 54. _Opposite:_ In the 1920s, Winchester ventured into other product lines.

With only a minor redesign and facelift, the Model 54 became the Model 70 in 1937. The Model 21 made its debut in 1931. However, firearms sales were not enough to keep the sinking ship afloat and by February of 1929 the Winchester Company was dissolved and a new company, The Winchester Repeating Arms Company of Delaware, took over all the old obligations of the old company.

The dealer agents were disbanded and all products were to be sold on the open market. Within two years, the debt service had become totally debilitating at nearly a million dollars a year, and the company was propelled into bankruptcy on 21 January 1931. Winchester had gone down with the Great Depression. It was to rise again less than one year later on the shoulders of the Western Cartridge Company, which acquired it on 22 December 1931.

THE
WINCHESTER
HERALD
New WINCHESTER PADLOCKS Modern Protection
WINCHESTER
"AS GOOD AS THE GUN"

WINCHESTER
TRADE MARK
TOOLS
Largest and most complete line of tools offered by any manufacturer under one brand—
WINCHESTER
Fine tools made for exclusive distribution to the retail trade through the stores of Winchester Dealers
WINCHESTER
BIT BRACES

The "Young Idea"
Turns to the Sport of Roller Skating
At the time when the fisherman feels the Izaak Walton rising in him and the shooter grows impatient under the lure of target and trap, the active "young idea" turns to strenuous days in the open. With increasing thousands all over America each year this means that a large outlet for their energy is in the sport of roller skating.
With vigorous municipal and recreation center promotion this healthful, joy-filled sport is growing in popularity every year. Besides the thousands of initiates who will be in the market for the best in roller skates as their first equipment there is that army of old timers to whom new skates will be necessary or who will be ready for better ones this year.
Yours is the opportunity, Mr. Winchester Agent, to profit by this 1922 demand. The sturdiness of Winchester girder frame skates, that means safety and satisfactory service, the long wearing, easy running disc rolls, the resilient rubber cushioned frames are some of the features that combine to make a roller skate you can offer to youngster and grown up alike with pride and utmost confidence in their selling qualities. Even in the lower priced Winchester skates there is a Winchester quality that means the fullest value.
The demand for
WINCHESTER
TRADE MARK
ROLLER SKATES
In 1922 was more than 50% greater than in 1921

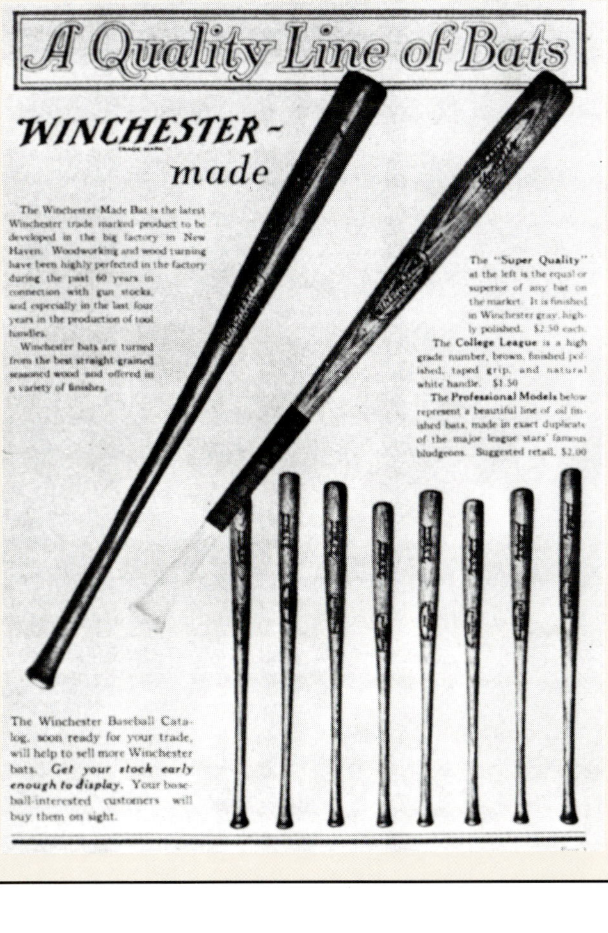
A Quality Line of Bats
WINCHESTER-
TRADE MARK
made
The Winchester Made Bat is the latest Winchester trade marked product to be developed in the big factory in New Haven. Woodworking and wood turning have been highly perfected in the factory during the past 60 years in connection with gun stocks, and especially in the last four years in the production of tool handles.
Winchester bats are turned from the best straight grained seasoned wood and offered in a variety of finishes.
The "Super Quality" at the left is the equal or superior of any bat on the market. It is finished in Winchester gray, highly polished. $2.50 each.
The College League is a high grade number, brown, finished polished, taped grip, and natural white handle. $1.50
The Professional Models below represent a beautiful line of oil finished bats, made in exact duplicate of the major league stars' famous bludgeons. Suggested retail, $2.00
The Winchester Baseball Catalog, soon ready for your trade, will help to sell more Winchester bats. Get your stock early enough to display. Your baseball-interested customers will buy them on sight.

The Cartridge

The Western Cartridge Company had its roots in Franklin W Olin, who founded, in 1892, the Equitable Powder Manufacturing Company of East Alton, Illinois. Initially that company had produced black powder for use in southern Illinois coal mines, but by 1894 had switched its emphasis to production of 'sporting powder' for ammunition. Aware of the growing popularity of factory loaded ammunition, Olin began work on a machine that would load shotgun shells and this invention established the Western Cartridge Company.

Olin believed in 'hands on' involvement in the important elements of developing the company's various product lines and Western's reputation for manufacturing quality products grew until, by the turn of the century, it was a major force in the ammunition business. The reliability of its ammunition earned the Western Cartridge Company commendations from the US and Allied governments during World War I.

Franklin Olin was succeeded by his son, John, who himself was gifted with an inventive mind. Young John shared his father's interest in the technical side of the business, and his interests in the development of smokeless powder for commercial use resulted in the introduction of Western's Super-X ammunition, which is still available today. The demand for these Super-X shells was so great among hunters and sportsmen that the Western Cartridge Company soon rose to a position of absolute dominance in the ammunition industry.

With the purchase of Winchester, the Winchester-Western Company became the largest owner of patents on ammunition and firearms in the world. Relying on the same innovative spirit that started the company, John Olin took an active interest in the development of the ammunition and firearms now produced by Winchester. By 1940, Winchester-Western had introduced 23 new guns to its line and was in a solid position to serve the country once more as World War II approached. By that war's end the company had produced more than 15 billion rounds of ammunition and 1.5 million military arms.

Following the war, Winchester-Western continued to remain on the leading edge of ammunition technology, with a list of innovative firsts that included Ball Powder propellant in 1946, the Baby Magnum shotshell in 1954, the .22 Winchester Magnum Rimfire cartridge in 1959, the Mark 5 shotshell in 1962, the Compression-Formed plastic shotshell in 1964, the Double A target load in 1965, the Super Double X 10 gauge shotshell in 1968, the Silvertip hollow-point load in 1979 and the Super-X 10 gauge Magnum steel shot load in 1982.

Western Company

Introduced in 1924, the Model 54 Rifle *(above)* marked Winchester's entry into the heavy caliber, bolt action field. In 1980, Winchester introduced the Model 23 Shotgun *(below)*, which is manufactured by a subsidiary in Japan. It was the first side-by-side shotgun produced by Winchester in 20 years.

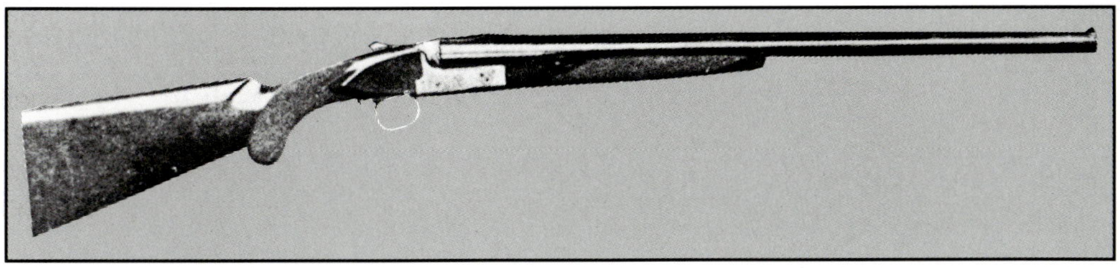

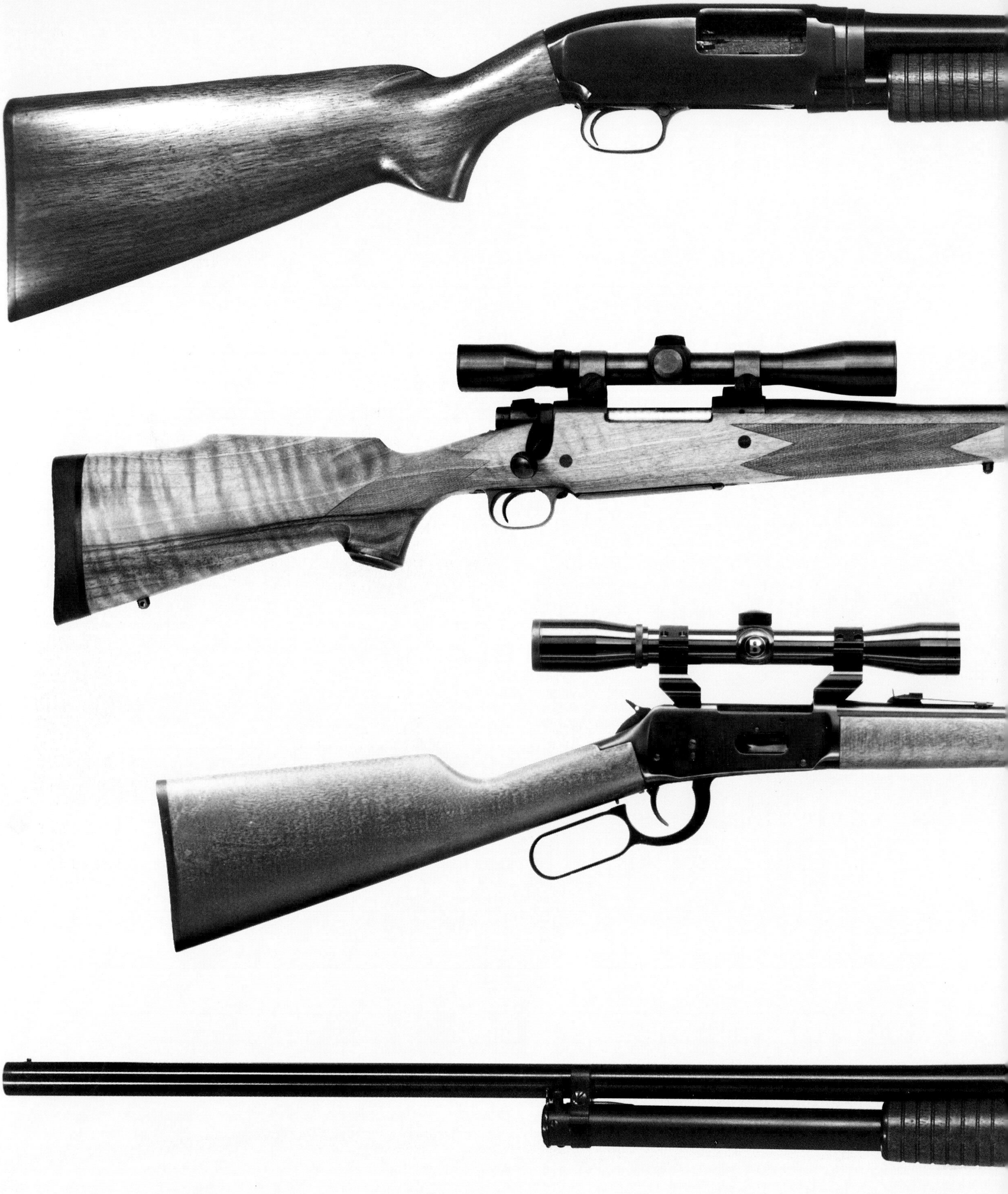

At top and bottom: **Two views of the Model 1912 Shotgun. Priced at $20, this gun was an immediate best seller. General Curtis E LeMay** ***(above)*** **fires his Model 1912 Trap Gun.** ***Center, above and below:*** **The Model 70 Magnum Bolt Action Center Fire Rifle—and the Model 94 Ranger Carbine with Bushnell Sportview 4X scope and see-through mounts.**

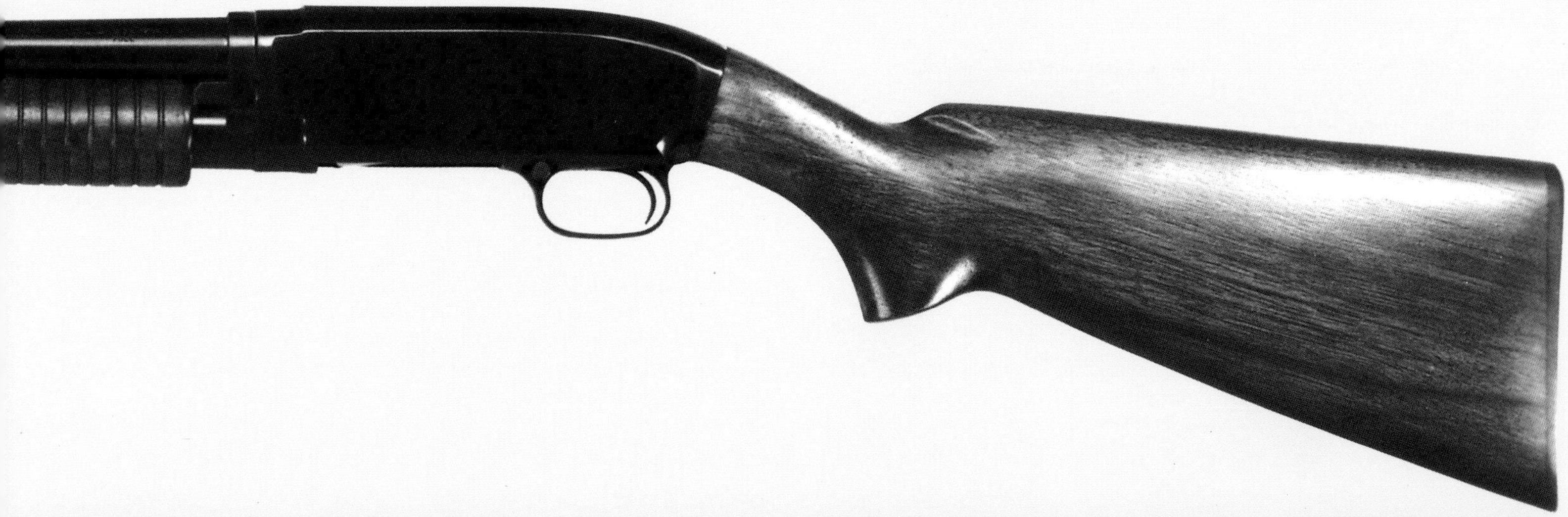

Winchester

From the days of the Winchester Repeating Arms Company's Repeating Rifle manufactured by (as seen in the advertisement *at right*), to the present, Winchester firearms have consistently ranked among the best in the world. The Winchester Model 9422 .22 Caliber Rifle *(above)* typifies modern day gun making at its finest.

Today

In August 1954, Olin merged with Mattheson Chemcal Corporation to form Olin Mattheson, one of America's largest industrial complexes. In December 1980, Olin's board of directors authorized the disposal of the company's Winchester Sporting Arms business in the United States, and on 20 July 1981 Winchester was sold to the US Repeating Arms Company, which was actually a group of former employees, investors and bankers. Today the firm, though currently under bankruptcy court protection, is still making the famed Winchester rifles under a license from Olin. (It is interesting to note that in January of 1988 Browning acquired 37 percent interest in Winchester arms.)

Olin's Winchester Operations branch continues to manufacture sporting and defense ammunition and market its Japanese-produced line of high-quality over-and-under and side-by-side shotguns. The worldwide operations of today's Winchester include headquarters and an ammunition manufacturing plant (complimented by Olin's brass mill) in East Alton, Illinois; a ball powder propellant manufacturing plant in St Mark's, Florida; and a defense products manufacturing facility at Marion, Illinois.

Winchester operations also include the Lake City Army Ammunition Plant at Independence, Missouri; a Winchester shotshell plant at Anagni, Italy; and another ammunition plant in Australia. Olin-Kodensha (OK Firearms Company) at Tochigi, Japan produces the popular Classic Doubles line of Winchester shotguns. Whatever the future may bring, it is clear that when you load up with Winchester, you load up with a legend.

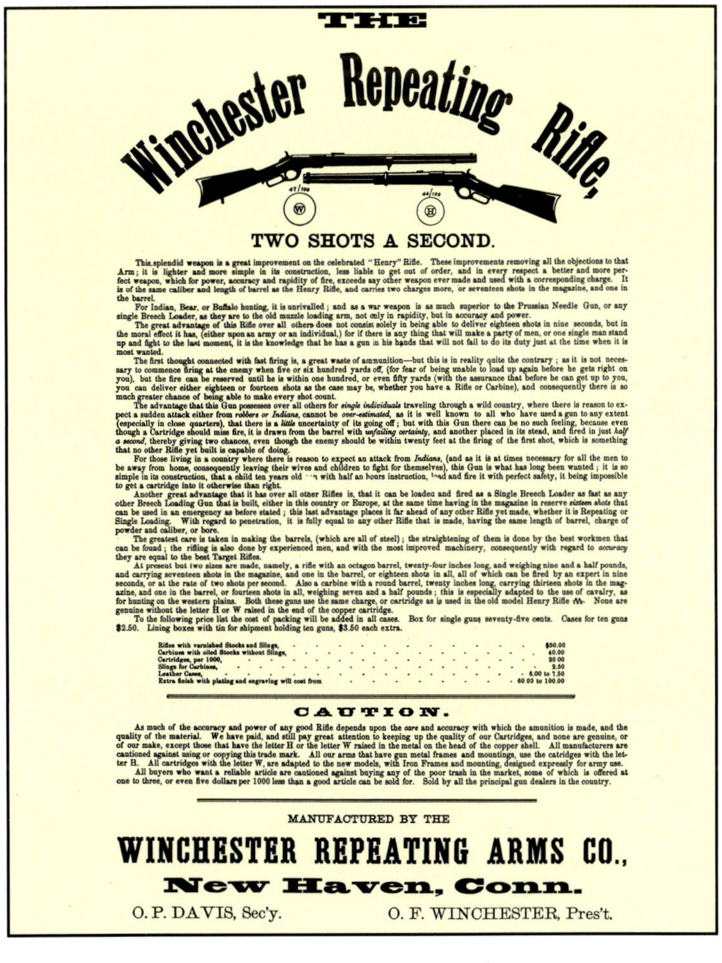

THE

Winchester Repeating Rifle,

47/100 (W) 44/100 (H)

TWO SHOTS A SECOND.

This splendid weapon is a great improvement on the celebrated "Henry" Rifle. These improvements removing all the objections to that Arm; it is lighter and more simple in its construction, less liable to get out of order, and in every respect a better and more perfect weapon, which for power, accuracy and rapidity of fire, exceeds any other weapon ever made and used with a corresponding charge. It is of the same caliber and length of barrel as the Henry Rifle, and carries two charges more, or seventeen shots in the magazine, and one in the barrel.

For Indian, Bear, or Buffalo hunting, it is unrivalled; and as a war weapon is as much superior to the Prussian Needle Gun, or any single Breech Loader, as they are to the old muzzle loading arm, not only in rapidity, but in accuracy and power.

The great advantage of this Rifle over all others does not consist solely in being able to deliver eighteen shots in nine seconds, but in the moral effect it has, (either upon an army or an individual,) for if there is any thing that will make a party of men, or one single man stand up and fight to the last moment, it is the knowledge that he has a gun in his hands that will not fail to do its duty just at the time when it is most wanted.

The first thought connected with fast firing is, a great waste of ammunition—but this is in reality quite the contrary; as it is not necessary to commence firing at the enemy when five or six hundred yards off, (for fear of being unable to load up again before he gets right on you), but the fire can be reserved until he is within one hundred, or even fifty yards (with the assurance that before he can get up to you, you can deliver either eighteen or fourteen shots as the case may be, whether you have a Rifle or Carbine), and consequently there is so much greater chance of being able to make every shot count.

The advantage that this Gun possesses over all others for *single individuals* traveling through a wild country, where there is reason to expect a sudden attack either from *robbers or Indians*, cannot be *over-estimated*, as it is well known to all who have used a gun to any extent (especially in close quarters), that there is a *little* uncertainty of its going off; but with this Gun there can be no such feeling, because even though a Cartridge should miss fire, it is drawn from the barrel with *unfailing certainty*, and another placed in its stead, and fired in just *half a second*, thereby giving two chances, even though the enemy should be within twenty feet at the firing of the first shot, which is something that no other Rifle yet built is capable of doing.

For those living in a country where there is reason to expect an attack from *Indians*, (and as it is at times necessary for all the men to be away from home, consequently leaving their wives and children to fight for themselves), this Gun is what has long been wanted; it is so simple in its construction, that a child ten years old [illegible] with half an hours instruction, load and fire it with perfect safety, it being impossible to get a cartridge into it otherwise than right.

Another great advantage that it has over all other Rifles is, that it can be loaded and fired as a Single Breech Loader as fast as any other Breech Loading Gun that is built, either in this country or Europe, at the same time having in the magazine in reserve *sixteen shots* that can be used in an emergency as before stated; this last advantage places it far ahead of any other Rifle yet made, whether it is Repeating or Single Loading. With regard to penetration, it is fully equal to any other Rifle that is made, having the same length of barrel, charge of powder and caliber, or bore.

The greatest care is taken in making the barrels, (which are all of steel); the straightening of them is done by the best workmen that can be found; the rifling is also done by experienced men, and with the most improved machinery, consequently with regard to *accuracy* they are equal to the best Target Rifles.

At present but two sizes are made, namely, a rifle with an octagon barrel, twenty-four inches long, and weighing nine and a half pounds, and carrying seventeen shots in the magazine, and one in the barrel, or eighteen shots in all, all of which can be fired by an expert in nine seconds, or at the rate of two shots per second. Also a carbine with a round barrel, twenty inches long, carrying thirteen shots in the magazine, and one in the barrel, or fourteen shots in all, weighing seven and a half pounds; this is especially adapted to the use of cavalry, as for hunting on the western plains. Both these guns use the same charge, or cartridge as is used in the old model Henry Rifle. None are genuine without the letter H or W raised in the end of the copper cartridge.

To the following price list the cost of packing will be added in all cases. Box for single guns seventy-five cents. Cases for ten guns $2.50. Lining boxes with tin for shipment holding ten guns, $3.50 each extra.

Rifles with varnished Stocks and Slings,	$50.00
Carbines with oiled Stocks without Slings,	40.00
Cartridges, per 1000,	20 00
Slings for Carbines,	2.50
Leather Cases,	6.00 to 7.50
Extra finish with plating and engraving will cost from	60.00 to 100.00

CAUTION.

As much of the accuracy and power of any good Rifle depends upon the *care* and accuracy with which the amunition is made, and the quality of the material. We have paid, and still pay great attention to keeping up the quality of our Cartridges, and none are genuine, or of our make, except those that have the letter H or the letter W raised in the metal on the head of the copper shell. All manufacturers are cautioned against using or copying this trade mark. All our arms that have gun metal frames and mountings, use the catridges with the letter H. All cartridges with the letter W, are adapted to the new models, with Iron Frames and mounting, designed expressly for army use.

All buyers who want a reliable article are cautioned against buying any of the poor trash in the market, some of which is offered at one to three, or even five dollars per 1000 less than a good article can be sold for. Sold by all the principal gun dealers in the country.

MANUFACTURED BY THE

WINCHESTER REPEATING ARMS CO.,

New Haven, Conn.

O. P. DAVIS, Sec'y. O. F. WINCHESTER, Pres't.

Theodore Roosevelt

Theodore Roosevelt was born in New York on 27 October 1858. By the time he graduated from Harvard in 1880, he had become both an excellent boxer and an avid sportsman. In 1884, he became a rancher in North Dakota, where he served as a local deputy sheriff. Roosevelt captured these western experiences in his book *Hunting Trips of a Ranchman*, which was published in 1885. It was in this volume that he first expressed his enthusiasm for Winchester rifles.

The Sharps and English Express rifles of his time were noted for their vicious recoil, but when Teddy came into contact with a .45-75 Winchester Model 76 Half Magazine, his lifelong love affair with Winchesters was born. The Model 76 was a pleasure to shoot, it was accurate and handy, and was quite equal to any kind of hunting to be found in North America. In short order, Teddy also acquired a .44 caliber WCF Winchester Model 73, a .45-75 caliber WCF Winchester Model 76, and a Hammerless Top Lever Breechloading Double Shotgun.

When Roosevelt's Rough Riders went to Cuba during the Spanish-American War, Teddy brought along his .30 caliber Winchester Model 95. His exploits as Colonel Roosevelt of the Rough Riders brought him such notoriety that in 1898 he was elected Governor of New York. Roosevelt was elected Vice President of the United States under President McKinley in 1901 and became the 26th President of the United States when the latter was assassinated. He served the remainder of McKinley's term and was returned to the presidency in 1904 by a large majority.

It was during his last year in office that Roosevelt began extensive preparations for his now famous African trip with his son, Kermit, to gather specimens for the Smithsonian Institution. Naturally Teddy wanted to use Winchester rifles and ammunition on the hunt, and so entered into extensive correspondence with the Winchester Company to procure weapons to his exacting specifications.

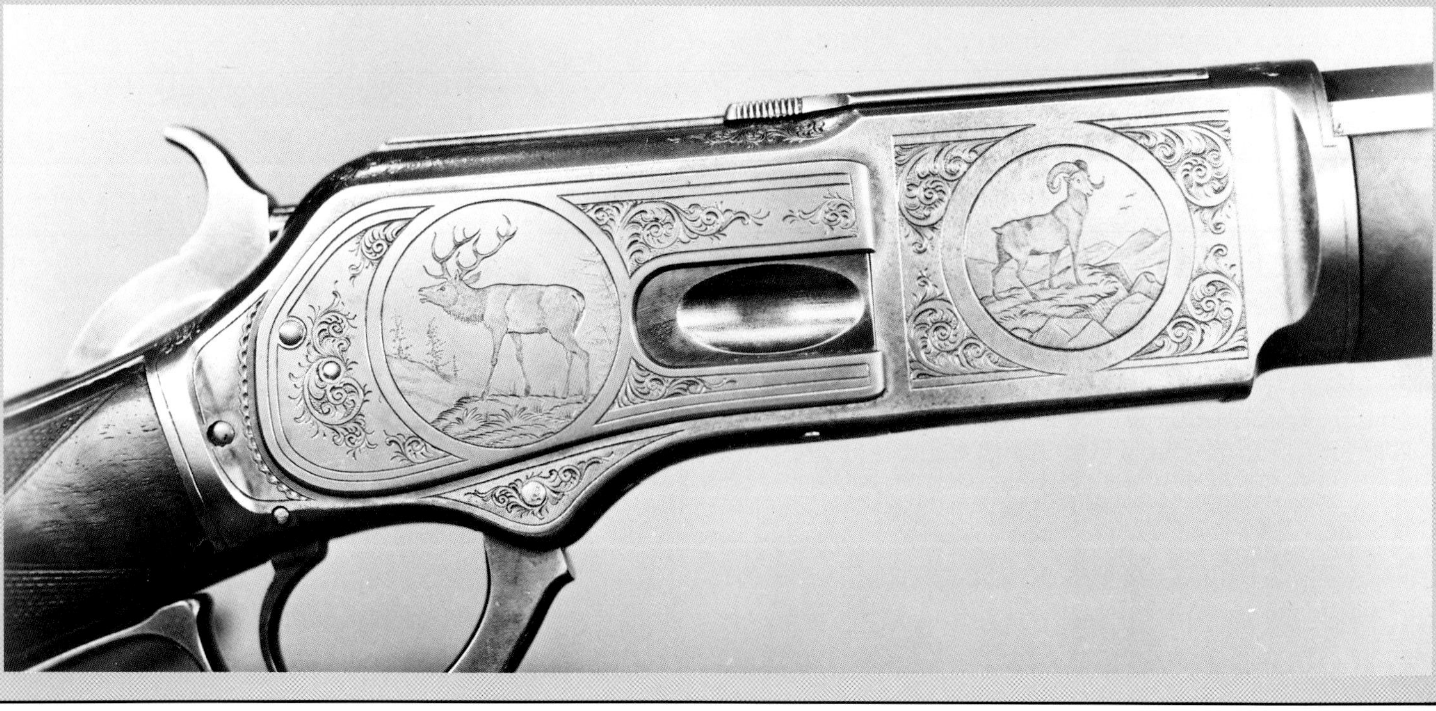

In his many letters to Winchester, Teddy showed himself to be both impersonal and difficult to please. He became very upset over the way the guns were first made even though he was himself chiefly responsible for the confusion. The management of Winchester, however, saw the inestimable worth of having the President of the United States use their weapons in such a public setting, and so handled the matter with both tact and diplomacy by sparing no effort to give Roosevelt exactly what he wanted.

Teddy's initial choice of weapons was as follows: a .30-40 caliber Model 95, two .405 caliber Model 95s and a .45-70 caliber Model 86. After considerable discussion, it was decided that the company would supply two .405 caliber Model 95 rifles and one .30 caliber Model 95, chambered for the US Government ammunition, as well as all of the ammunition needed for the trip.

The President's great African hunting trip began on 23 March 1909 when he, his son Kermit and a group of naturalists sailed from New York for Mombasa, British East Africa. The party landed in April of that year and spent the next 11 months hunting wild animals. They sent back to the United States a total of 4897 mammals, more than 4000 birds, 2000 reptiles and approximately 500 fishes, besides numerous other specimens. Accounts of the trip written by Roosevelt ran in *Scribner's Magazine* during the years 1909 and 1910 and were later incorporated into his book entitled *African Game Trails.*

Teddy lavishly praised his Winchester weapons in all of these accounts, and Winchester lavishly quoted him in their advertising campaigns. One example read 'Tarlton took his big double-barrel and advised me to take mine as the sun had just set and it was likely to be close work; but I shook my head, for the Winchester .405 is, at least for me personally, the "medicine gun" for lions.'

Far left: **Theodore Roosevelt the hunter, in 1883 with his Model 1876.** ***At bottom:*** **Two views of Roosevelt's finely engraved Model 1876 in .40-60 caliber.** ***At above left:*** **'Teddy' and his hunting companions Wilmont Dow (photo left) and Bill Sewell (photo right).** ***Left, center:*** **The Winchester ammunition wagon for Roosevelt's famed African Safari.**

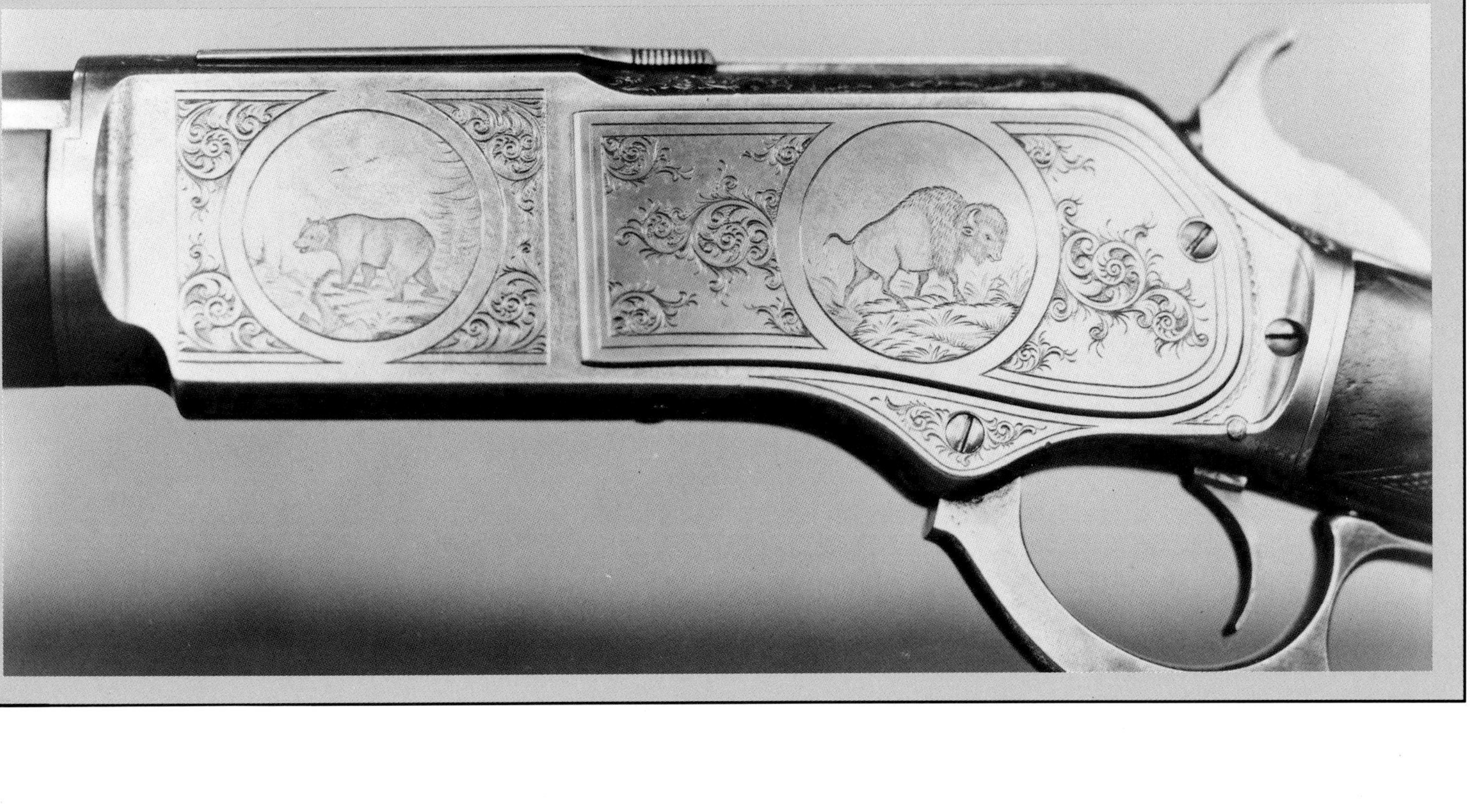

'Buffalo Bill' Cody

William Frederick Cody promoted himself into the ranks of such legendary Americans as Kit Carson, Daniel Boone, Jim Bridger and 'Wild Bill' Hickok. He was both a superb rider and marksman and, between 1872 and 1916, he recreated the atmosphere of the American West before European and American audiences principally through his now famous Wild West Show.

Cody was never employed by the Winchester company to publicize its products, but Winchesters were associated with him and many of his fellow marksmen in the Wild West Show from the very beginning. Cody was featured in over 200 'nickel novels' (the forerunners to modern comic books) and, either directly or indirectly, was always associated with Winchester firearms, as is evidenced by the following quote from one of those cheap thrillers. 'Buffalo Bill turned in his saddle and sent a dozen shots from his Winchester rattling back up the hill at the savages...Crack! Crack! went Buffalo Bill's Winchester, and howls and yells followed the reports.'

One of Cody's personal Winchester favorites was his smoothbore .44 Caliber Model 73 with which he used shot shells. These shells were necessary for safety reasons, because the shot would disperse and drop harmlessly within the grounds of the exhibition centers. However, this in no way detracted from Cody's marksmanship. He was known to have terrified his wife by shooting coins from between the fingers of his own children (who of course had complete confidence in their father's acumen). Winchester never failed to publicize the fact that its guns were the first choice of such star performers. This semi-elitism became the hallmark of Winchester advertising. A typical example would read:

'Look all the makes over, but if you are not swayed from your purpose of getting the gun with the maximum of strength, safety, ease and certainty, good shooting and good wearing qualities, you will surely select a Winchester. There are other makes, but the Winchester is the only one that has successfully stood every conceivable test that sportsmen could put to it, and also the rigid technical trials of the US Ordnance Board, embracing strength, accuracy, penetration, endurance, excessive loads, defective shells, rust and dust.

'Its popularity with sportsmen and its official endorsement by Government Experts are convincing proof of its reliability and wearing and shooting qualities. Stick to a Winchester and you won't get stuck!'

Far right: **Buffalo Bill Cody, the showman of the American frontier, did much both directly and indirectly to spread the fame of Winchester firearms. In his famous Wild West Show, he and his fellow sharpshooters—including Annie Oakley—used Winchester rifles and ammunition. As the hero of Western nickel novels *(at right, above and below)*, Buffalo Bill was armed with Winchester rifles in his battles against Indians and outlaws.**

Robert Peary

Admiral Robert Peary, had long claimed to be the first man to reach the North Pole on 6 April 1909. While controversy has raged around Peary's achievement one thing is certain: he carried with him a Winchester Model 92. Advertisements such as the following were circulated by Winchester in 1909, under the heading 'The Rifle That Helped Peary Reach the North Pole.' Peary is quoted as saying—

'Personally I always carry a Winchester rifle. On my last expedition I had a Model 1892 .44 caliber Carbine, and Winchester cartridges, which I carried with me right to the North Pole. After I left the ship, I depended upon it to bring down the fresh meat that we needed. Since 1888, both in Nicaragua and in the Arctic regions, I have always used the Winchester Repeaters.

'Each of my Arctic expeditions since '91 has been fitted with these arms. The last expedition carried the .44-40 Carbine, for use on deer, seals, hare and the like, and the .40-82 for use on musk-oxen, walrus and polar bears. In facing the polar bears, in gathering a herd of musk-oxen with the least expenditure of time and priceless ammunition, and in securing the greatest number of walrus out of an infuriated herd in the least time, I desire nothing better than a Winchester Repeater.'

Adolph and 'Plinky' Topperwein

In the early 1900s, Winchester employed the son of a German gunsmith named Adolph Topperwein to represent the company as an exhibition shooter. In 1903, Topperwein married Elizabeth Servaty, who worked in the ammunition loading room at the Winchester plant at New Haven. Until she was married, Mrs Topperwein's acquaintance with shooting had not extended beyond the loading of ammunition, but she quickly proved to have an exceptional talent as a markswoman.

She set her first world's record in trap shooting in 1904 at the World's Fair in St Louis by breaking 967 clay targets out of a possible 1000 and was ever after known as 'Plinky' Topperwein. Winchester immediately arranged to have the Topperweins travel as a team, and they took their place among the world's finest shooters. The couple's feats are indeed impressive.

Plinky once 'shot trap' for a total time of five hours using a pump gun, and hit 1952 clays out of 2000 thrown. Adolph, firing a .22 caliber Winchester rifle at 2.5 inch wooden blocks tossed into the air, shot steadily, eight hours a day for 10 consecutive days, hitting a total of 72,491 blocks, missing only nine. Of the first 50,000 blocks, he missed only four, and had a number of runs of more than 10,000 without a miss, and one perfect run of 14,540.

Even more amazing, Adolph specialized in targeting playing cards held edge-on at a distance, and one of his most astonishing feats involved extinguishing lighted matches that were held by assistants—by shooting backward from a prone position using a mirror to sight the target! He could also hit potatoes thrown directly toward him, break balls thrown over his head from directly behind, and break targets thrown directly in front of him.

His most famous shot was billed as never having been accomplished by any other shooter in the world. In this, he threw balls into the air and broke them, using a rifle with solid bullets while riding a bicycle at full speed. The Topperweins retired from travelling for Winchester in 1940, still retaining their status as excellent mark shooters—despite the fact that Adolph was 70 years old and his wife but a few years younger. They had done much to keep the name of Winchester before the public.

Opposite, above: **Admiral Robert Peary carried a Winchester Model 92 with him on his historic expedition to the North Pole.** ***Opposite, below:*** **The midnight sun on the horizon above the Arctic.** ***Below, left and right:*** **'Plinky' and Adolph Topperwein. For 36 years, the Topperweins represented Winchester as exhibition shooters. Their fancy shots did much to promote the Winchester name.**

Major Winchester

The Winchester Repeating Arms Company put John M Browning *(far right)* to work redesigning the repeating action of the Models 73 and 76. The end result was the Model 1886 *(above)*, a rifle with an exceptionally smooth operating action—capable of handling the heavier, more powerful ammunition loads.

Browning Models

Rifles

Single Shot Rifle. This was John M Browning's first firearm model, invented in 1878 when he was 23 years old. The patent was filed on 12 May 1879, and US Patent Number 220,271 was granted on 7 October 1879. Production by the Browning Brothers in Ogden, Utah Territory, began about 1880 and continued until 1883, with a total of approximately six hundred rifles manufactured. Manufacturing and sales rights were sold to the Winchester Repeating Arms Company in 1883 and the arm appeared in 1885 as the Winchester Single Shot Model 1885.

The Single Shot is a lever action, exposed hammer, fixed barrel single shot rifle. The hammer drops down with the breechblock when the rifle is opened and is cocked by the closing movement. It can also be cocked by hand. The Single Shot has been adapted to over 33 different calibers, more than any other single shot or repeating rifle known. Including both rimfire and center fire types, its loads range from the .22 Short to the .50-90 Sharps. It was the first Winchester rifle capable of handling the most powerful metallic cartridges of the period.

Barrel lengths vary depending on the model, from the light carbine, with a 15-inch barrel, to the 30-inch Schuetzen. Barrel styles are round, octagon, or half octagon. The weight of this arm ranges from 4.5 to 13 pounds, depending on specifications. Model styles include sporting and special sporting rifles, special target rifles, Schuetzen rifle, carbine, musket and shotgun. Stock types are many and various.

Through the years, the Single Shot was produced in a variety of models. The light carbine (called the 'Baby Carbine') appeared in 1898. The takedown model was

introduced in 1910. A special military target version was introduced in 1905; in 1914 it was revamped as the Winder Musket, named in honor of Colonel CB Winder, and was used for training troops in World War I. In 1914 the Single Shot was also made into a shotgun, chambered for the three inch, 20 gauge shell. The Single Shot was discontinued in all models in 1920. Total production of all models was approximately 140,325, which includes the 600 unit production by the Browning Brothers.

Single Shot Rifle

Winchester Single Shot Rifle

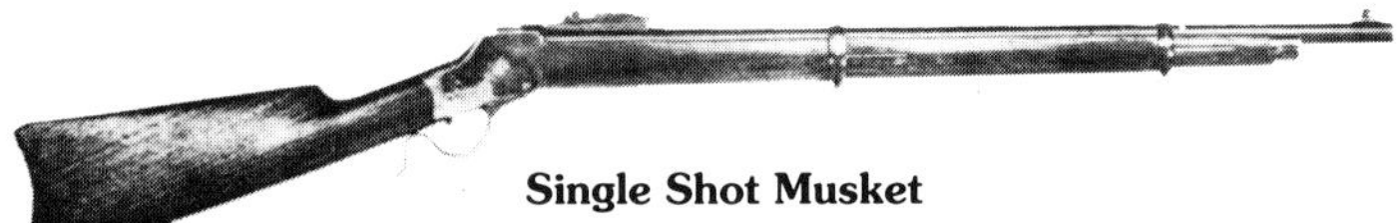

Single Shot Musket

Single Shot, Baby Carbine

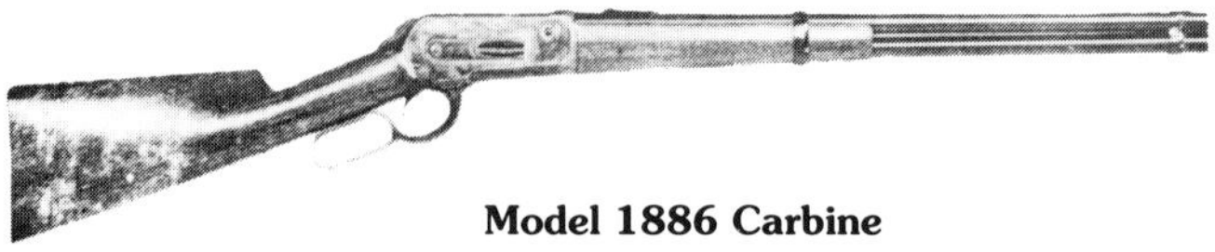

Model 1886 Carbine

Model 1886 Lever Action Repeating Rifle. Invented in 1882–83, this was the first Browning-designed repeating rifle to be manufactured. It was also the first repeating rifle to successfully employ sliding vertical locks, which effectively sealed the breech and barrel of the gun; as such it was the forerunner of all later Browning lever action repeating rifles. The patent was filed on 26 May 1884, and the US Patent No 306,577 was granted on 14 October 1884. Purchased by Winchester in October 1884, it appeared in 1886 as Model 1886.

The 1886 Lever Action is a tubular magazine, fixed barrel repeating rifle in a wide variety of calibers, including .45-70 US Government, .40-82 WCF, .45-90 WCF, 40-65 WCF, 38-56 WCF, .50-110, .40-70 WCF, .38-70 WCF, .50-100-450, .33 WCF. Options included a choice of full or half length tubular magazine of varying capacities, depending on the ammunition used.

Safeties on this firearm are manual and mechanical, and barrels include 26-inch round, octagon or half octagon, and 22-inch round. Special barrels and magazines finished to specifications were available until 1908. Stock types range from the sporter with straight or pistol grip, to extra

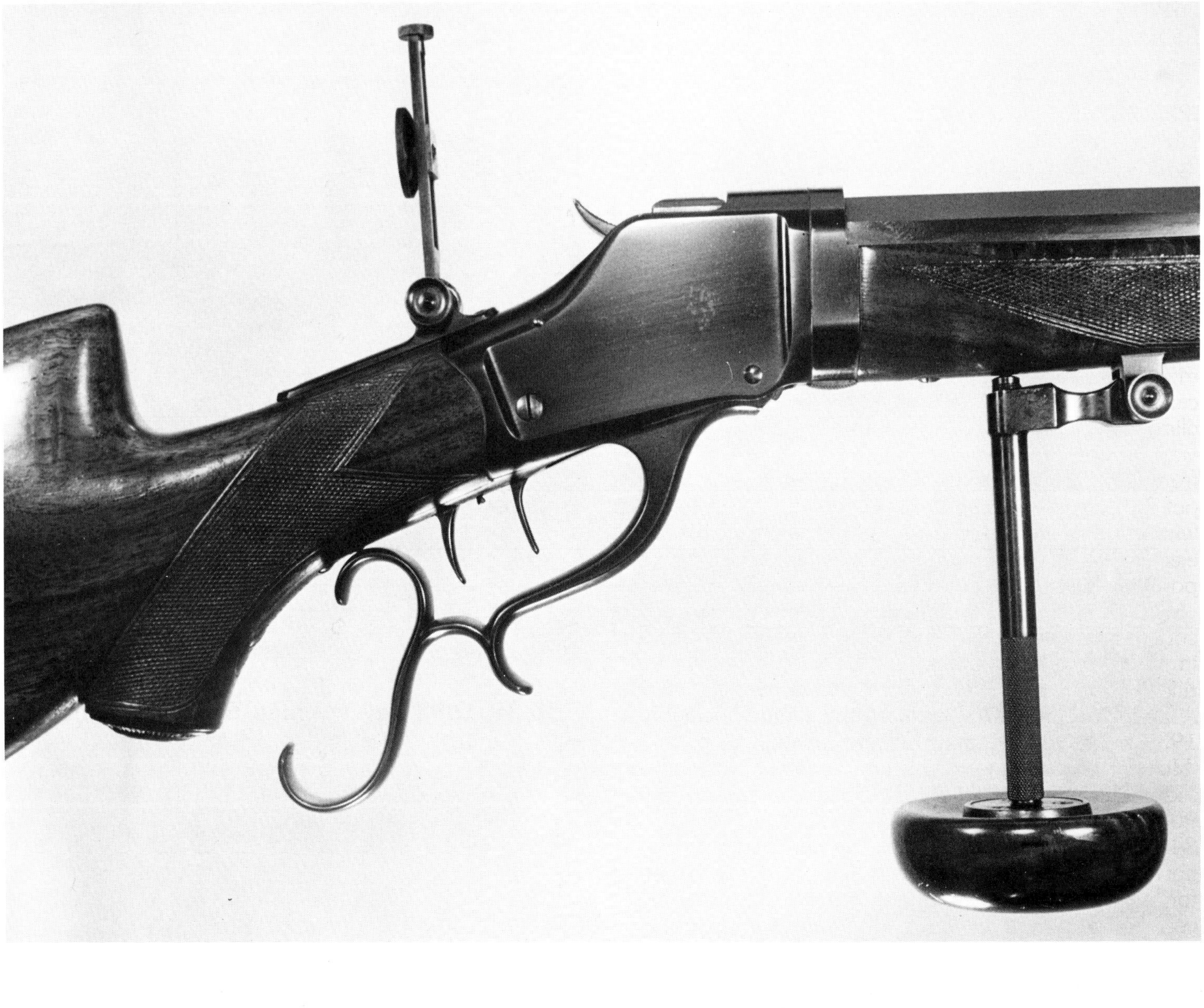

lightweight, to shotgun, carbine and musket type stocks. The weight varies widely, depending on specifications and caliber.

In 1894, it was converted to a takedown model. In 1936 the Model 1886, slightly modified to handle the .348 Winchester cartridge, became the Model 71. The Model 1886 was discontinued in 1935 with 159,994 produced; the Model 71 was discontinued in 1957 with 43,267 produced—making the total for this gun 203,261 units during a production life of 71 years.

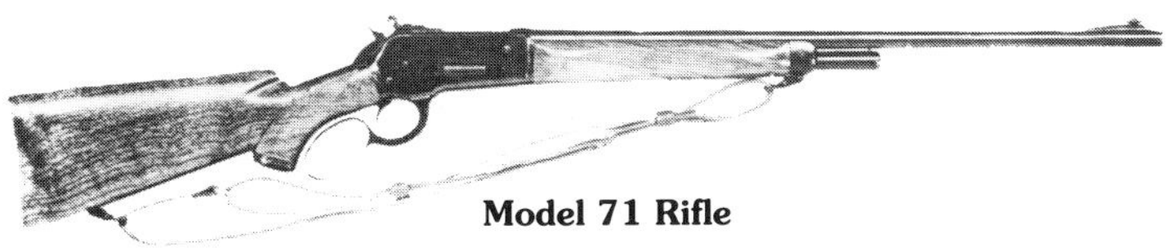
Model 71 Rifle

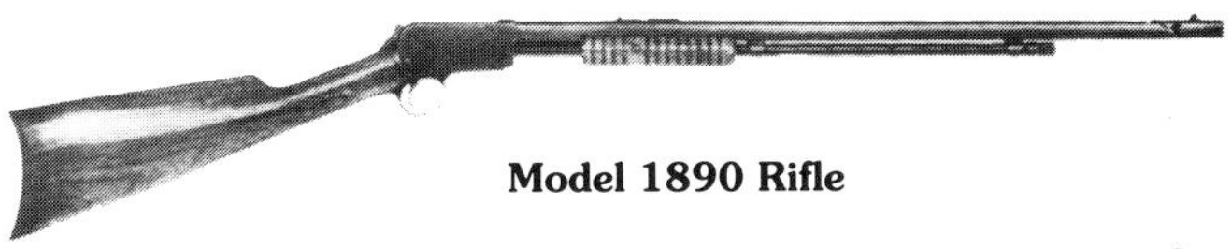
Model 1890 Rifle

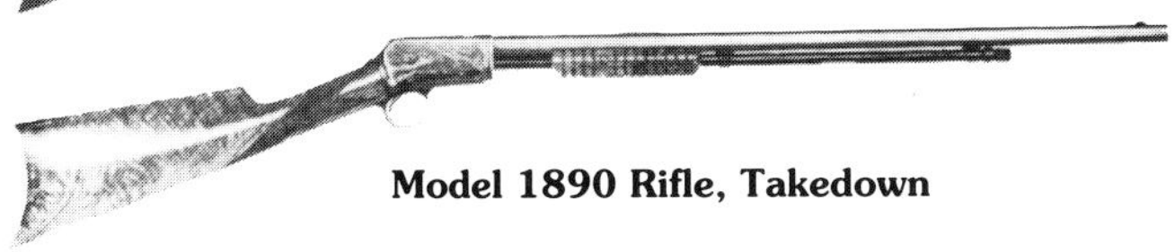
Model 1890 Rifle, Takedown

Model 1890 .22 Caliber Pump Action Repeating Rifle. The patent application for this gun was filed on 13 December 1887, and US Patent Number 385,238 was granted on 26 June 1888. It appeared in 1890 as the Winchester .22 Caliber Repeating Rifle Model 1890, and was the first repeating pump action gun manufactured by Winchester.

The Model 1890 is a tubular magazine repeating rifle of .22 caliber (.22 short, long rifle and WRF; not originally interchangeable) with a tubular magazine of varying capacity (from 15 shorts to 11 long rifles). It has a sliding breechblock, operated by forearm slide, and both manual and mechanical safeties. It has a 24-inch octagon barrel and weighs from 5.75 to six pounds. Available stocks include a standard rifle type, with curved steel butt plate, and straight grip and optional pistol grip stocks.

The Model 1890 has been called 'the most popular .22 caliber pump action rifle ever made.' The radical improvement in this rifle over previous .22 caliber repeaters was the carrier mechanism. Previously no positive method of handling the .22 caliber short cartridges had been developed. Browning suceeded by installing a fingerlike cartridge stop in front of the carrier—this metered one cartridge at a time onto the carrier from the magazine. At the correct instant, when the spent cartridge from the chamber had been ejected, the carrier raised and held the new cartridge in positive alignment with the chamber for loading.

First manufactured with its barrel fixed to the frame, it was converted to takedown in 1893. The Model 06, introduced in 1906, incorporated a modification which enabled one rifle to accept all .22 caliber cartridges, except the .22 WRF. A 20-inch round barrel replaced the 24-inch octagon. In 1932 the Models 90 and 06 were renamed as combined 'Model 62,' with the introduction on both of a barrel with slightly different specifications and new sights. The Models 90 and 06 were discontinued in 1932 with 849,000 and 848,000 produced respectively; the Model 62 was discontinued in 1958 with 409,475 produced—making the total for this gun 2,106,475 units, with a production life of 69 years.

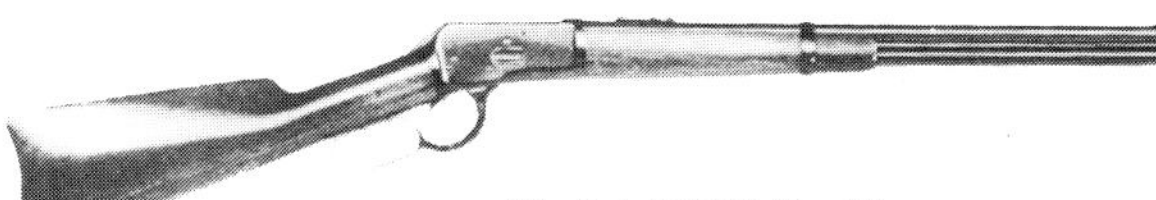
Model 1892 Carbine

Model 1892 Rifle, Takedown

Model 1892 Lever Action Repeating Rifle. This model, first manufactured by Winchester in 1892 and known as the Winchester Model 92, has the same basic design as the Model 1886, and incorporates many of its special features, including the double locking system, covered under US Patent Number 306,577. Two additional patents covered it—Number 465,339, filed on 3 August 1891 and granted on 15 December 1891, and Number 499,005, filed on 19 September 1892 and granted on 6 June 1893.

The Model 1892 is a simplified, lighter version of the Model 86, specifically designed for smaller calibers including .44-40, .38-40, .32-20 and .25-20, with a tubular magazine capacity of from five to 17 rounds. This firearm has both manual and mechanical safeties, and weighs from 5.5 to eight pounds, depending on model and caliber. Barrel lengths and styles include 24-inch round, octagon or half octagon for rifles; 20-inch round for carbines; and 30-inch round for muskets. Shorter barrels from 14 to 20 inches and special lengths up to 36 inches are also available. Stock types include sporting, carbine and musket with straight grips and fancy models with a pistol grip.

Originally, the 1892 was made with its barrel fixed to its frame, but became available in a takedown model in 1893. A modified version with a decreased magazine capacity was introduced in 1924 as the Model 53. Its successor, the Model 65, was introduced in 1933. The Model 53 was discontinued in 1932 with a total production of 24,916 units; the Model 65 was discontinued in 1947, with a total of 5704 units; the Model 92, though not produced except in the carbine model for several years after the introduction of the Model 53, was not officially discontinued until 1941, at which time 1,004,067 units had been manufactured. The manufacturing total for all variants combined stands at 1,034,687 units.

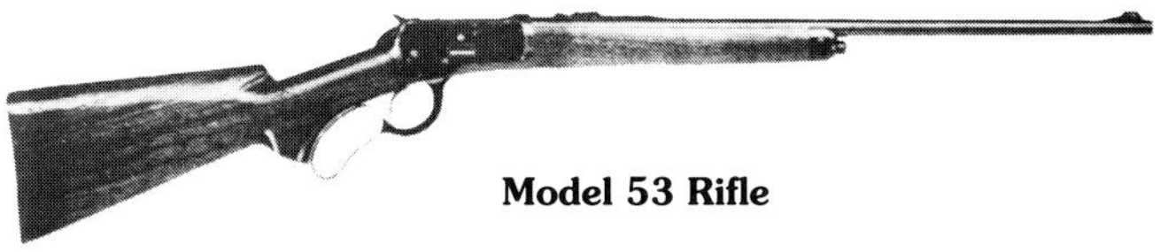
Model 53 Rifle

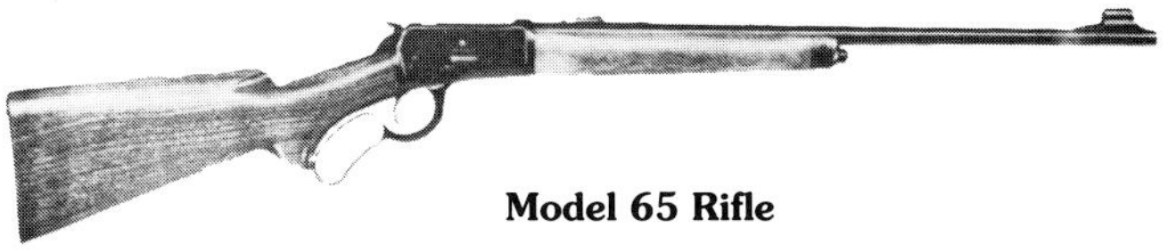
Model 65 Rifle

Model 1894 Lever Action Repeating Rifle. The patent for this gun was filed on 19 January 1894, and US Patent Number 524,702 was granted on 21 August 1894. It was first manufactured by Winchester in 1894 and was known as the Winchester Model 1894. Often called 'the most famous sporting rifle ever produced,' the Model 94 is

Far left: **The Model 1885 Single Shot Schuetzen Rifle. Although repeating rifles were gaining in popularity during the 1880s, such high-quality single shots as this have never lost their loyal following.**

Above, from top to bottom: A handsomely engraved Model 1886, an unadorned variant (like the Model 1876 pictured on page 45, the Model 1886 was a favorite of Theodore Roosevelt) and the Model 1906 Slide Action Repeater, which Winchester introduced when it learned that Stevens Arms Company was planning to bring out a new line of repeating rifles chambered for .22 caliber cartridges. *At right:* An advertisement for the Winchester Repeating Arms Company.

WINCHESTER REPEATING
Fire Arms,
MANUFACTURED BY THE
WINCHESTER
Repeating Arms Company,
NEW HAVEN, CONNECTICUT.
CARTRIDGE
H
TRADE MARK
44/100.
CARTRIDGE
W
TRADE MARK
47/100
Punderson & Crisand, New Haven, Ct

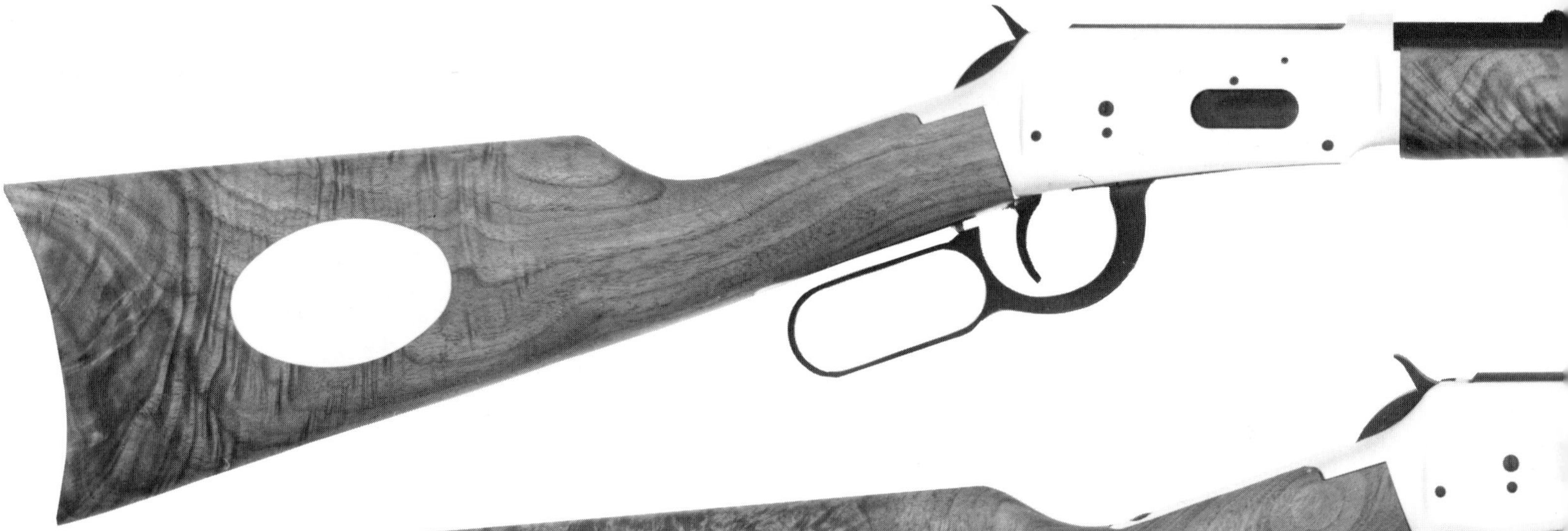

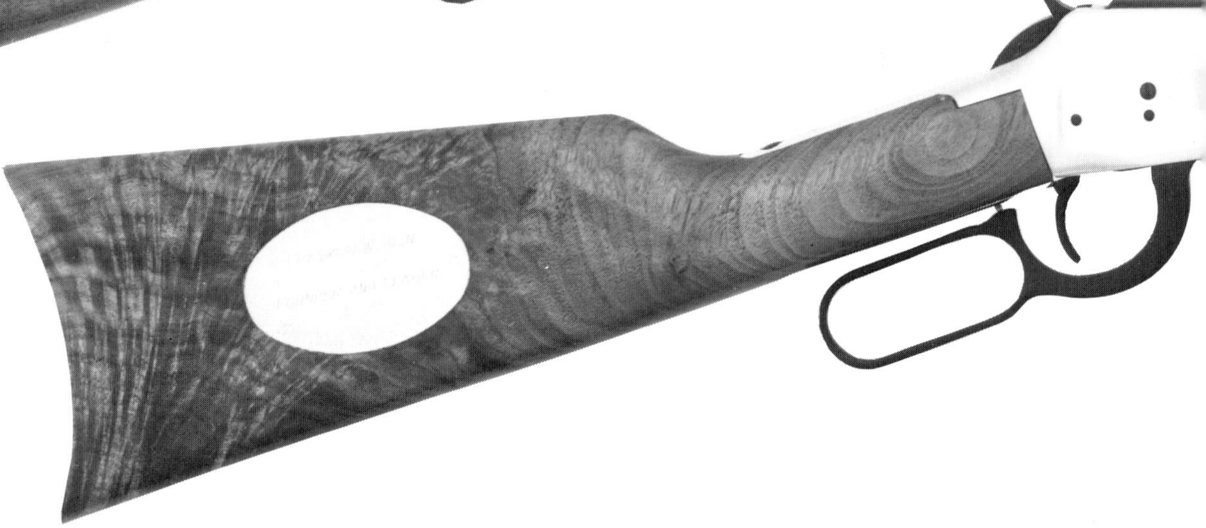

perhaps best known as the 'Winchester .30-30.' It was revolutionary in that it was the first sporting repeating action rifle to handle smokeless powder cartridges.

It is a lever action, tubular magazine, repeating rifle in .32-40 and .38-55 (both black powder) calibers. In 1895, .25-35 and .30-30 were added, and .32 Special in 1902, all three using smokeless powder. This firearm has a tubular magazine of various capacities, ranging from three to eight cartridges, manual and mechanical safeties, and adjustable sights. Barrel lengths and styles are 20-inch round, 22-inch round, octagonal or half octagonal, and weights range from 5.75 to 6.25 pounds for carbine models, to seven to 7.75 pounds for other variants. Model styles include sporting rifle, fancy sporting rifle, extra lightweight rifle and carbine.

First manufactured as a repeater, the Model 94 became available in a takedown model in 1895. Modified versions include the Model 55, introduced in 1924 (the principal differences being a shorter barrel, a redesigned stock and a

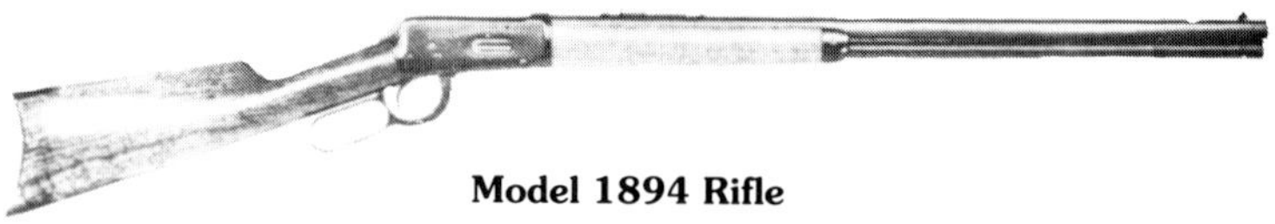

Model 1894 Rifle

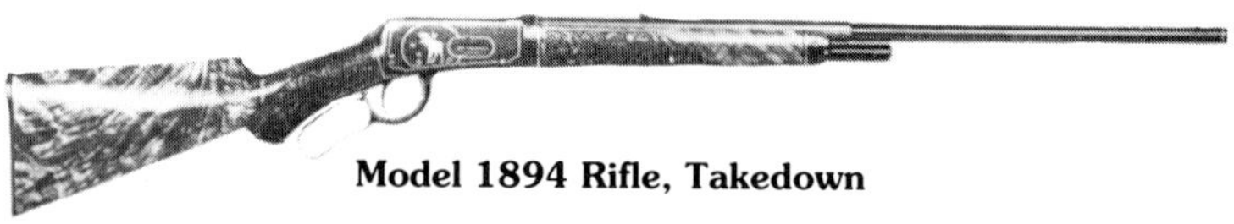

Model 1894 Rifle, Takedown

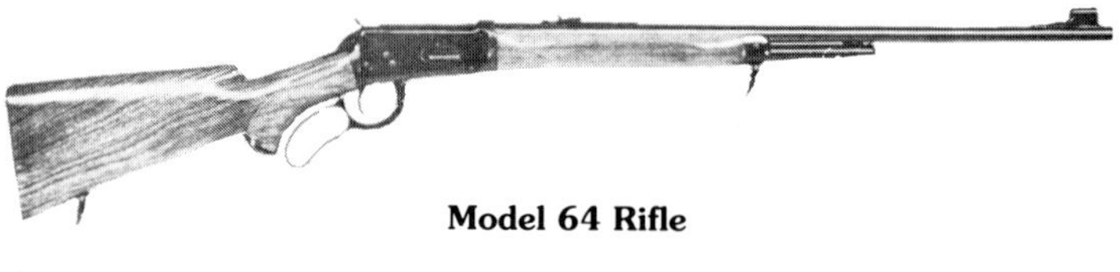

Model 64 Rifle

***At top, above and below:* The Centennial Model 1894 Rifle and Carbine honoring Oliver F Winchester and Franklin W Olin, respectively, two men who shaped the history of Winchester firearms. *At bottom:* The Model 55.**

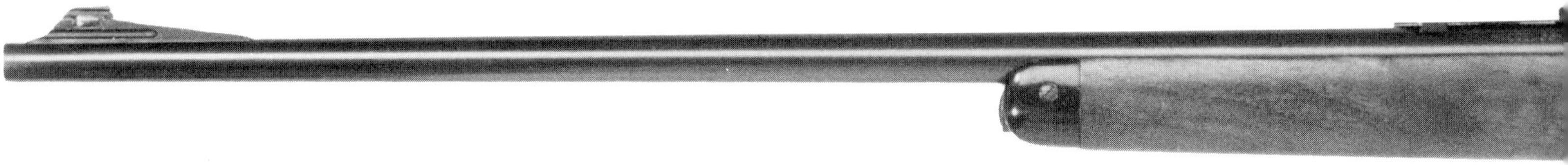

switch to half magazine) and the Model 64, introduced in 1933 (the main difference being the steel used). The Model 55 was discontinued in 1932 and the Model 64 in 1957. Still in production as the Model 94 carbine, this rifle has outsold any other manufactured by the Winchester Repeating Arms Company. Over two and a half million had been produced by 1962.

Model 1895 Lever Action Repeating Rifle. The patent application on this gun was filed on 19 November 1894, and US Patent Number 549,345 was granted on 5 November 1895. It was first manufactured by Winchester in 1896 and was known as the Winchester Model 95. This was the first nondetachable box type magazine rifle designed to handle the jacketed sharp nosed bullets.

It is a lever action rifle, with a wide range of calibers—.30 US Army (Krag), .38-72, .40-72 Winchester, .303 British, .35 Winchester, .405 Winchester, .30 Government 1903, .30 Government 1906, 7.62mm Russian. This firearm has a box magazine of from four to six rounds capacity, and manual and mechanical safeties. Barrel lengths are varied, from 22 to 36 inches in round, octagon or half octagon styles. Weight also varies, depending on barrel and caliber. Available stock types include sporting and fancy sporting, carbine and musket.

Four slightly differing versions of the musket appeared between 1895 and 1908. One, the Musket .30 Army Model 1895 US Army Pattern, was adopted by the US Army in 1895. The same year some 10,000 muskets chambered for the .30-40 Krag cartridge were purchased by the US Army for use in the Spanish-American War. Prior to America's entry into World War I, 293,816 of these guns, chambered for the 7.62mm Russian cartridge, were sold to Russia. A takedown version of the rifle appeared in 1910. Model 95 was discontinued in all models in 1931 with a total production of 425,881 units.

Above: Winchester Model 94 Rifle in .357 caliber 'big bore.' *Below:* Two variants of the Model 95 Lever Action Repeating Rifle. The Model 95 was introduced to meet the demand for a big game weapon and was widely used by hunters in both North America and Africa. *Far right:* John M Browning and his brother (photo right) Matt on an elk hunting trip in Montana.

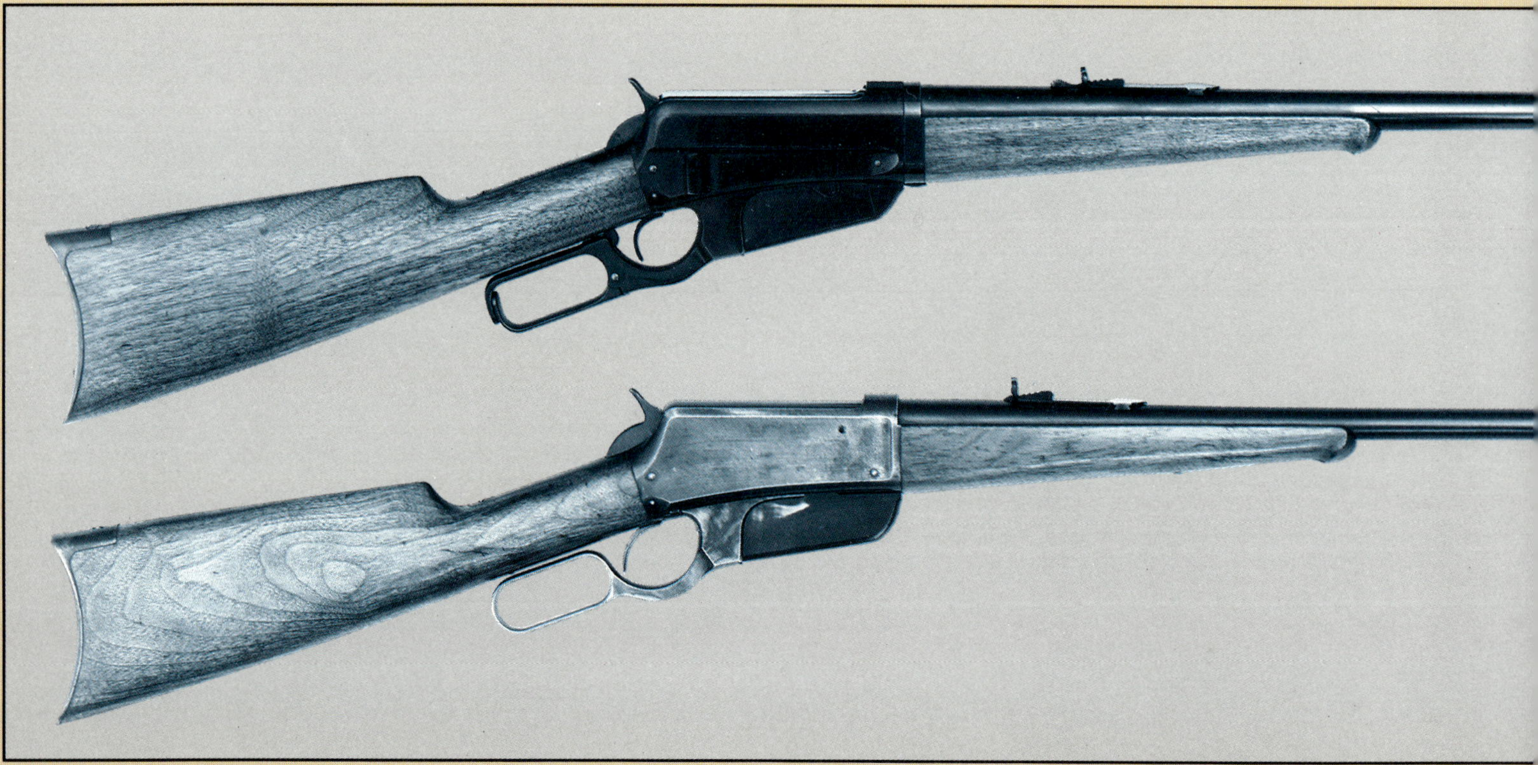

Below, from top to bottom: **Modifications on the Model 1900 Bolt Action Single Shot Rifle—The Model 1902 Rifle, featuring a different trigger guard shape and a short trigger pull; the Model 1904 Rifle with a longer, heavier barrel; and the Model 99 Thumb Trigger Rifle, which uses a button to release the firing pin.**

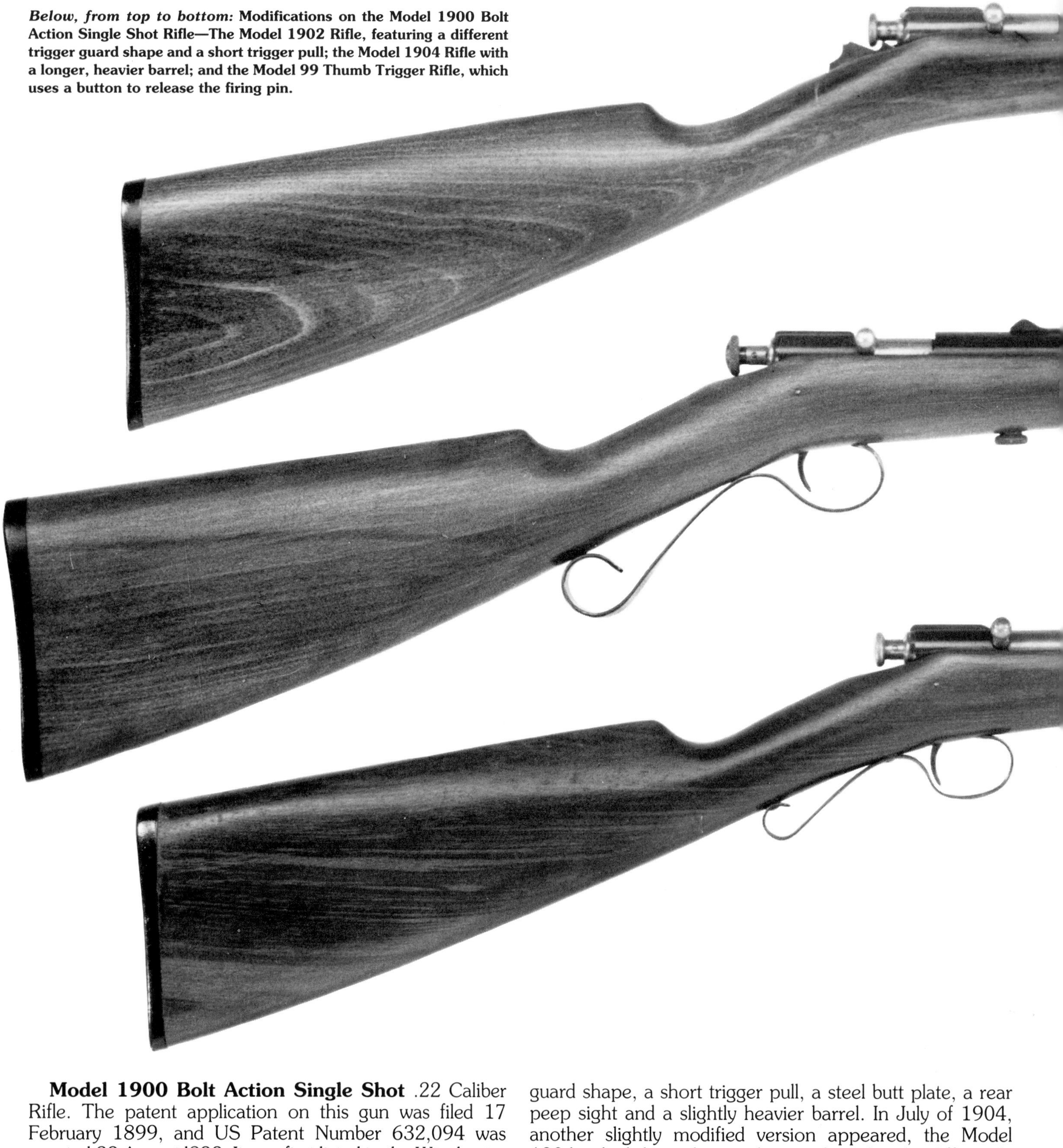

Model 1900 Bolt Action Single Shot .22 Caliber Rifle. The patent application on this gun was filed 17 February 1899, and US Patent Number 632,094 was granted 29 August 1899. It was first listed in the Winchester 1899 catalogue as the Winchester Model 1900 Single Shot Rifle. Designed as a low priced, single shot 'plinking' rifle, it has an especially simple construction and has been widely copied.

It is a bolt action, single shot, takedown rifle of .22 caliber (short and long, interchangeable), with a manual safety. This Single Shot Rifle weighs 2.75 pounds, has an 18-inch round barrel, and is available with a straight grip.

The Model 1900 was discontinued in 1902; the Model 1902, announced the same year, has a modified trigger guard shape, a short trigger pull, a steel butt plate, a rear peep sight and a slightly heavier barrel. In July of 1904, another slightly modified version appeared, the Model 1904, which has a longer, heavier barrel and a differently shaped stock.

An interesting modification is the Model 99 Thumb Trigger Rifle, which also appeared in 1904. This rifle is void either of trigger or trigger guard. Just behind the cocking piece on the bolt is a button called the thumb trigger. When in shooting position, the shooter merely presses downward on this button with the thumb to release the firing pin.

In 1928 and the years following, Winchester brought out other variations, the Models 58, 59, 60 and 68. In 1920, a shotgun version similar to the Model 1902 was announced;

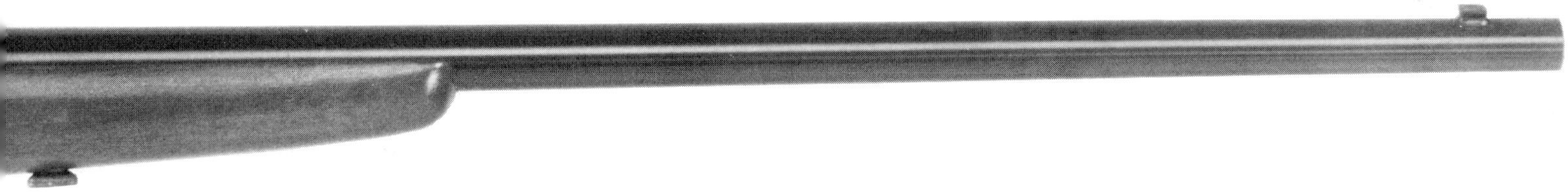

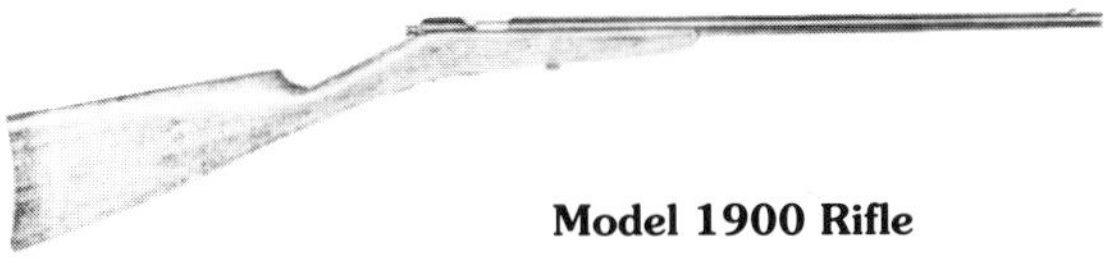

Model 1900 Rifle

this was the Winchester Model 36 Single Shot Shotgun. This is the only American made shotgun chambered for 9mm paper shells; it was discontinued in 1927. The last model, the 68 (introduced in 1934) was discontinued in 1946. Production totals are as follows: Model 1900, 105,000; Model 02, 640,299; Model 04, 302,859; Model 99 Thumb Trigger, 75,433; Model 36 Shotgun, 20,306; Model 58, 38,992; Model 59, 9293; Model 60, 165,754; and Model 68, 100,730 for a total of 1,458,666 units.

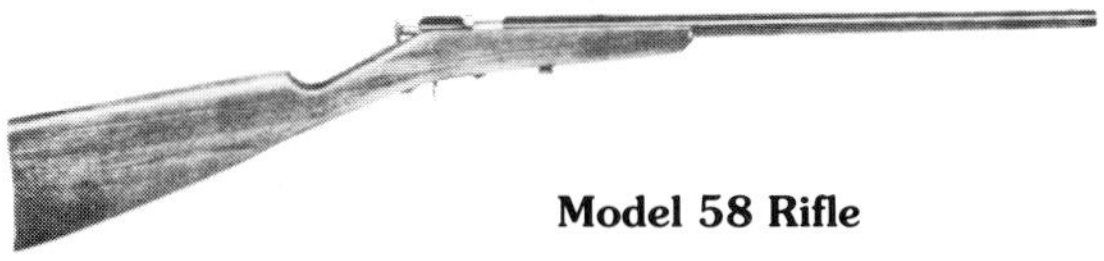

Model 58 Rifle

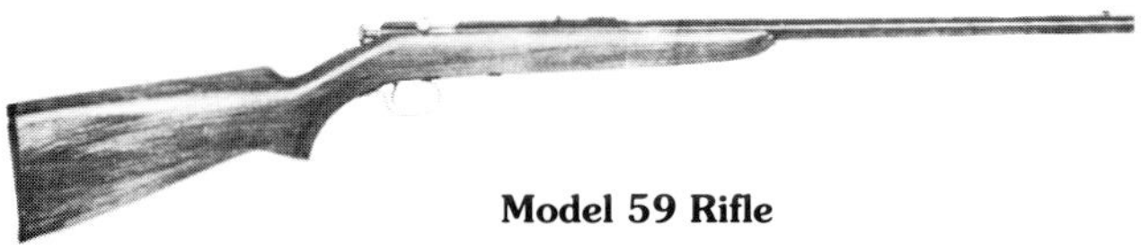

Model 59 Rifle

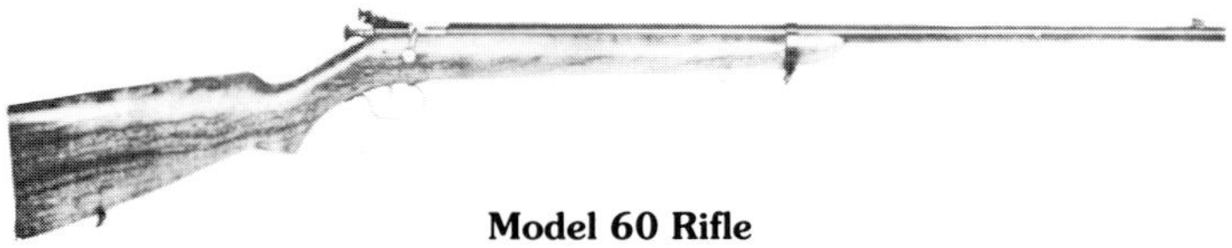

Model 60 Rifle

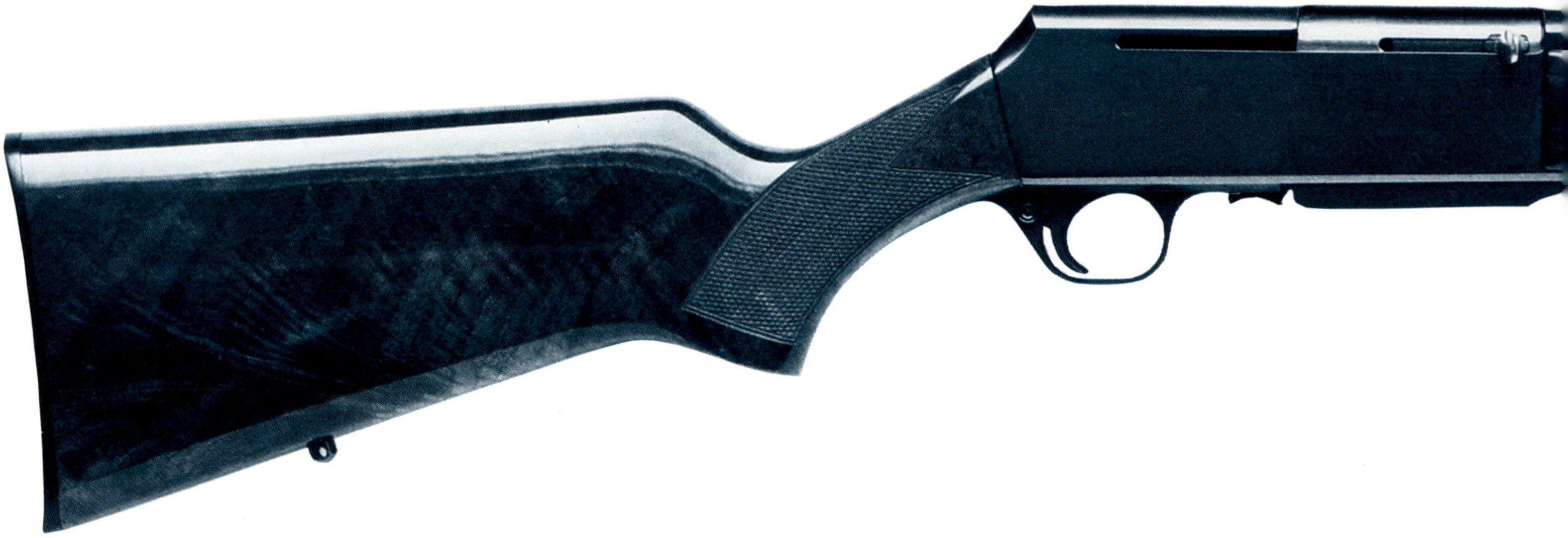

The Browning Automatic Rifle. The Browning Automatic Rifle was invented prior to 1917. The patent application on this gun was filed on 1 August 1917, and US Patent Number 1,293,022 was granted on 4 February 1919. Best known as the BAR, it is also known as the Browning Light Machine Rifle Model 1917, the Light Browning, the Colt Automatic Machine Rifle, and the Fusil Mitrailleur Browning. The BAR was officially adopted by the United States government in 1917 and first saw combat use in July of 1918.

The specifications that follow refer to the Colt Model 1917. It is an air cooled, gas actuated, automatic machine rifle. The BAR has a caliber of .30-06, with a detachable box magazine of either 20 or 40 rounds, staggered arrangement. The safety is a fire control change lever. When the change lever is in its forward position, marked with the letter 'F,' the rifle will shoot one shot with each pull of the trigger. In vertical position, marked with the letter 'A,' the rifle will fire full automatic. In the rearward position, marked by the letter 'S,' the rifle is safe. On some models, the 'F' position, when the lever is all the way forward, merely reduces the rate of fire in such a way that single shots may be fired by quickly pulling and releasing the trigger. It weighs 17.37 pounds with full magazine, and has a 24-inch round barrel. Stock type is standard rifle only, with pistol grip. A takedown, its 70 pieces can be completely disassembled and reassembled in 55 seconds.

A lever on the receiver permits fully automatic or semiautomatic firing. At full automatic, it can be fired at a maximum rate of 480 rounds per minute, emptying a 20 round magazine in two and one-half seconds. This rifle has a bolt lock which pivots to the rear of the bolt, and rises in and out of locking engagement with a shoulder on the receiver. The rear of the bolt lock is attached to the slide by a link, which is free to reciprocate backward and forward. Attached to the forward part of the barrel is a gas piston which derives its energy from a gas port drilled through the barrel wall. In operation, the piston sends a slide to the rear, and, in turn, the slide, through its link connection with the bolt lock, pivots the bolt lock downward out of locking contact with the receiver.

During World War I approximately 52,000 were manufactured by Colt, Winchester, and Marlin-Rockwell. After World War I, production rights reverted to Colt and, by arrangement with John M Browning, Fabrique Nationale began European production in 1920, calling their model the Fusil Mitrailleur Leger. Large quantities of the rifle have since been manufactured for various European countries. It was made in 6.5mm, 7mm, 7.62mm, 7.9mm and .30-06 caliber. It has been widely copied; many nations historically have had the BAR or a similar gun in reserve.

In 1922 the US Army brought out its Cavalry Model. In 1933, Colt produced the 'Colt Monitor' for police and bank guard use. In November 1939, there were approximately 87,000 in our war reserve. Approximately 177,000 were produced in this country during World War II. In comparison with earlier models, the World War II BAR, the M1918-A2, is slightly heavier and equipped with flash hider and bipod. It carries the conventional stock without pistol grip. A decelerating device permits a cyclic rate of fire of 350 to 550 rounds per minute. No mechanical provision is made for semiautomatic fire, but, at a low rate of fire, single shots can be discharged by pulling and quickly releasing the trigger.

The Fabrique Nationale version differed from the Colt model chiefly in having a quicker takedown mechanism which allowed the barrel to be removed easily for replacement. Total production by FN to the end of 1961 was 67,310 units.

At top: **The Browning Automatic Rifle—aka BAR.** ***At right:*** **The original Browning Brothers Store in Ogden, Utah, circa 1882—and the staff of 'The Largest Arms Factory Between Omaha and the Pacific.'**

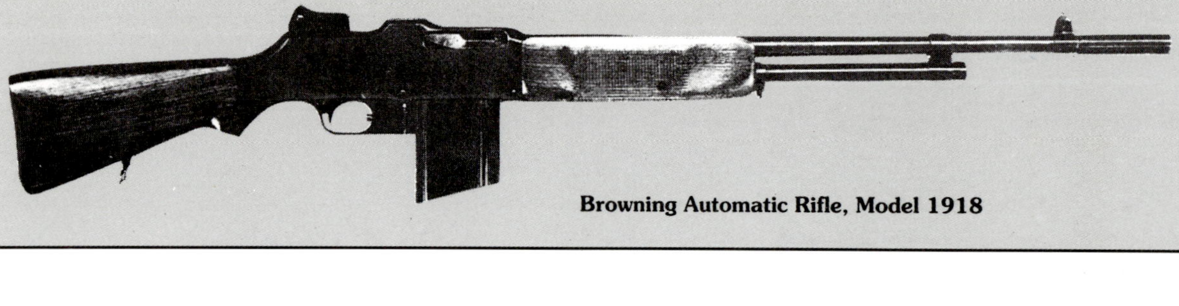

Browning Automatic Rifle, Model 1918

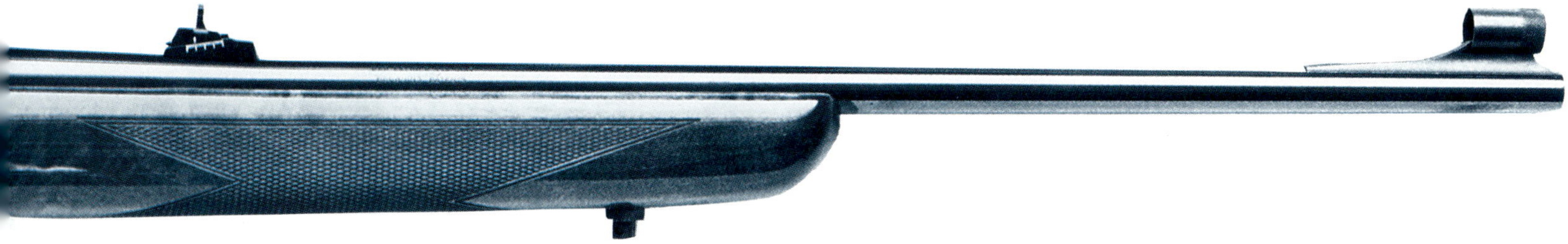

J.M. BROWNING & BRO.
GUNS, PISTOLS,
AMUNITION & FISHING TACKLE

Shotguns

Model 1887 Lever Action Repeating Shotgun. This was the first lever action repeating shotgun made in the United States and has been called 'the first really successful repeating shotgun.' The patent application on this gun was filed on 15 June 1885 and US Patent Number 336,287 was granted on 16 February 1886. Manufacturing and sales rights were sold to the Winchester Repeating Arms Company in 1886, and it appeared in June 1887 as the Winchester Model 1887 Shotgun.

It is a lever action repeating shotgun in 10 and 12 gauge, with a tubular magazine that holds four shells in the magazine and one in the chamber. In 1898, 10 and 12 gauge riot guns were added. Barrel lengths are 30 and 32 inches for both the 10 and 12 gauge, with full chokes and 20 inches for the 10 and 12 gauge riot gun, with cylinder bore. The 10 gauge weighs about nine pounds; the 12 gauge, about eight pounds. The standard stock is plain with a pistol grip and a hard rubber butt plate.

The model 1887 was discontinued in 1899. Redesigned to handle the smokeless powder loads, it reappeared in 1901, in 10 gauge only, as the Model 1901. This model was discontinued in 1920. 64,855 of the Model 1887 were produced and 13,500 of the Model 1901—for a total of 78,355.

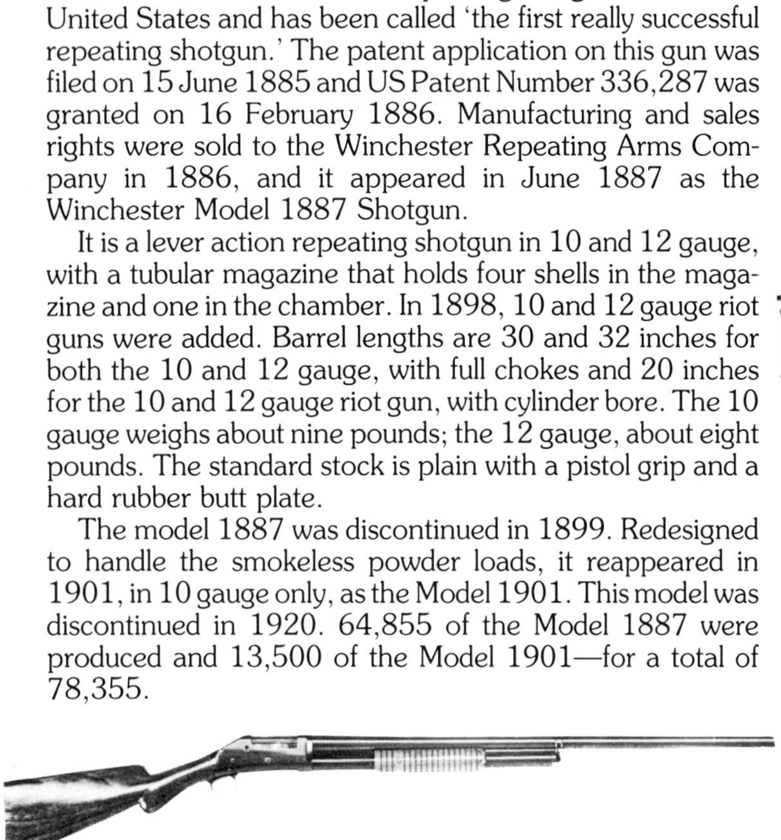

Model 1893 Shotgun

Model 1893 Pump Action Repeating Shotgun. The patent application on this gun was filed on 30 June 1890, and US Patent Number 441,390 was granted on 25 November 1890. Manufacturing and sales rights were sold to the Winchester Repeating Arms Company in 1890; the gun was announced in April 1894 as the Winchester Model 1893. This was the first shotgun with a sliding forearm of pump action manufactured by Winchester.

It is a pump action repeating shotgun in 12 gauge with a five shot, tubular magazine. Barrel lengths are 30 and 32 inches with a full choke—modified choke or cylinder bore specials being available. The Model 1893 weighs about 7.75 pounds and is available in plain stocks with pistol grip and a hard rubber butt plate.

The Model 1893 was discontinued in 1897 when the Model 1897, a modified takedown version of the Model 1893, was introduced. Total production was 34,050 units.

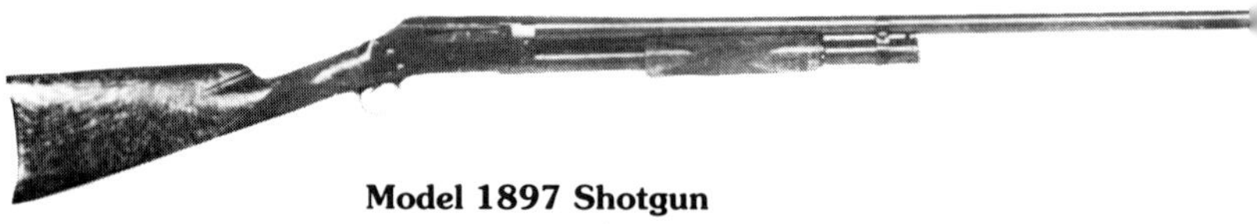

Model 1897 Shotgun

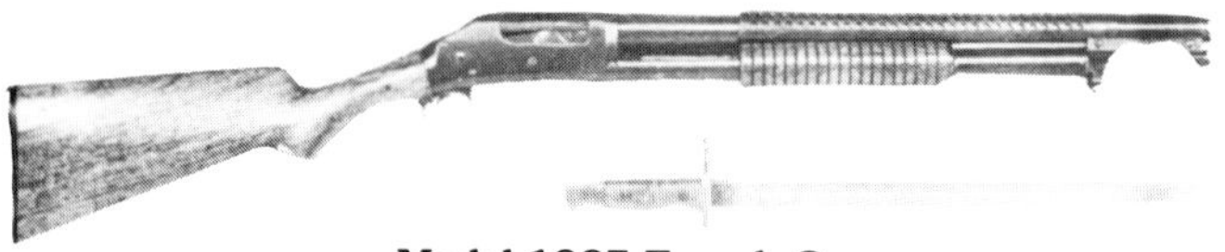

Model 1987 Trench Gun

Model 1897 Pump Action Repeating Shotgun. The Model 1897 is a modified takedown version of the Model 1893, with a stronger frame and side ejection. Introduced in November of 1897, it soon became one of the most popular shotguns in America. It is a pump action repeating shotgun in 12 and 16 gauge (takedown exclusive on the 16, and optional on the 12) with a five shot, tubular magazine. Variant examples have barrel lengths of 20, 22, 26, 28, 30 and 32 inches, with cylinder bore, modified, intermediate, full or Winchester skeet chokes. The weights of the various examples of the Model 1897 are from 7.1 to 7.9 pounds, and standard stocks are plain, with pistol grip and hard rubber butt plate, plus optional checkering and other specialties having been available.

In addition to its great popularity as a sporting arm, the 97 saw other uses. A short barrel version was widely used as a riot gun by law enforcement agencies; also for a time the American Express Company armed its messengers with this

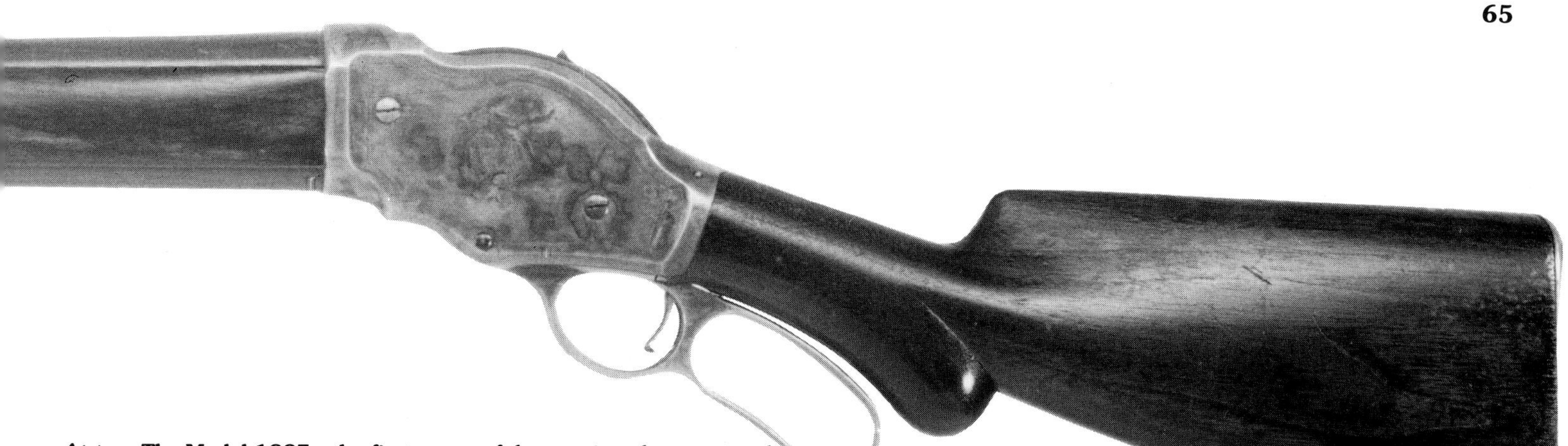

At top: The Model 1887—the first successful repeating shotgun—and a modification, the Model 1901 *(at bottom)*. *Below:* A Hollywood depiction of a stagecoach guard and his trusty Winchester. In the movies, it was usually a rifle, but in reality a shotgun—especially a sawed-off shotgun good for short-range intimidation—did more to discourage would-be bandits.

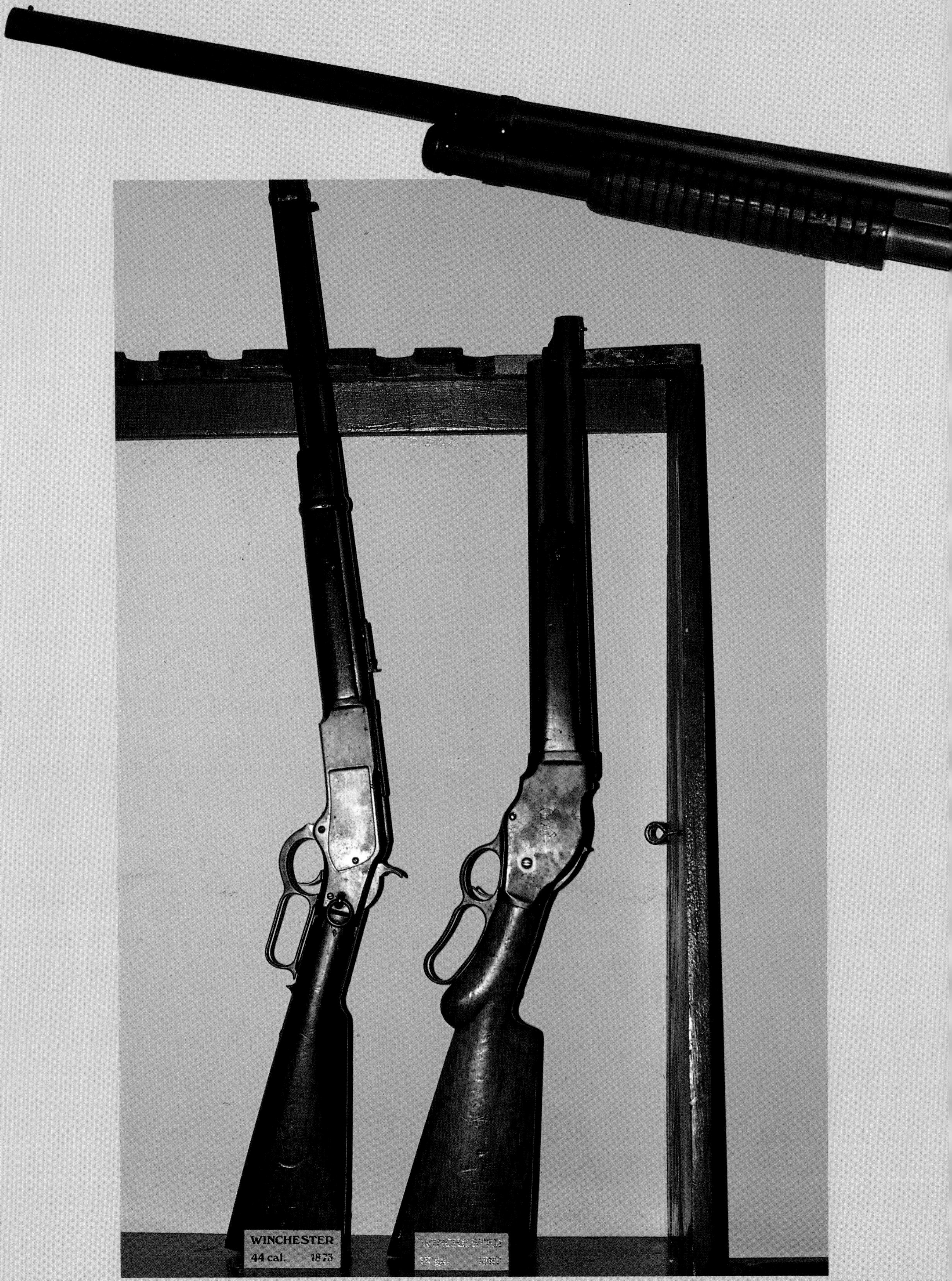
WINCHESTER
44 cal. 1873

Winchester firearms responded to diverse situations. During World War I, a later variant of the Model 1897 *(at left)* was used to combat German infantrymen (as seen in the painting below) as they charged American troops in the trenches. *Far left:* John M Browning's creativity allowed Winchester to expand its product line with a lever action repeating shotgun—a short-barrel Model 1887 (photo right). Designed to use a center fire cartridge, the Model 1873 Rifle (photo left) strengthened the company's nonmilitary market.

firearm. During World War I the 97 was used by American troops as a trench gun, with considerable success.

The standard, trap, pigeon and brush guns were introduced in 1897, followed by the riot gun, in 1898; the tournament, in 1910, and the trench gun, in 1920, (but previously manufactured for the US Army use in World War I). The trap gun was discontinued in 1931 and was succeeded by the special trap gun, which was discontinued in 1939. Other models were discontinued as follows—the pigeon gun was discontinued in 1939, the brush gun in 1931, the riot gun in 1935 and the trench gun in 1935.

The tournament gun was discontinued in 1931 and was succeeded by the standard trap, which was discontinued in 1939. The standard Model 1897 was discontinued in 1957. Total production for all models stands at 1,240,700.

Winchester's Rare Brownings

John M Browning sold Winchester a total of 44 firearms—31 rifles and 13 shotguns. Of this number, only seven rifles and three shotguns were actually manufactured. Most of the remaining 34 arms, comprising 24 rifles and 10 shotguns, exist only as one-of-a-kind prototype specimens in either the Winchester or Browning Museums.

Among the rarest guns in the world, they are unique in design, functionality and construction. The Winchester Museum also contains three other Browning rifles and one other shotgun that were neither bought by Winchester nor patented for manufacture principally because they infringed previously existing patents.

The following is a listing of these rarest-of-the-rare American firearms.

Rifles

Repeating Rifle in .38 Caliber. The patent application on this gun was filed on 6 March 1884, and US Patent number 312,183 was granted on 10 February 1885. This .38 caliber rifle has a 28-inch octagon barrel and weighs 9.25 pounds. In this lever action, tubular magazine rifle, the locking arrangement of the breechblock is greatly simplified, inasmuch as the lever itself, having a seat in the receiver, acts as the locking lug.

The lever is spring loaded in such a way as to allow the lever to snap in and out of engagement with its socket, or locking shoulder, in the receiver.

.38 Caliber Repeating Rifle

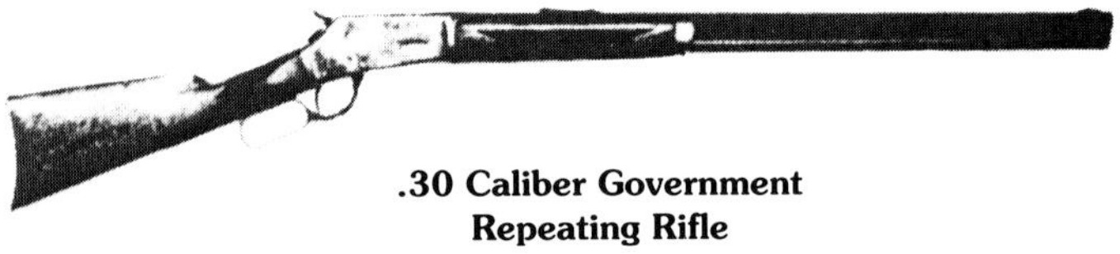

.30 Caliber Government Repeating Rifle

Lever Action .30 Government Caliber Repeating Rifle. The patent application for this gun was filed on 5 March 1885, and US Patent number 324,296 was granted on 11 August 1885. This lever action, .30 Government caliber, tubular magazine rifle has a 28-inch octagon barrel and weighs 9.25 pounds.

The main novelty of this gun is its locking lug, which is pivoted on the rear of the sliding breechblock in such a manner that the front end rises in and out of locking engagement with the receiver and breechblock. The locking lug also serves as the link between the rotary motion of the lever, and the longitudinal motion of the breechblock.

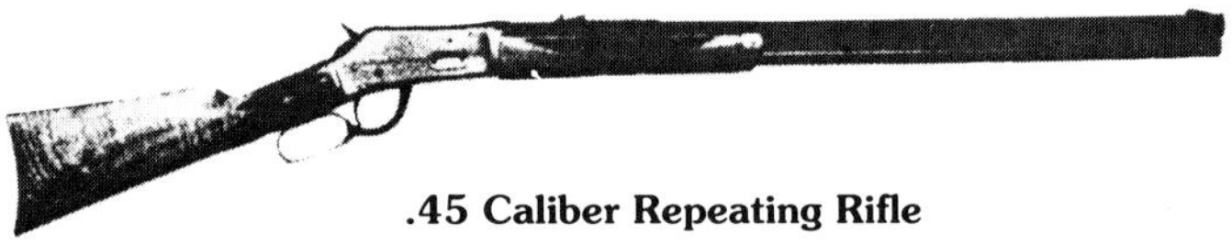

.45 Caliber Repeating Rifle

Lever Action Repeating Rifle in .45 Caliber. The patent application for this gun was filed on 26 May 1885, and US Patent number 324,297 was granted on 11 August 1885. It has a 28-inch octagon barrel and weighs 9.25 pounds. This .45 caliber, lever action, tubular magazine rifle features a toggle locking system, wherein the lever is the front part of the toggle, which 'bears' in a socket in the breechblock.

The rear half of the toggle pivots at the rear, against the receiver, and houses the trigger. Opening the lever flexes the toggle joint and allows the bolt to slide to the rear.

As in many of John M Browning's designs, one part has several functions: the links of the toggle joint serve to form a stout breech locking system, and act as the linkage necessary to reciprocate the breechblock. The action also features a firing pin block which renders the gun safe until the lever piece is fully closed.

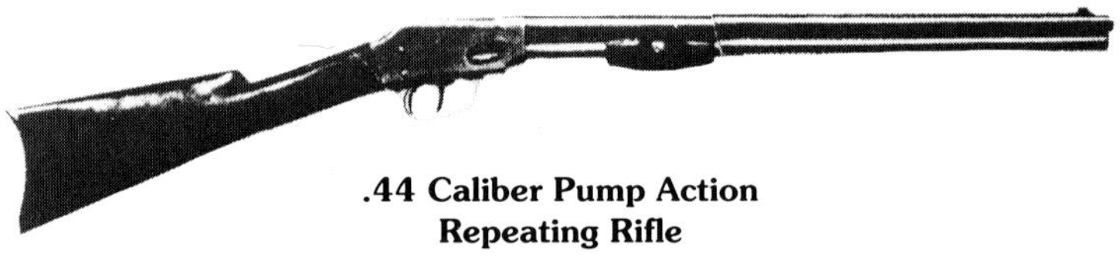

.44 Caliber Pump Action Repeating Rifle

Pump Action Repeating Rifle in .44 Caliber. The patent application on this gun was filed 12 July 1886, and US Patent number 367,336 was granted 26 July 1887. This .44 caliber firearm has a 20-inch round barrel and weighs close to six pounds. It is a pump action rifle having a tubular magazine and a pivoting breechblock, the rear end of which rises into locking engagement with the receiver.

Instead of being placed to the rear of the breechblock, as is most common, the hammer works through a recess nearly in the middle of the breechblock, allowing for a very short receiver. The tail end of the hammer projects into the trigger guard forward of the trigger, allowing the hammer to be cocked or uncocked manually.

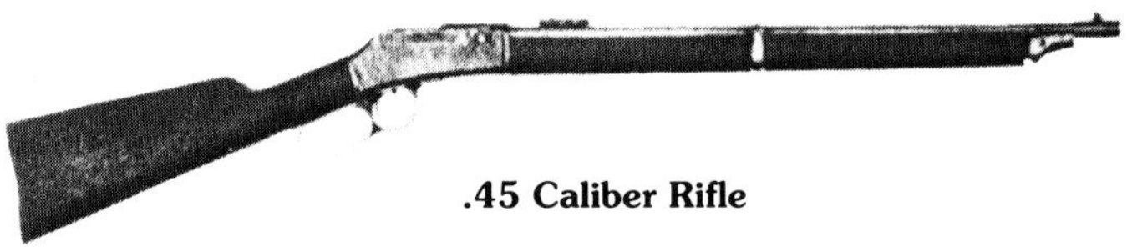

.45 Caliber Rifle

Lever Action Repeating Rifle in .45 Caliber. The patent application on this gun was filed 21 November 1887, and US Patent number 376,576 was granted 17 January 1888. This lever action, tubular magazine .45 caliber rifle has a 22-inch round barrel and weighs 7.2 pounds. It loads through the bottom and ejects from the top of the receiver.

The forward end of the operating lever contains the lock mechanism. The operating lever is hung to the receiver by a link, which extends to the rear. The forward end of the lever is guided by channel cuts in the receiver. The sliding firing pin acts as a hammer and is cocked by the closing movement of the lever.

Lever Action Repeating Rifle in .45-70 Caliber. The patent application on this gun was filed on 18 November 1889, and US Patent number 428,887 was granted on 27 May 1890. This .45-70 caliber, box magazine rifle has a 28-inch round barrel and weighs 8.1 pounds.

In this unique firearm the breechblock, magazine and lever are one unit. With the lever closed the assembly is in locking engagement with the receiver and comprises an effective breech closure. The cartridges ride in the magazine recess in a 'bullet end down position,' with magazine spring pressure urging them forward. Opening the lever turns this whole assembly and brings the cartridges in line with the bore. This rifle can be operated either as a repeater or as a single shot firearm.

A selector lever on the side of the magazine portion urges the top cartridges out of the magazine into loading position. Closing the lever completes the loading cycle. Extraction is to the side and is effected by a combination extractor and pivot slide attached to the breech assembly.

Another interesting feature of this rifle is the firing pin, which acts as its own pivot sear. The front of the firing pin is latched in cocked position by a hardened screw in the receiver. A lever attached to the trigger pushes the rear of the firing pin upward, pivoting the striker out of engagement with the hardened screw.

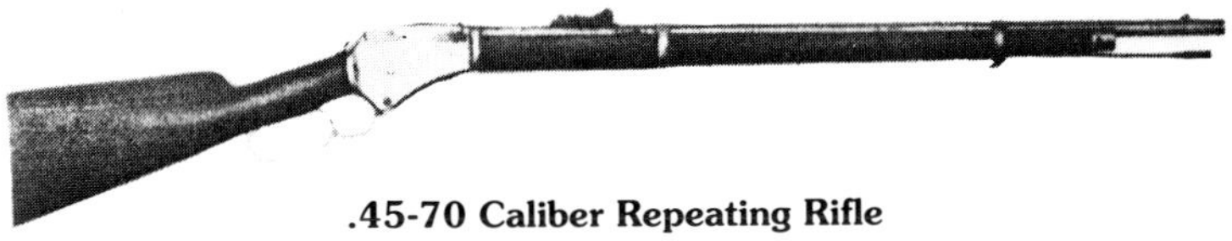

.45-70 Caliber Repeating Rifle

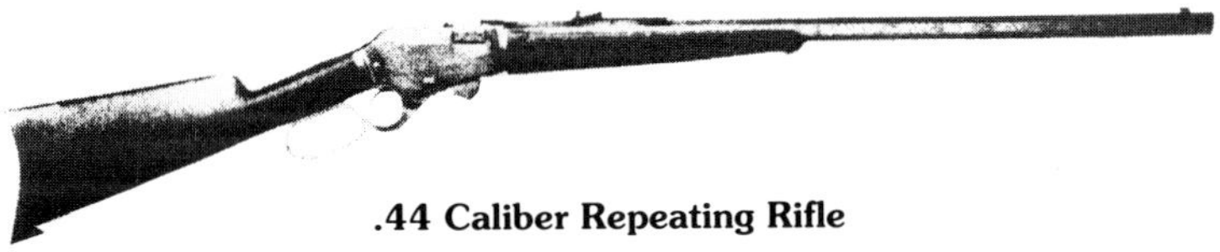

.44 Caliber Repeating Rifle

Lever Action Repeating Rifle in .44 Caliber. This is a lever action, integral revolving magazine rifle, and is very similar to the .45-70 Caliber Lever Action Repeating Rifle. The lever, magazine and breechblock are essentially one piece; the cartridges ride 'bullet down' in the magazine; the magazine is loaded from the bottom and the cartridges are inserted upward, rim first.

The unique feature of this rifle is the arrangement of the firing pin and the method for inserting the cartridges.

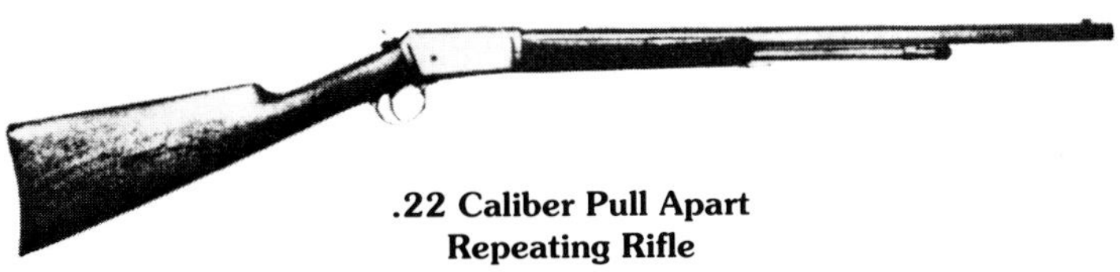

.22 Caliber Pull Apart Repeating Rifle

Pull Apart Repeating Rifle in .22 Caliber. This firearm is of the pull apart variety. Operation of the action is effected by literally pulling it open to its full extension of seven-eighths of an inch, just far enough for its .22 caliber cartridges, which are fed by a carrier from a tubular magazine.

Ignition is by a striker, the rear end of which projects from the rear of the receiver. The two main parts are unlocked from each other by pulling the trigger.

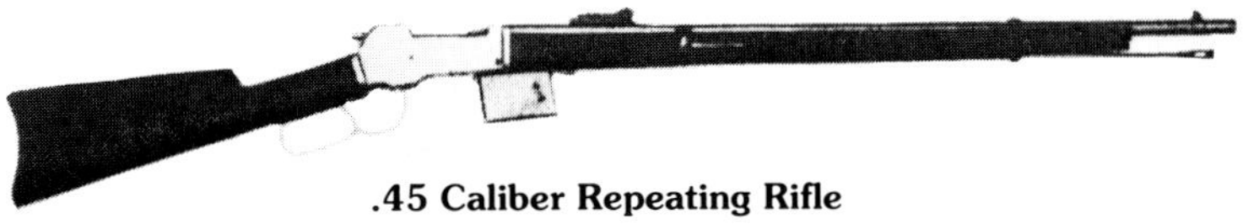

.45 Caliber Repeating Rifle

Lever Action Repeating Rifle in .45 Caliber. This military type rifle, with detachable box magazine, features a locking system with vertically rising locking lugs that are similar to the Winchester 86 and 94 models, but utilizes a striker rather than a hammer.

The novelty in this firearm is the magazine, which is positioned for the most part under the barrel forward of the breech face. The cartridges are pulled rearward out of the magazine onto a carrier by the breech bolt during its rearward movement. The carrier then lifts the cartridges into position for loading by the breech bolt during its forward movement.

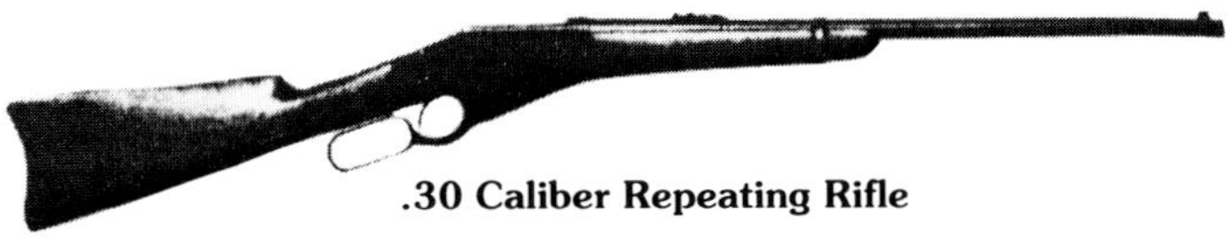

.30 Caliber Repeating Rifle

Lever Action Repeating Rifle in .30 Caliber (Number One). In this lever action box magazine rifle, the locking block is pivoted to the receiver immediately to the rear of the hammer, and encloses the hammer on both sides. Initial motion of the lever pivots the locking block downward, allowing the breechblock to slide to the rear. Ejection and loading of the magazine are through the top.

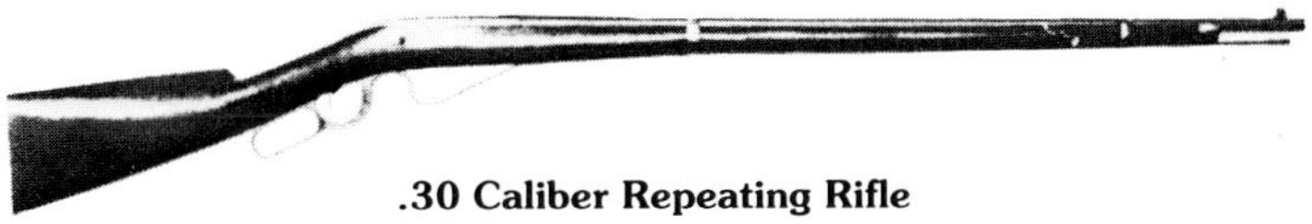

.30 Caliber Repeating Rifle

Lever Action Repeating Rifle in .30 Caliber (Number Two). This military type, box magazine lever action rifle features a novel hammer arrangement. The hammer does not pivot, as is usual in lever action rifles; it is essentially a striker which works in a recess in the upper tang of the receiver, and has an exposed ear for manual cocking. As is the case in most of Browning's lever actions, cocking is automatic with the operation of the lever. Loading is from the top by means of a cartridge clip.

.30 Caliber Pull Apart Repeating Rifles

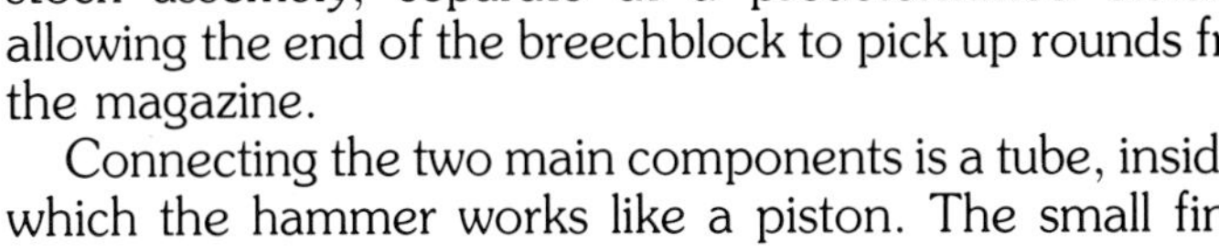

Pull Apart Repeating Rifle in .30 Caliber. This pull apart musket type rifle, with box magazine, operates in the manner common to pull-apart designs. The receiver and barrel assembly, and the breechblock, trigger guard and stock assembly, separate at a predetermined distance, allowing the end of the breechblock to pick up rounds from the magazine.

Connecting the two main components is a tube, inside of which the hammer works like a piston. The small finger

Above: This Charles Russell painting has forever captured Buffalo Bill Cody and his Winchester in a duel to the death with Yellow Hand at War Bonnet Creek.

piece at the front of the trigger guard is a sear block safety. The breechblock locks at the rear on a shoulder in the receiver.

A second variant of this design was also sold to Winchester. This model has a safety which locks the sear with the hammer cocked, and also locks the gun against accidental operation.

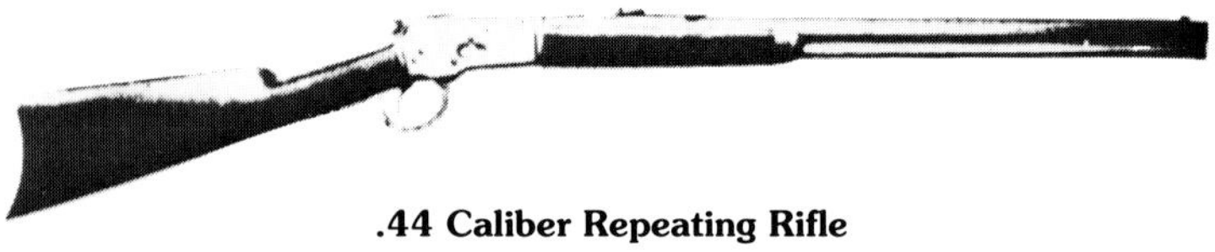

.44 Caliber Repeating Rifle

Lever Action Repeating Rifle in .44 Caliber (Number Three). This lever action, tubular magazine repeating rifle has the same action as the Winchester Model 92. It is identical in principle and differs only in minor detail.

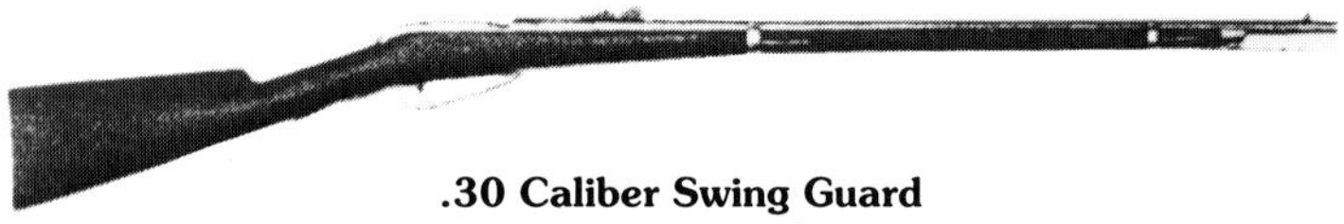

.30 Caliber Swing Guard Repeating Rifle

Swing Guard Repeating Rifle in .30 Caliber. This novel firearm works like a lever action with the lever mounted backward. The trigger is pivoted to the frame at its rear. The front of the guard is latched to the rear of the box magazine by a spring latch.

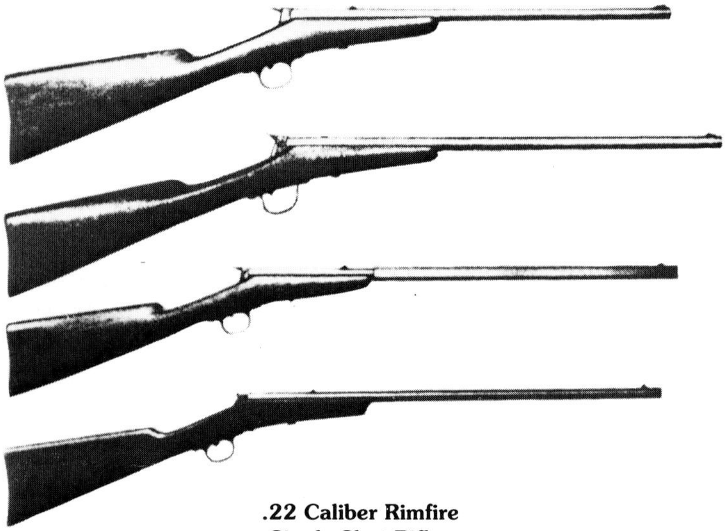

.22 Caliber Rimfire Single Shot Rifles

Rimfire Single Shot Rifle in .22 Caliber. This rifle, like the three models which follow, is of extremely simple design. The breechblock, hammer and trigger are one piece, and operate up and down at about 20 degrees from the vertical. In loading, the breech bolt is pushed down until the tail of the breechblock extends into the trigger guard, and is latched there against the force of the mainspring, which forces the breechblock upward into a locked position with the barrel.

The firing pin is a hardened pin installed rigidly on the face of the breechblock. A thumbpiece projects from the rear of the breechblock for the purpose of pushing it downward into locked position. The tail of the breechblock acts as a trigger. The gun is ready to fire the moment a fresh cartridge is placed in the chamber.

Pulling the trigger allows the breechblock assembly to spring forcibly upward into locked position. The built in firing pin ignites the cartridge simultaneously. Extraction is manual with two clearance cuts on the rear of the barrel to allow the fingers to pick out the cartridge.

A second version of this design differs in the use of a simple pushrod type extractor and a different spring arrangement on the breechblock. The third variant uses a different type of mainspring, and incorporates various minor detail changes. The fourth, and final, variant is unique only in that its replaceable firing pin is screwed into the back of the breechblock.

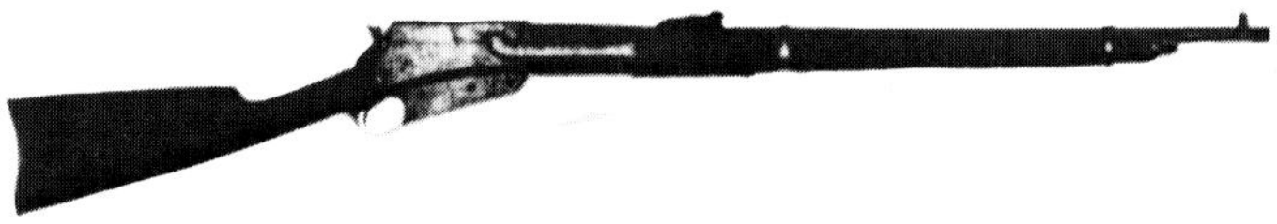

.30 Caliber Pump Action Repeating Rifle

Pump Action Repeating Rifle in .30 Caliber. This rifle has a box magazine which loads from the bottom. The breechblock is locked into a recess in the left side of the receiver, and is positively held in locking engagement with the receiver by a locking cam on the slide.

The breechblock, instead of rising into a vertical position, moves laterally into a locking position with the receiver. This gun cannot be fired until it is completely locked. The action is very smooth and is suitable for relatively low pressure cartridges.

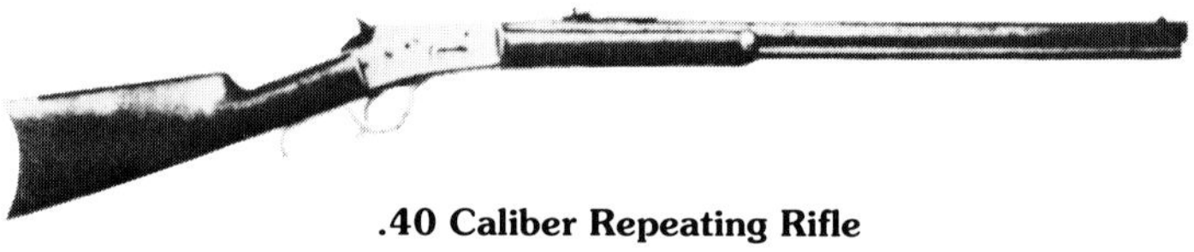

.40 Caliber Repeating Rifle

Lever Action Repeating Rifle in .40 Caliber. This tubular magazine rifle features a one piece locking block, which lifts vertically as it closes the lever into a recess at the rear of the bolt. The locking block is raised in and out of locking position by a link which also serves as a trigger housing. This arrangement disconnects the trigger from the sear until the action is fully closed.

.236 Caliber Repeating Rifle

Lever Action Repeating Rifle in .236 Caliber. This rifle has a box magazine, and loads and ejects obliquely out the top of the receiver. Its tilting breechblock is guided at the front only, with the rear being left free to follow the lever through its downward arc.

This downward motion of the lever allows for a short receiver. The actuating lever carries the trigger and hammer as a unit. The hammer is cocked by closing the lever. A projection on the rear of the mainspring guide latches the lever in closed position.

.30 Caliber Repeating Rifle

Bolt-sear Lever Action Repeating Rifle in .30 Caliber. In this lever action rifle, the sear is part of the bolt assembly, and acts on a striker, which allows the trigger to pivot as a unit with the lever. The box magazine is attached with a screw and is not freely detachable. The receiver is cut away to conform to a one piece stock. The safety on this is on the top tang to the rear of the receiver.

A second variant of this design has a two piece stock and the magazine is inside the receiver. Its magazine loading arrangement features staggered double rows of cartridges.

Shotguns

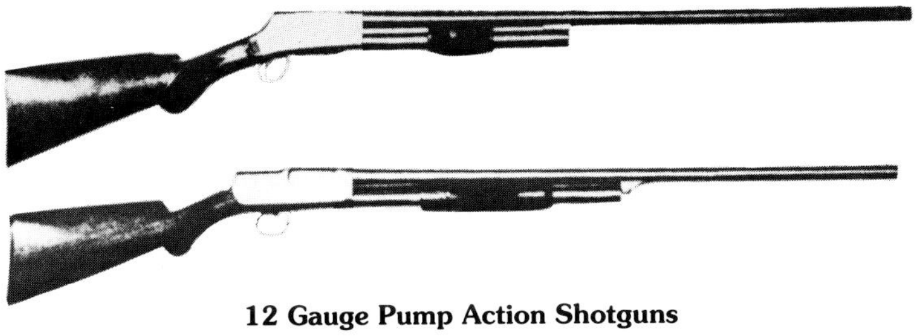

12 Gauge Pump Action Shotguns

Pump Action Shotgun in 12 Gauge. This 12 gauge, pump action shotgun is locked by a turning breechblock which is actuated by a cam slot in the slide. The slot in the receiver to the rear of the ejection opening is the passage or clearance for the large locking lug on the bolt.

The long, rail type locking lug acts as a guide for the cylindrical breechblock as it reciprocates. A standard type carrier elevates the cartridges from the tubular magazine into loading position. On the front of the carrier, however, is a simple dog which serves as a cartridge stop. A second, similar design was also sold to, but not manufactured by, Winchester. A third variant has a pivoting breechblock which locks at the rear of the side of the receiver. The slide which manipulates the breechblock is mounted on the opposite side of the receiver in such a way as to completely close the ejection opening when the gun is closed. The rear end of the magazine can pivot downward free from the receiver, allowing the tube and handle to be used as a wrench for unscrewing the barrel from the receiver.

A fourth variant has a locking system that is unusual but exceptionally strong. Instead of rotating, or pivoting, or being locked by a separate member, the whole breechblock raises vertically in and out of locking engagement with a series of locking lugs spaced along the top of the receiver. Both ends of the breechblock are raised by two links pivoted fore and aft on the slide. The extractor is pivoted to the breechblock to allow for its vertical movement.

The fifth variant incorporates many of the features which later appeared in John M Browning's automatic shotguns and in many of the modern day shotgun designs. The locking block, assembled to and pivoting from the breechblock, is locked to the upper wall of the receiver. As with most modern shotguns, the hammer and trigger mechanism are part of an assembly which is fastened inside an opening at the bottom of the receiver.

The gun has a barrel takedown using interrupted threads with a takeup ring very similar to that used in the Browning .22 Semiautomatic Rifle. The magazine tube pivots to the barrel. When the rear of the magazine is disengaged from the receiver, the tube swings down and is used as a handle to thread the barrel in and out of the receiver.

Pump Action Shotgun in 10 Gauge. This model has a tilting breechblock, which is pivotally mounted at the rear to the receiver. The front of the breechblock tilts down so far that the breechblock itself is used as a carrier, picking the cartridges up from tubular magazine with a 'tray' on top of the breechblock.

The breechblock pauses in its upward movement long enough for the extracting slide, which reciprocates longitudinally, to pick the cartridge off the top of the breechblock and force it into the chamber. The breechblock then completes its upward motion, ready for firing.

A second design, similar to this but differing in minor details, was also sold to, but not manufactured by, Winchester.

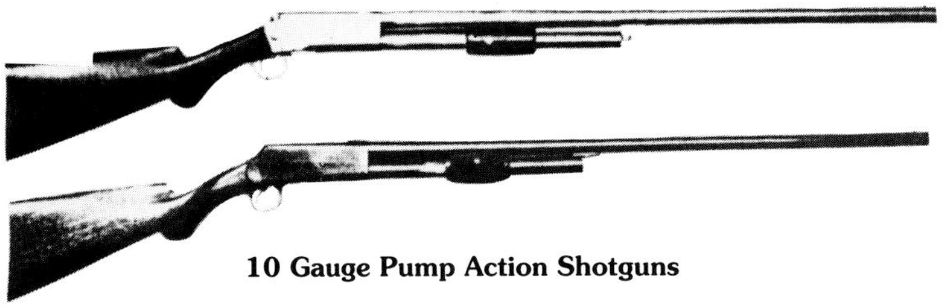

10 Gauge Pump Action Shotguns

10 Gauge Lever Action Shotgun

Lever Action Shotgun in 10 Gauge. This lever action shotgun has a tubular magazine and pistol grip. The finger lever, carrying the entire locking mechanism, is hung to the receiver by a link on the left hand side. The forward end of the link is hung on a pivot in the finger lever; the rear of the link on a pivot in the frame. The upper portion of the finger lever is guided by the receiver.

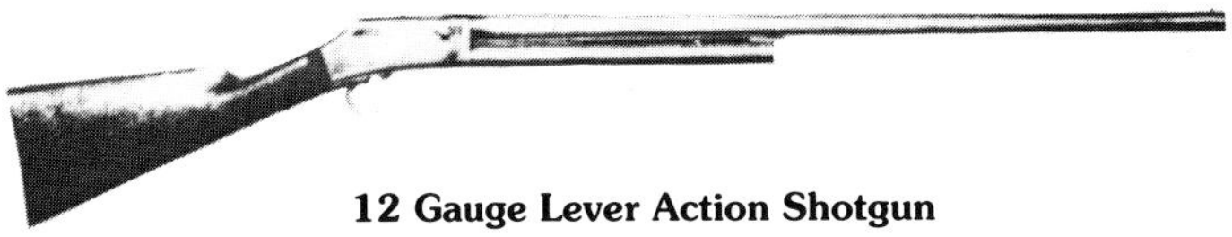

12 Gauge Lever Action Shotgun

Lever Action Shotgun in 12 Gauge. This shotgun has a tubular magazine and a one piece breechblock, trigger guard and lever combined. The breechblock works along a track on the side of the receiver, by means of a round pin visible at the front of the breechblock.

In working the lever, the greater part of the insides of the gun come out of the receiver with the lever. This, and the long lever throw, are two disadvantages of this extremely simple, rugged gun.

12 Gauge Pull Apart Shotgun

Pull Apart Shotgun in 12 Gauge. Another of John M Browning's pull apart firearms, it only handles the 12 gauge cartridge. A latch is positioned at the front of the trigger guard, to prevent accidental operation. The rear unit, which includes the trigger guard, has a lug projecting forward into the top of the receiver. The lug works on the rear of the breech bolt in such a way as to unlock it from the back of the frame.

In this model, the hammer and mainspring work inside a long tube attached to the receiver. The tube acts as a guide to keep the two essential parts—the stock and trigger assembly and the barrel and receiver assembly—in alignment when the gun is pulled apart.

Major
Through the

Western pioneers preferred the Model 1873 *(above)* for its rapid fire, rugged construction and reliability in all kinds of weather—qualities that made it ideal for short range hunting and skirmishes with Indians.

Winchesters Years

Oliver F Winchester knew that he had the first and best lever-action repeater in the world and did not mind extolling its virtues. In one of his letters, he asks the following historically pertinent questions.

'What would be the value of an army of one hundred thousand infantry and cavalry, thus mounted and armed with a due proportion of artillery, each artilleryman with a repeating carbine slung to his back?

'Certainly the introduction of repeating guns into the army will involve a change of the Manual of Arms. Probably it will modify the art of war; possibly it may revolutionize the whole science of war. Where is the military genius that is to grasp this whole subject, and so modify the science of war as to best develop the capacities of this terrible engine—the exclusive control of which would enable any government (with resources sufficient to keep half a million of men in the field) to rule the world?'

The Model 1866. This gun, the first truly operant lever action repeater, was invented by B Tyler Henry and is also known as the Henry Rifle. Various loading methods were developed and patented for the Model 1866 in both 1865 and 1866. Collectors have determined that at least four types of the 1866 were manufactured.

The first model has the Henry drop in the receiver ahead of the hammer, no flare to accommodate the fore end, an additional screw in the upper tang and an inside serial number. The second model has less drop ahead of the hammer and has the fore end flare. The third model has the drop ahead of the hammer but is less pronounced than the preceding two models and has an outside serial number usually in block numerals. The fourth model has slightly less drop in the receiver ahead of the hammer, and the serial number is usually in script numbers between the lever latch and the lower tang screw.

Model 1866 Carbine

Model 1866 Rifle

Model 1866 Musket

Winchester submitted a specially made Model 1866 to the Army trials in February of 1873. Although this Winchester did not pass all of the tests satisfactorily, it should be noted that none of the repeaters present passed the test. When one considers the details of the testing procedure, one can see why. The first test examined rapidity with aim—the number of shots fired in one minute that strike a target six feet by two feet, at a distance of 100 feet.

Winchester Experimental Rifle

The second tested rapidity at will—the number of shots that can be fired in one minute, irrespective of aim. The third tested endurance. Each gun had to fire 500 continuous rounds, without cleaning, and then the state of the breech mechanism was examined at the end of every 500 rounds. The fourth tested performance with defective cartridges. Each gun was fired once with cartridges that had been cross-filed on the head to nearly the thickness of the metal, cut at intervals around the rim and had a longitudinal cut the whole length of the cartridge from the rim up.

The fifth tested performance under dusty conditions. The gun was placed in a box and exposed to a blast of fine sand dust for several minutes; it was removed from the box, fired 50 rounds, replaced for 5 minutes, removed and fired 50 rounds more. The sixth test examined performance under rusty conditions. The breech mechanism and receiver were cleaned of grease; the chamber of the barrel was then greased and plugged, and the butt of the gun inserted to the height of the chamber in brine for 10 minutes, exposed for 2 days to the open air standing in a rack, and then fired 50 rounds.

The seventh, and final test, examined performance firing overloads. The gun was fired once with 86 grains of powder and one lead ball weighing 450 grains; and again, with 90 grains and one ball; and once again with 90 grains and two balls. The firearm was closely examined after each discharge.

Benito Juarez bought at least 1000 Model 1866s for use in his war with Emperor Maximilian of Mexico. Turkish contracts in 1870 and 1871 accounted for 46,000 muskets and 5000 carbines. The French government also bought 3000 muskets and 3000 carbines from Winchester, and Chili and Peru cooperatively bought a large consignment of 1866 Winchesters at a cost of about $90,000. The Model 1866 was officially discontinued in 1898. Peak production of over 35,000 units had been achieved in 1871.

Model 1873 Carbine

The Model 1873. The Model 1873 is the Winchester best known to collectors and the public alike. Although a tremendous number of variations were produced, collectors have designated at least four separate model types of the '73,' each distinguished by minor structural alterations. The first Model 1873s were manufactured with an iron frame

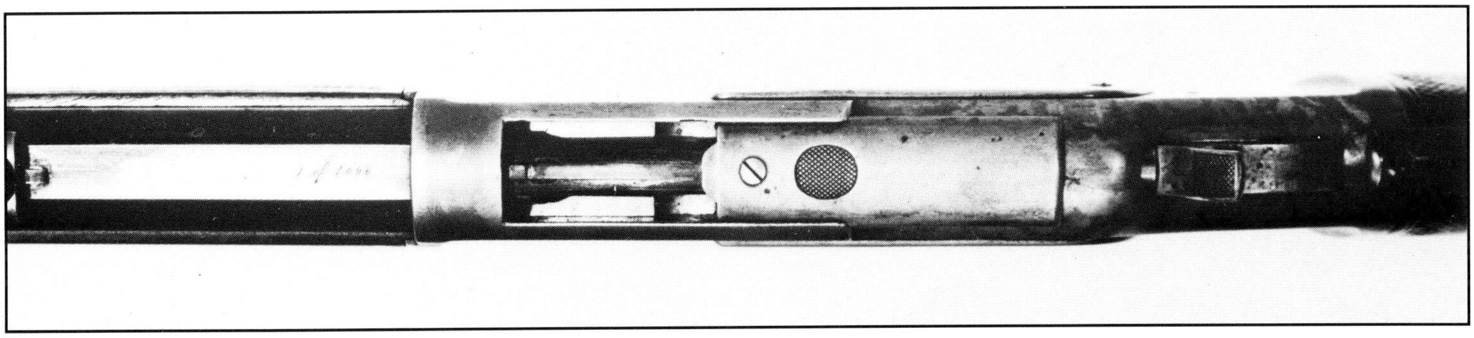

which was later replaced with one of steel, resulting in a lighter gun and lower production costs. A bright blue finish was the standard for the Model 73, with trigger, hammer, lever and internal parts casehardened for greater durability and to minimize wear.

Of particular interest to collectors is a 'cutaway' display Model 73 which was produced in the Winchester Model Shop. This 'cutaway' version featured sectional cuts that enabled Winchester salesmen to show the inner workings of the gun at fairs, exhibits and other public gatherings. Of the few that were produced, no two were sectioned in the same manner.

An interesting, if often misunderstood, variation of the Model 1873 is the 'One of One Thousand.' This version was announced as follows in the 1875 catalog:

'It is the purpose of the manufacturers of these arms to introduce a greater variety than has heretofore been made, to meet the different purposes and uses to which they are applicable, whether for sporting or war. Among these, the demands of amateur sportsmen are the most exacting for an arm that will shoot with unerring accuracy.

'With the perfect machinery and great skill of the men we employ in boring, rifling, straightening, polishing and finishing our barrels, we can always count with confidence upon any

***At bottom:* The Model 66 Carbine. *At top:* The Model 1873 Special Sporting Rifle. For shooters who wanted a premium gun—the Model 1873 One of One Thousand. To collectors of antique firearms, this model is probably the most valuable of all American shoulder arms. *Above:* Detail of barrel marking on a Model 1873 One of One Thousand.**

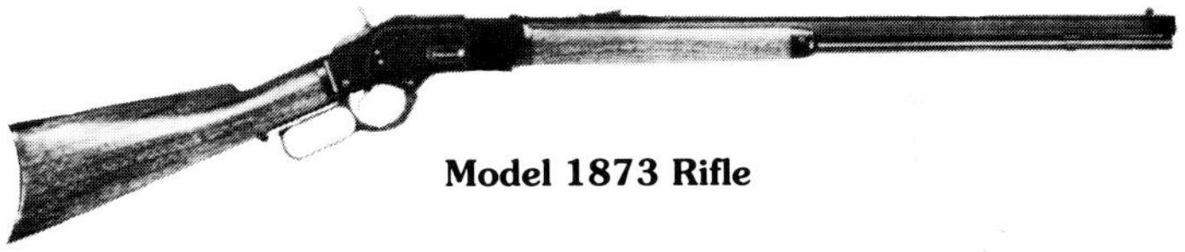

Model 1873 Rifle

Model 1873 Musket

Model 1873 Rifle

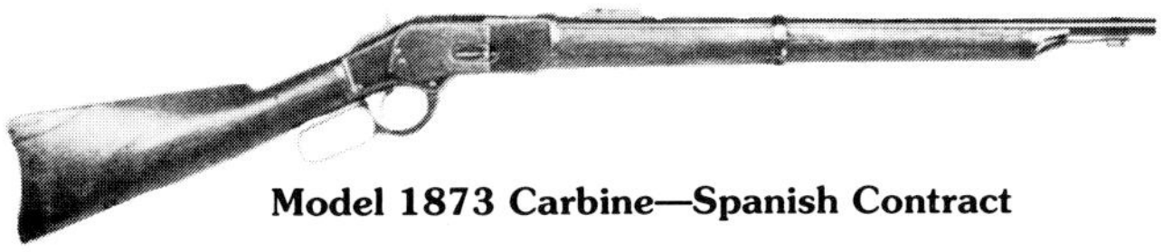

Model 1873 Carbine—Spanish Contract

Above: **Winchester also produced a One of One Thousand variant for the Model 76.**

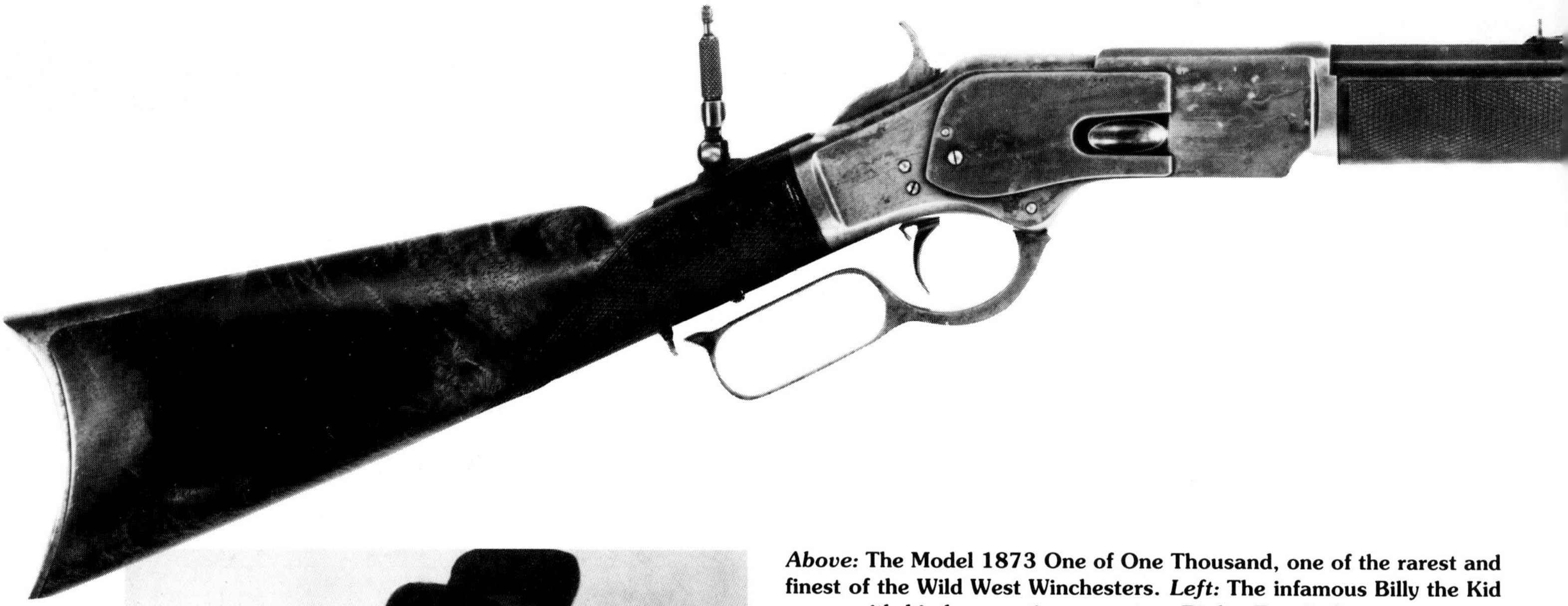

Above: **The Model 1873 One of One Thousand, one of the rarest and finest of the Wild West Winchesters.** ***Left:*** **The infamous Billy the Kid poses with his lever action repeater.** ***Right:*** **Two Indian scouts—one holding a Model 1876—and an Indian school boy, circa 1880.**

barrel shooting with accuracy; but in this as in all other cases, the degree of accuracy will vary. The barrel of every sporting rifle we make will be proved and shot at a target, and the target will be numbered to correspond with the barrel and be attached to it.

'All of the barrels that are found to make targets of extra merit will be made up into guns with set triggers and extra finish and marked, as a designating name, One of One Thousand.'

By 1877, the One of One Thousand was dropped from the catalog but not before a total of 136 of these firearms were produced. Although only 36 of these guns have been found to date, it is believed by most collectors that others are still somewhere in circulation.

The year 1891 saw the greatest Model 73s produced, when over 41,000 were manufactured. Production ceased in 1923 after over 700,000 had been produced.

Model 1876 Carbine

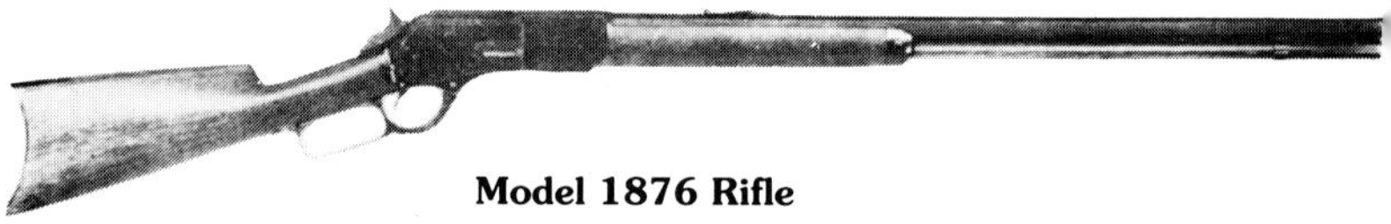

Model 1876 Rifle

The Model 1876. After the introduction of the Model 1873, Winchester conceded that 'the constant calls from many sources, and particularly from the regions in which the grizzly bear and other large game are found, as well as the plains where absence of cover and shyness of game require the hunter to make his shots at long range, made it desirable to build a still more powerful gun than the Model 1873.'

In 1876, at the Philadelphia Centennial Exposition, the Model 1876 first appeared. It was immediately christened the 'Centennial Model,' commemorating the anniversary of the Revolutionary War. The Model 1876 is essentially the same as the Model 73, but is built heavier, to handle the .45-75 WCF cartridge.

In 1886, production of the Model 76 was discontinued, but the last rifle did not leave the factory until over 10 years later. Production figures indicate that a little over 63,000 of

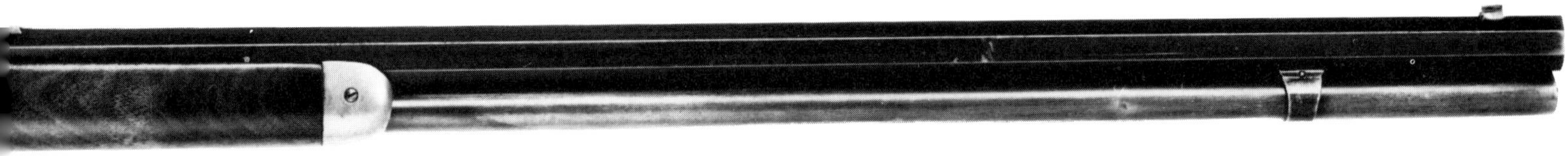

these rifles were manufactured, with most of them having been sold to the Royal Canadian Mounted Police, who used them in the Indian conflicts of Western Canada around the turn of the century. By 1905, the Model 76 had been retired from duty with the Mounties, but not before it had carved a record for dependability and ruggedness. The peak production year was 1884, when over 12,000 were manufactured.

The Model 71. The Winchester 1871, a continuation of the Model 1886, commenced production in 1935. This rifle was chambered only for the .348 Winchester, for which varying bullet weights of 150, 200 and 250 grains were offered. A 24-inch barrel, an open sporting or peep rear sights and hooded front ramp sights were standard. The Model 71 was available in 'Standard Rifle' and 'Deluxe Rifle' grades with the 'Deluxe' having sling loops and slings, a pistol grip cap and checkering. By the time the Model 71 was discontinued in 1958, over 47,000 had been produced.

The Model 53. The Model 53 was introduced in 1924 as a continuation of the Model 1892. Chambered for .25-20, .32-20 and .44-40 cartridges, this rifle has a 22 inch round barrel, a six shot magazine, straight grip and shotgun style butt plate. The Model 53 is considered by collectors to be a rare gun since it was discontinued in 1932 and only about 25,000 were actually produced over a period of 10 years.

The Model 65. Another continuation of the Model 1892, the Model 65 features a shotgun butt stock, uncapped pistol grips and a semi beavertail fore end. The barrel is tapered, generally 22 inches long and the magazine holds seven shots. The Model 65 is chambered for the .218 Bee, the .25-20, and .32-20 cartridges. A total of less than 6000 were manufactured from 1933 to 1947.

The Model 1901. The Model 1901 is a lever action shotgun made for smokeless powder loads and available only in 10 gauge. Its barrel length is 32 inches, with a standard blued overall finish. The Model 1901 did not sell well, principally because the relatively new slide action shotguns of the period were proving themselves far more popular.

The Model 1901 has some safety features, among them a trigger block and a mechanically operated firing pin retractor, both of which prevent accidental discharge. Manufacture of the Model 1901 ceased in 1920, and the remaining guns on hand were shipped to Mexico in the early 1930s.

The Model 64. The Model 64 is a long-lived and very popular continuation model which utilized John M Browning's Model 1894 action. It was introduced in 1933, and was chambered for various cartridges including the .25-35, the .30-30, the .32 Winchester Special and the .219 Zipper. A rapid taper 24-inch barrel is standard, with ramp type front sights. Manufacture of the Model 64 ceased in 1956 but was resumed in 1970.

The Lee Model Winchester. The Lee Winchester is a bolt action rifle which uses a slight upward and then rearward

***Left:* A serious Gary Cooper (photo far left), appearing in the 1950 movie *Dallas*, keeps his Winchester Model 1876 close by his side. The Model 76 was introduced to fill the need for a powerful, long range rifle.**

W.R.A
TRADE
Firestone

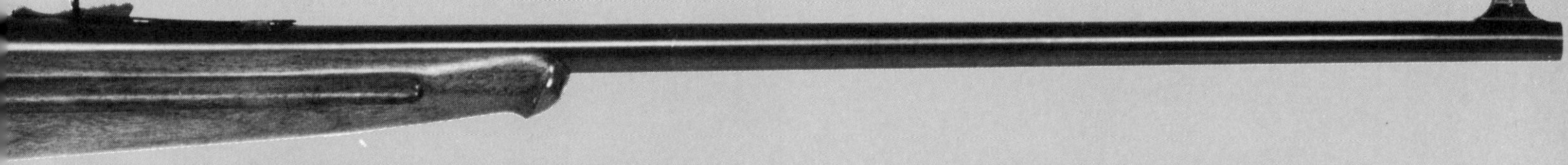

Counterclockwise from top: The rare Model 65 Lever Action Repeater—less than 6000 units were produced; the Model 98 Breechloading Cannon, popular for starting yacht races and off-stage sound effects; and the Lee Model Winchester—a bolt action, high velocity, small caliber rifle—far ahead of its time and consequently did not sell well; the *Maine.* Most of the Lee Winchesters were sold to the navy and 50 units went down with the *Maine* during the Spanish American War.

Above: **The wreck of the *Maine*, with Winchesters aboard.** *At left:* **For over 50 years, the Model 73 Lever Action Repeating Rifle was one of the most popular rifles produced by Winchester.**

pull of the bolt. This type of action is both fast and dependable. Only about 20,000 Lee 'straight pull' models were produced and of these only a small number were fitted as sporting rifles.

Although it had been in use by US Armed forces for many years, sportsmen found it less desirable than most lever actions. The majority of Lee Winchesters—in musket configuration—were sold to the Navy and saw duty in the Spanish-American War. Apparently, a large number of these Lee muskets were on board the *Maine* when it was sunk in Havana Harbor. About 50 of these rifles were recovered from the ship, and were later sold by a New York arms dealer. Manufacture of the Lee Model was discontinued in 1902.

The Model 1898 Winchester Cannon. While the Winchester Cannon is not a true gun because it does not fire projectiles, it has nonetheless proved to be a crowd pleaser for the general public, as well as being a sought-after collectors' item. The cannon is made for 10 gauge black powder blanks only, and the barrel is marked 'Not for Ball.' The earliest of these cannons were made with enamelled metal surfaces and had steel wheels. On later models, rubber tires and chrome plated metal parts were also available at extra cost. The cannons were designed primarily as a starter or salute guns and so were in limited demand. However, nearly 19,000 had been manufactured before they were discontinued in 1958.

Winchester-Western Rifles

Winchester Model 73 Lever Action Repeating Rifle. The Model 73 is chambered for .32-20, .38-40 and .44-40 cartridges. Over 720,000 rifles of this model were manufactured from 1873 to 1924.

Winchester Single Shot Rifle. Designed by John M Browning, this firearm was manufactured from 1885 to 1920 in a variety of models and chambered for most of the popular cartridges of the period, rimfire and center fire, from .22 to .50 caliber. See also the description in the 'Major Browning Winchester Models' section of this text.

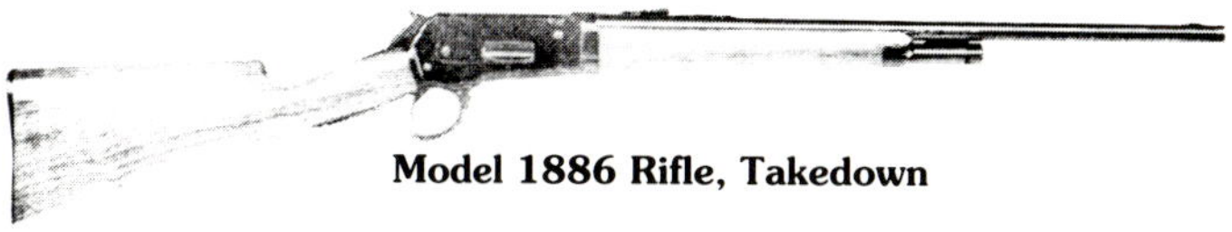

Model 1886 Rifle, Takedown

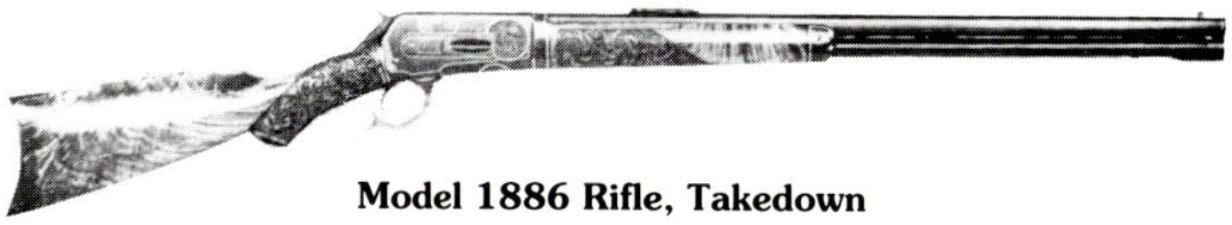

Model 1886 Rifle, Takedown

Winchester Model 86 Lever Action Repeater. Available in solid frame or takedown style, this rifle was made from 1886 to 1935. It is a lever action repeating rifle chambered for .45-70, .38-56, .45-90-300, .40-82-260, .40-65-260, .38-56-255, .38-70-255, .40-70-330, .50-110-300, .50-100-450 and .33 caliber. See also the description in the 'Major Browning Winchester Models' section of this text.

Winchester Model 90 Slide Action Repeater. The Model 90 is a pump action rifle that was chambered for the .22 short, long and .22 long rifle, and the .22 Winchester rimfire cartridge. It was manufactured from 1890 to 1932. See also the description in the 'Major Browning Winchester Models' section of this text.

Winchester Model 92 Lever Action Repeating Rifle. A solid frame or takedown, the Model 92 is chambered for .25-20, .32-20, .38-40 and .44-40 cartridges. It was made from 1892 to 1941. See also the description in the 'Major Browning Winchester Models' section of this text.

Winchester Model 53 Lever Action Repeating Rifle. A modification of the Model 92, this rifle of .25-20, .32-20 or .44-40 caliber was made from 1924 to 1932.

Winchester Model 65 Lever Action Rifle. Manufactured from 1933 to 1947, this design represented an improved version of the Model 53 in .25-20 and .32-20 calibers.

Ubiquitious—and useful—Winchesters, in real life as well as the movies—miners relax at home in Colorado *(left)*; a couple of prospectors and two cowhands during the short-lived gold rush in Weepah, Nevada in 1927 *(above)*; and Clint Eastwood in A Fistful of Dollars *(below)*.

Special Features

Winchester went to great lengths to please its customers by offering a variety of special order features for their guns in almost every conceivable price range and taste spectrum. Some of these special features were available for only a short time, while others were listed in Winchester catalogs for many years. Some features were standard on one type of gun but were listed as options on other types.

Variations in barrel style and length are just one example of the special features available. Round barrels were standard for all lever action Winchester rifles, but any customer could order an octagonal barrel at additional charge.

'Extra heavy' target barrels were provided for some models and these, whether round or octagonal in shape, were available in any length up to 36 inches. These rifles with heavy barrels were sometimes known as 'Buffalo Rifles.' For a time Winchester offered 'extra light weight' rifles in certain models but these did not prove to be as popular as the standard rifles. If the customer so desired, he could order his rifle with the front half of the barrel rounded and the rear portion octagonal in shape—which provided a finer overall balance in the gun.

The types, sizes, variations and designs of sights available for Winchester guns are no less than legion. They include 'The Winchester Express,' 'The Rocky Mountain Front Sight,' 'The Knife Blade,' 'The Marbles Improved Sight,' 'The Beach Combination Sight,' 'The Vickers-Maxim Sight,' 'The Globe Sight,' 'The Lymans Patent Windgauge Front Sight,' 'The Marbles Duplex,' 'The Caterpillar,' 'The Military Wind Gauge Sight,' 'The Flexible Rear Sight,' 'The Combination Tang Peep Sight,' 'The Mid Range Vernier Peep Sight' and 'The Spirit Lever Sight.'

Winchester even manufactured, for a while, telescopic scopes of high quality with five different reticles in three, four and five power. If a customer wanted a nonglaring sighting plane, he could order a matted barrel in either cross checkered or weaving lines design.

Smoothbore barrels could be ordered if the customer wanted to use shot cartridges. These smoothbore guns were mainly made for exhibition shooters, and were available in a wide variety of calibers. Various rifling twist combinations were also available upon request. Winchester, for many years, ran the following discussion of rifling in its catalogs.

'One of the most difficult things to determine in making rifle barrels is the twist, or rifling, required to shoot a given cartridge to best advantage. Cartridges of different or like caliber containing different weights of powder or lead require a different twist. A proper twist is one which will spin a bullet fast enough to keep it point on to the limit of its range, thus insuring the best possible accuracy.

'If the twist is too slow the flight of the bullet will be untrue, and it will "tumble" or "keyhole," as it is called when a bullet passes through the air in a lengthwise position instead of point on. On the contrary, if the twist is too quick or sharp the bullet will spin so rapidly that it is unsteady in its flight and wobbles like a top when it first begins to spin.

'The only sure way of ascertaining a perfect twist is by calculation and exhaustive practical tests. The Winchester Repeating Arms Company have complete facilities for verifying all calculations for twist, which enables them to determine with positive certainty the twist that will give best results with a given cartridge.'

These special order riflings could be ordered in basically three types—the Medford, the Whitworth or the Alexander Henry, as well as other more exotic styles. Winchester also offered a number of different devices intended to reduce the rifle's blast noise. Other devices were offered to reduce its recoil; these and other options were fitted upon request.

Most Winchesters had stocks made of selected straight grain American walnut. While American walnut was the standard, other woods such as English, Italian, or other imported walnuts, maple (either curly or bird's eye), orangewood or other fruitwoods such as cherry and peach, could be special ordered.

Winchester employed a rigid system of stock grading which included four basic categories—the grain flow of the wood (which was designated as either straight or fancy); the density of the wood (which had a great bearing on the kind of carving or checkering ultimately performed on it); the contrast or grain of the wood (which mainly had to do with its color and shading); and the fitting and finishing of the wood.

Winchester's checkering and carving were generally divided into eight different styles denominated A through H. Styles A and B consisted of carving, while a moderate amount of border carving was used with style C. Style D incorporated carving—usually of oak leaves and acorns—and style E was generally a tasteful combination of checkering and carving. Styles F, G and H carried progressively less carving, and style H (the lowest priced) carried only checkering.

In addition, Winchester offered color casehardening of receivers and butt plates as well as hammers and levers. During this process, the parts were packed in airtight cylinders with a combination of bone meal and leather dust heated to a red hot temperature. The parts were then quenched quickly in water. The quenching step actually controlled the colors that would appear, in an iridescent shimmer on the metal so tempered.

Plating in gold, silver, nickel and chrome was offered on many models. Winchester engraving was generally priced according to coverage and quality, and ranged through 10 grades, although the quality of the workmanship varied slightly from grade to grade. Various scenes were offered in standard patterns, but the customer could have an illustration from a photograph duplicated to his taste. Both American and English scrolls were employed in Winchester engraving, and inscriptions on the engraved gun were done in a variety of patterns consisting of names, dates or other pertinent information.

Also, gold, silver or platinum bands could be inlaid on engraved barrels or receivers if ordered. 'Engraving' means that the lines are cut into the metal, penetrating the surface. 'Inlay work' means that a precious metal is used to fill in the engraved grooves, and 'sculptured designs' refer to precious metal designs that are raised above the surface of the firearm. More often than not, the term 'inlay work' is used to include 'sculptured designs.' The engravers who worked for Winchester have in the past been allowed to choose their own patterns, provided the engravers had sufficient expertise to carry it off, or they could follow the basic styles that were offered in the current catalogs.

Figures of deer have been, by far, the most popular designs—with standing, drinking, listening and pausing stances generally the most used. The elk has also been a popular animal as well as moose, mountain goat, bear and antelope. Some kinds of buffalo and hunting dogs have also been pictured, but these are considered rare animals on older Winchesters, as are scenes which contained more than one animal.

Finally, Winchester has offered extra parts that could be special ordered for various firearms. For example, saber bayonets of 25 inches in length were offered for a number of Winchester muskets, as well as matching leather scabbards with brass fittings. Winchester has also offered saddle rings for firearms.

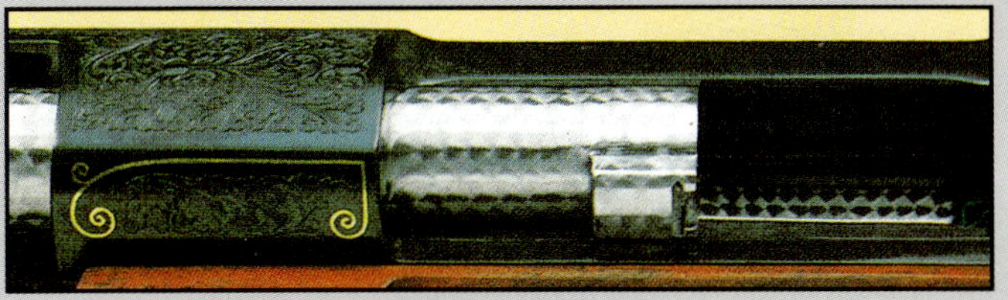

Custom work from Winchester—*right, from top down:* An engraved trigger guard and floor plate; a hand-jewelled bolt and magazine follower; and a hand-engraved receiver with gold inlay. *Below, left and right:* gold inlaid muzzle band and an engraved pistol grip cap. *At bottom, left to right:* Model 70 Exhibition Grade; Model 70 Custom Built; and a Super-X Model 1 Shotgun.

Winchester-Western Shotguns

Winchester Model 1887 Lever Action Repeater. Made from 1887 to 1901, the Model 1887 is a solid frame 10 or 12 gauge shotgun with a four shot tubular magazine. It has a plain 30- or 32-inch barrel, with full choke, and a plain pistol grip stock. It weighs nine pounds in 10 gauge and eight pounds in 12 gauge. See also the description in the 'Major Browning Winchester Models' section of this text.

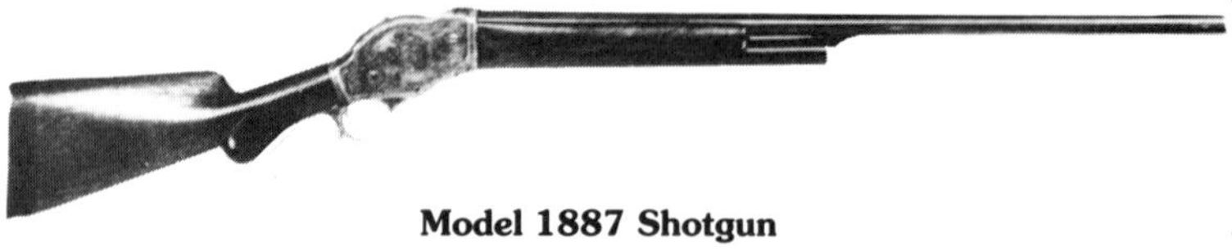

Model 1887 Shotgun

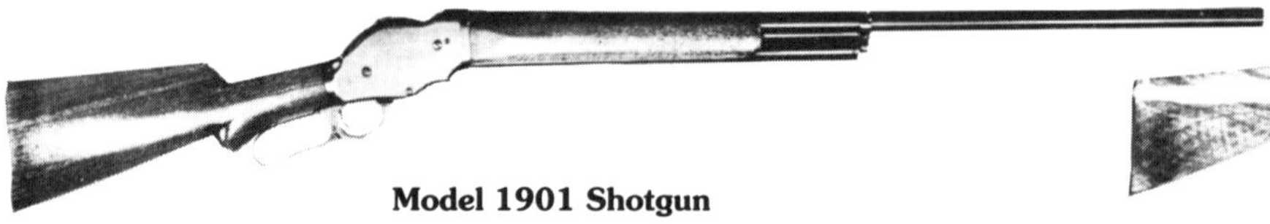

Model 1901 Shotgun

Winchester Model 1901 Lever Action Repeater. The Model 1901 is a redesigned version of the Model 1887, and has the same general specifications. It is available in 10 gauge only and was made from 1901 to 1920.

Winchester Model 97 Slide Action Repeating Shotgun. The Model 97 is a standard grade, takedown or solid frame pump action shotgun in 12 or 16 gauge, with a five shell tubular magazine. Available with barrel lengths of 26 to 32 inches, it weighs about 7.75 pounds and has a plain pistol grip stock and grooved slide handle. This firearm was manufactured from 1897 to 1957. See also the description in the 'Major Browning Winchester Models' section of this text.

Winchester Model 1911 Autoloading Shotgun. The Model 1911 is a hammerless, takedown semiautomatic shotgun in 12 gauge only, with a four shell tubular magazine. It weighs about 8.5 pounds and was made from 1911 to 1925. It should be noted that John M Browning invented the autoloading—or, 'automatic'—shotgun.

Model 1911 Shotgun

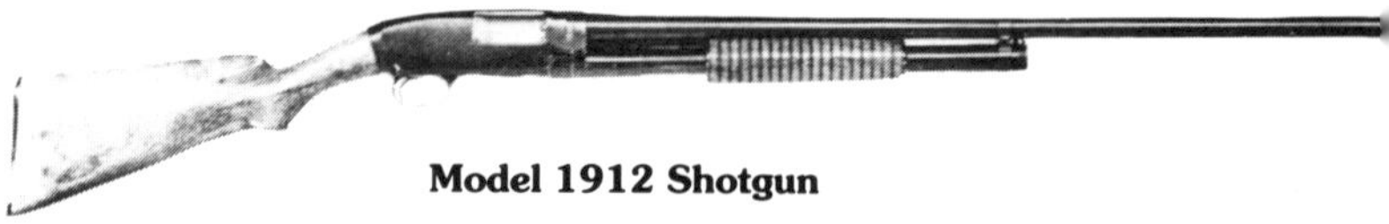

Model 1912 Shotgun

Model 1912 Trap Gun

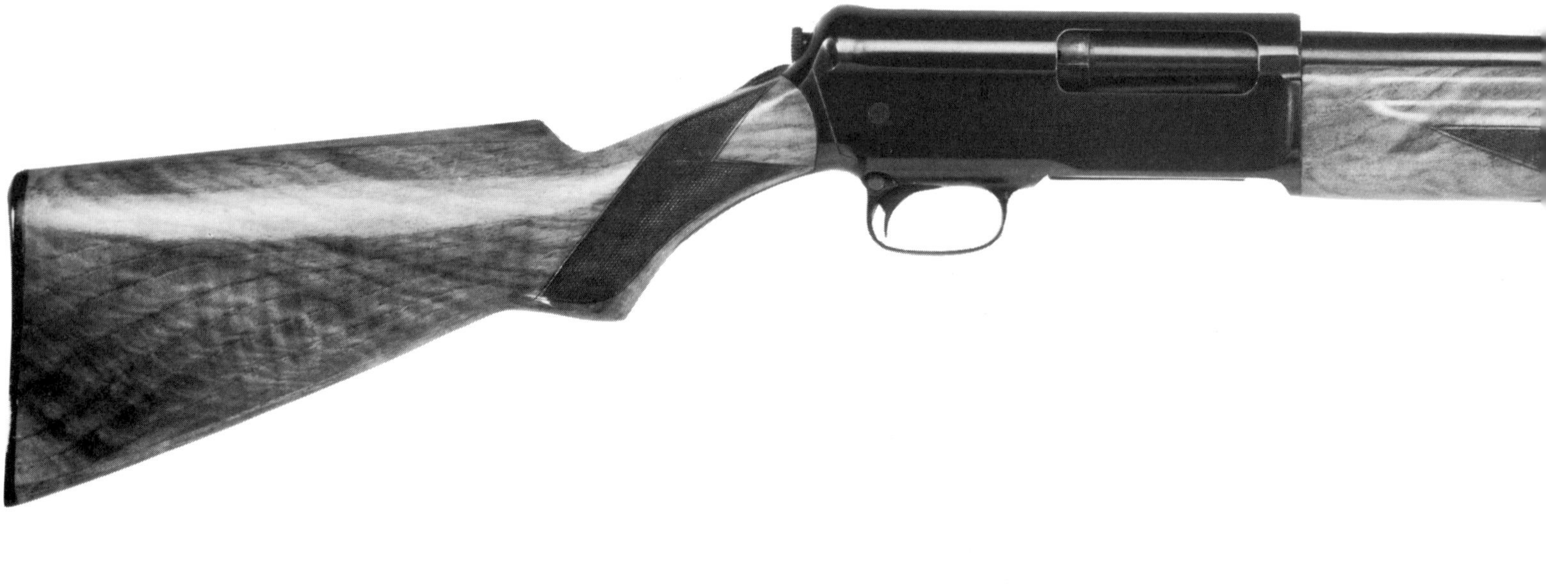

Winchester Model 12 Standard Slide Action Repeating Shotgun. The Model 12 is a hammerless, takedown pump action shotgun in 12, 16, 20 or 28 gauge, with a six shell tubular magazine and barrel lengths of from 26 to 32 inches with full to cylinder chokes. It weighs about 7.5 pounds and was made from 1912 to 1964.

Model 1912 Trench Gun

Winchester Single Shot Lever Action Shotgun. Like the Single Shot Rifle, this 20 gauge shotgun has a falling block action, with a high wall receiver. Available in solid frame or takedown, it has a 3-inch chamber, a 26-inch barrel and weighs about 5.5 pounds. This firearm was manufactured from 1914 to 1916.

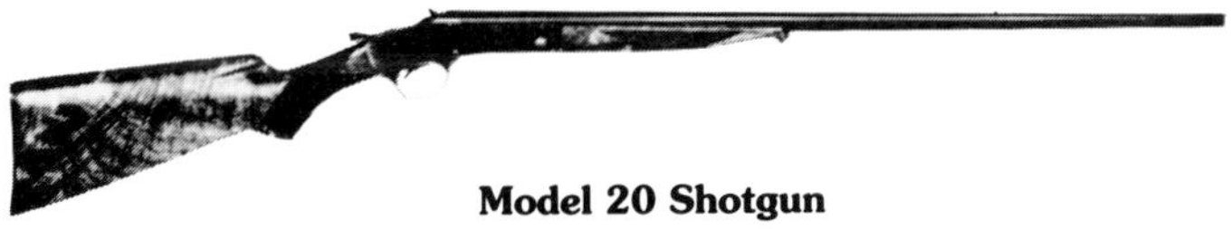

Model 20 Shotgun

Winchester Model 20 Single Shot Hammer Gun. The Model 20 is a takedown single shot shotgun chambered for a .410 gauge, 2.5 inch shell. It has a 2-inch barrel with a full choke and was made from 1919 to 1924.

Winchester Model 36 Single Shot Bolt Action Shotgun. The Model 36—a single shot, takedown firearm—uses 9mm short or long, shot shells or 'pumpkin ball' cartridges interchangeably. It weighs about three pounds and was made from 1920 to 1927.

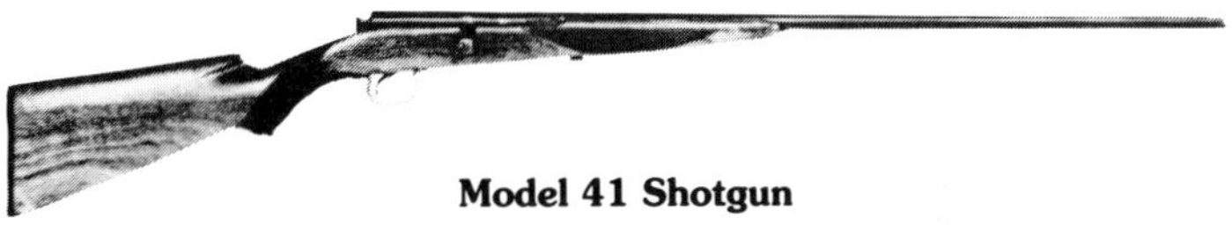

Model 41 Shotgun

Winchester Model 41 Single Shot Bolt Action Shotgun. The Model 41 is a single shot, takedown shotgun chambered for a .410 gauge, 2.5-inch paper shot shell. It has a 24-inch barrel with full choke and was made from 1920 to 1934.

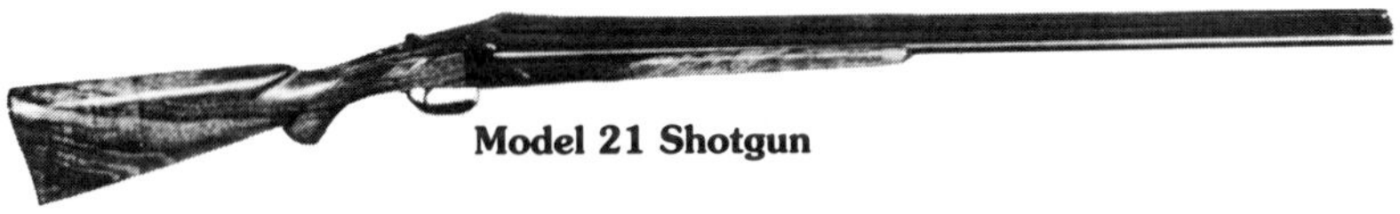

Model 21 Shotgun

Winchester Model 21 Double Barrel Field Gun. The Model 21 is a hammerless, box lock double barreled shotgun with an automatic safety. Made in 12, 16 and 20 gauge, it is available with double triggers or a selective single trigger, and selective or nonselective ejection. This gun was made from 1930 to 1958.

***At top:* The Model 97 became the standard against which other shotguns were judged. *At bottom:* The Model 1911 Autoloading Shotgun. John M Browning was the genius behind this revolutionary design.**

The Model 93 Shotgun *(far right)* was the forerunner of the Model 1897 Shotgun *(above and below)*. The Model 97's refinements corrected a number of weaknesses in the Model 93. The most notable modification was an improved slide lock which kept the gun locked until it was fired, thereby preventing the gun from jamming in case of a misfire.

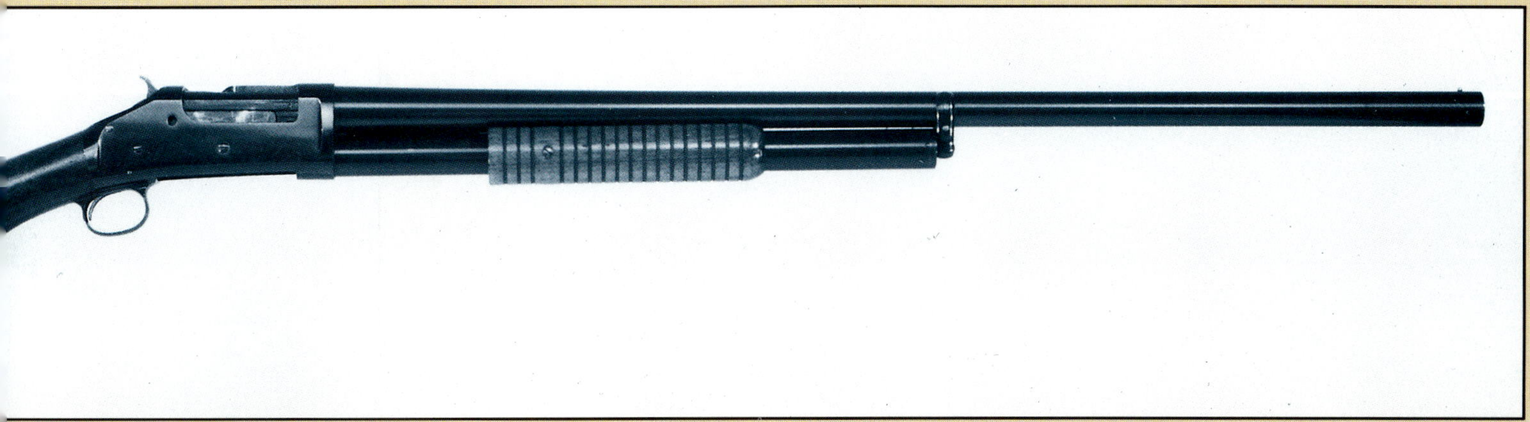

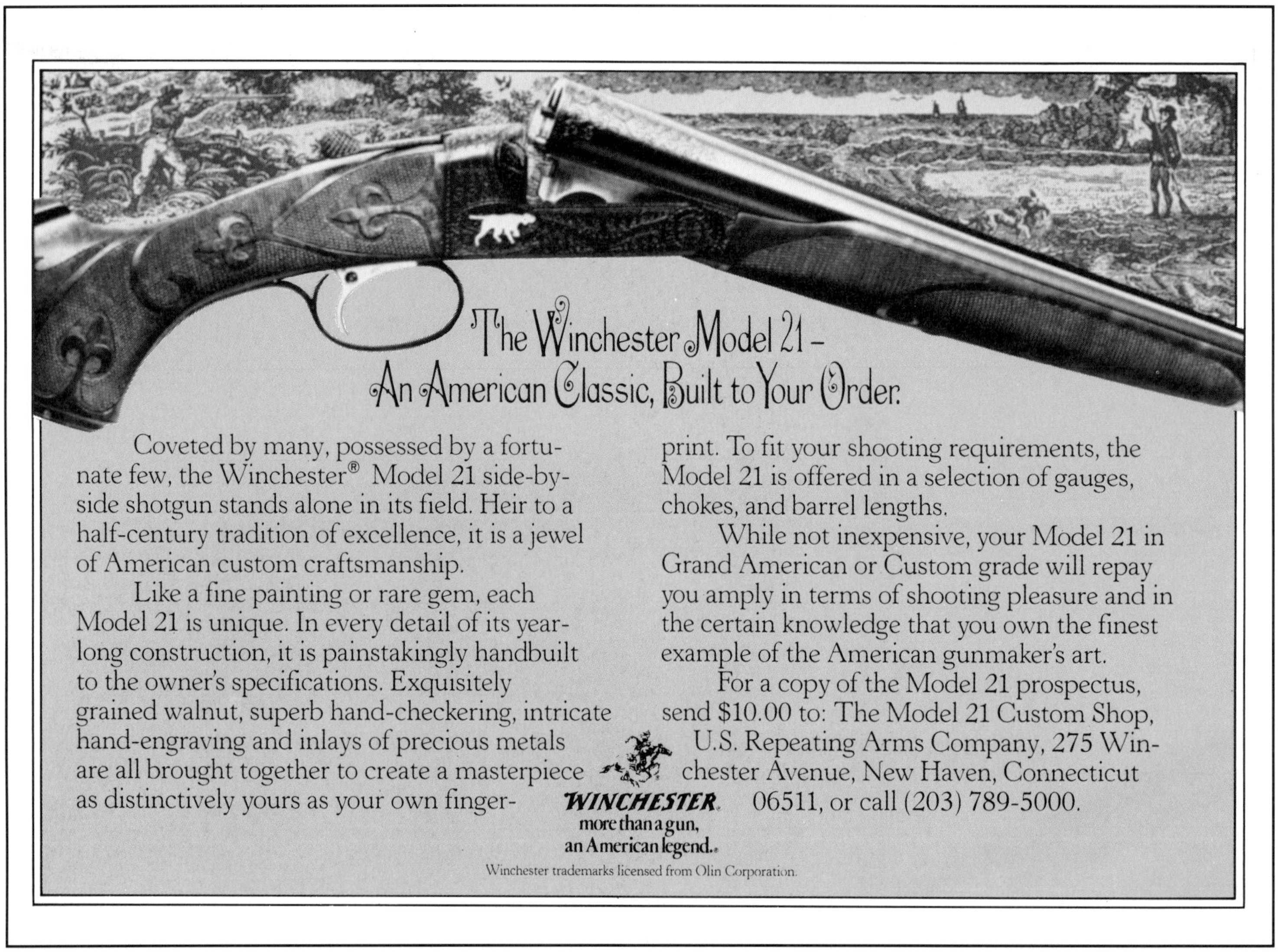

Winchester Model 21, Grand American. Since 1959, the Model 21 has been offered only in deluxe models on special order. Each of these custom guns has a full fancy American walnut stock and forearm with fancy checkering, finely polished and hand smoothed working parts with engraved inlays, carved stocks and other extras available at additional cost. Made from 1960, these have been among Winchester's presentation best at a cost of about $10,000.

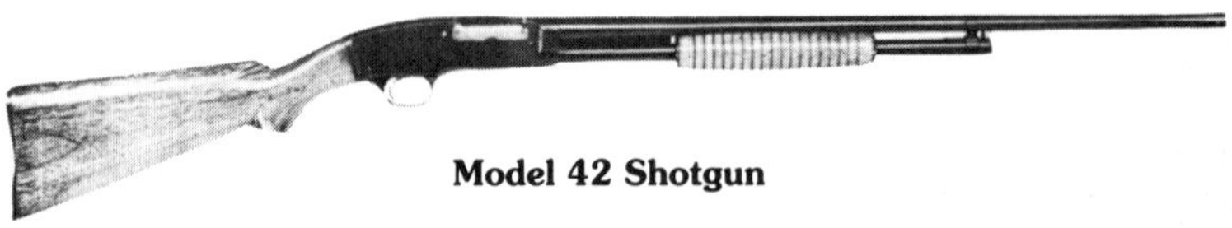
Model 42 Shotgun

Winchester Model 42 Standard Slide Action Repeating Shotgun. The Model 42 is a hammerless, takedown shotgun in .410 guage. The tubular magazine holds five 3-inch or six 2.5-inch shells. Made from 1933 to 1963, it weighs about six pounds.

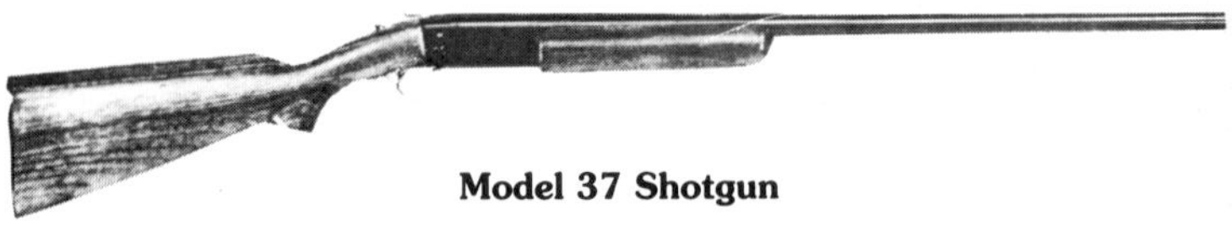
Model 37 Shotgun

Winchester Model 37 Single Barrel Shotgun. The Model 37 is semi-hammerless, takedown shotgun in 12, 16, 20, 28 and .410 gauge with automatic ejection. It was made from 1937 to 1963.

From the first firearms manufactured by the New Haven Arms Company *(right)*, Winchester has maintained a standard of excellence, as is illustrated by the custom built Model 21 seen in the advertisement *above*.

Winchester Model 370 Single Barrel Shotgun. The Model 370 is a takedown shotgun in 12, 16, 20, 28 and .410 gauge with automatic ejection. This firearm was produced from 1968 to 1973.

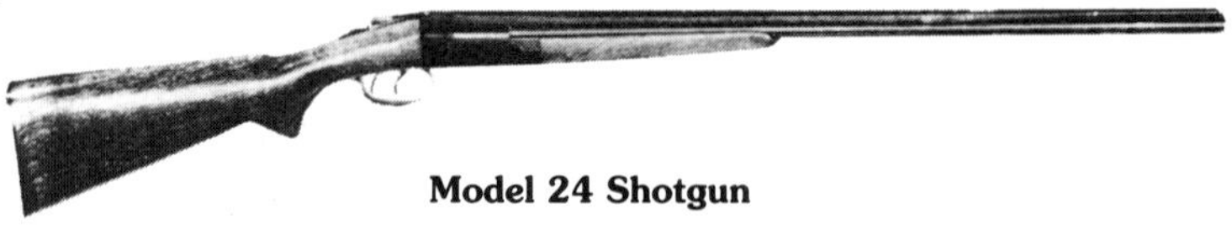
Model 24 Shotgun

Winchester Model 24 Hammerless Double Barrel Shotgun. The Model 24 is a double barreled box lock shotgun with double triggers, plain extractors and automatic safety. Made in 12, 16 and 20 gauge, it was manufactured from 1939 to 1957.

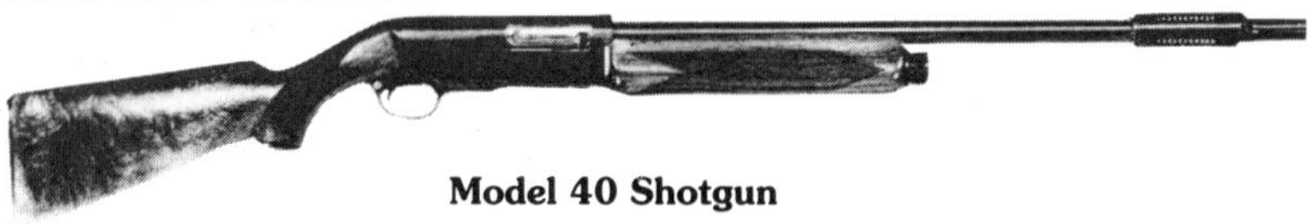
Model 40 Shotgun

Winchester Model 40 Standard Autoloading Shotgun. Made from 1940 to 1941, the Model 40 is an automatic repeating shotgun with a streamlined receiver. Hammerless and takedown-capable, it is available in 12 gauge only, with a four shell tubular magazine.

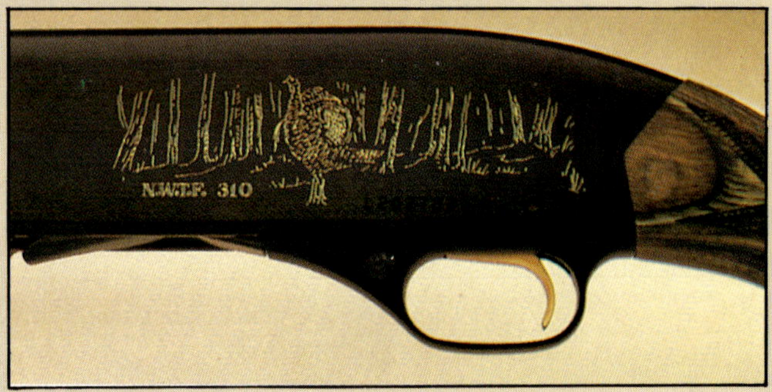

Named the 1987 Gun of the Year by the National Wild Turkey Federation, the Model 1300 Special Turkey Gun *(above)* was introduced as a tribute to the successful restoration of the wild turkey. This 12 gauge, pump action shotgun has a ventilated 22-inch rib barrel, Winchoke system, and a roll-engraved receiver with turkey scenes. It also features military-style lock-up of bolt and barrel *(far right)*. The Collector's Edition Model features an engraved and gold-filled receiver *(left)* and gold-plated trigger, middle and front sights. *Below:* The regular edition Model 1300 Turkey Gun has a satin-finished walnut or laminated WIN-CAM stock and forearm, with roll engraving on the receiver. *Below right:* The Model 1300 CamoPack combines all the features of the regular Turkey Gun with an extra 30-inch Waterfowl barrel.

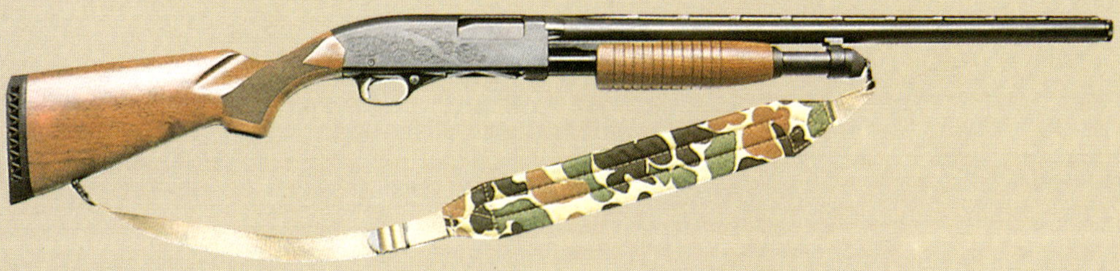

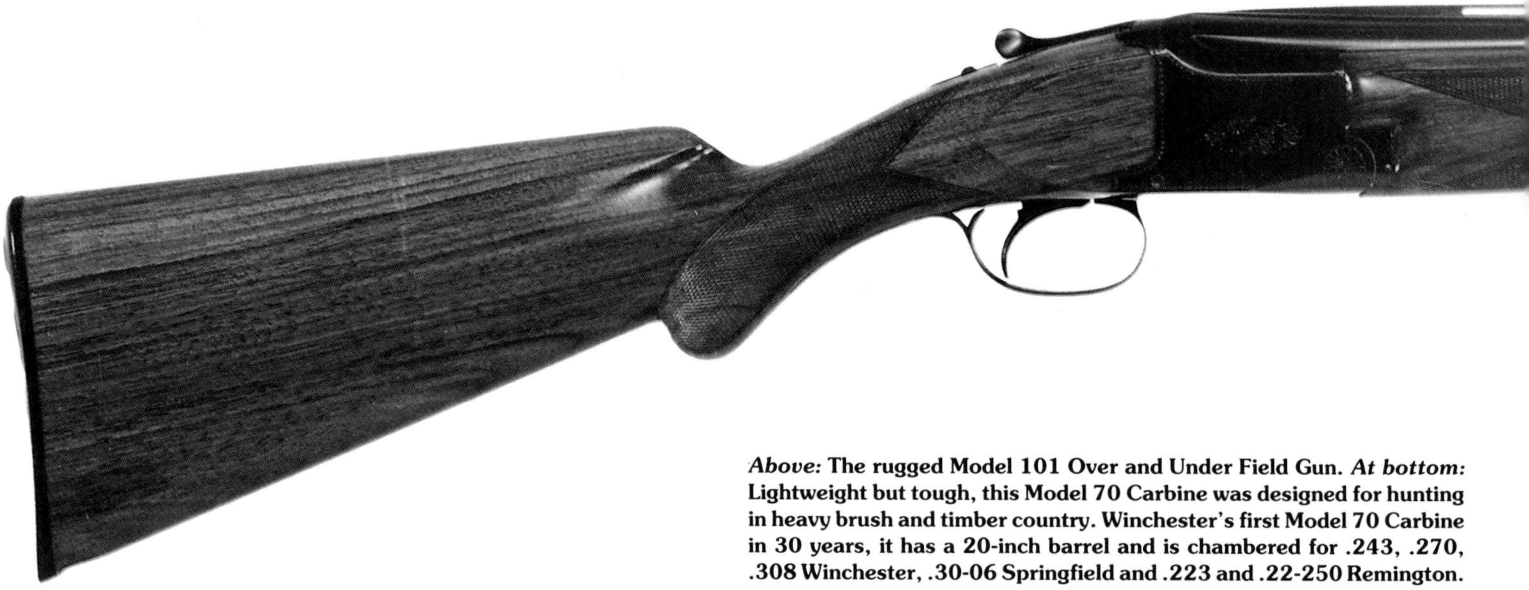

Above: The rugged Model 101 Over and Under Field Gun. *At bottom:* Lightweight but tough, this Model 70 Carbine was designed for hunting in heavy brush and timber country. Winchester's first Model 70 Carbine in 30 years, it has a 20-inch barrel and is chambered for .243, .270, .308 Winchester, .30-06 Springfield and .223 and .22-250 Remington.

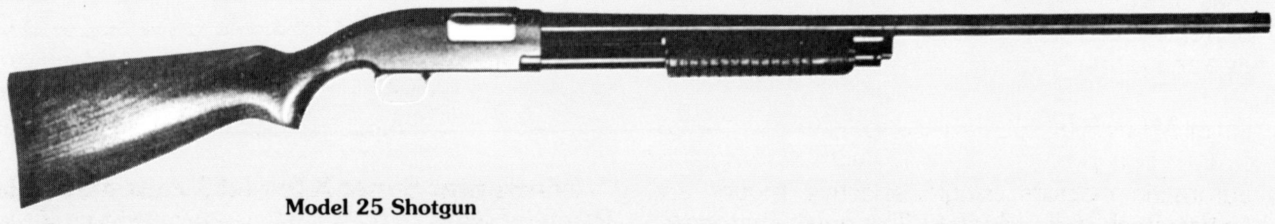

Model 25 Shotgun

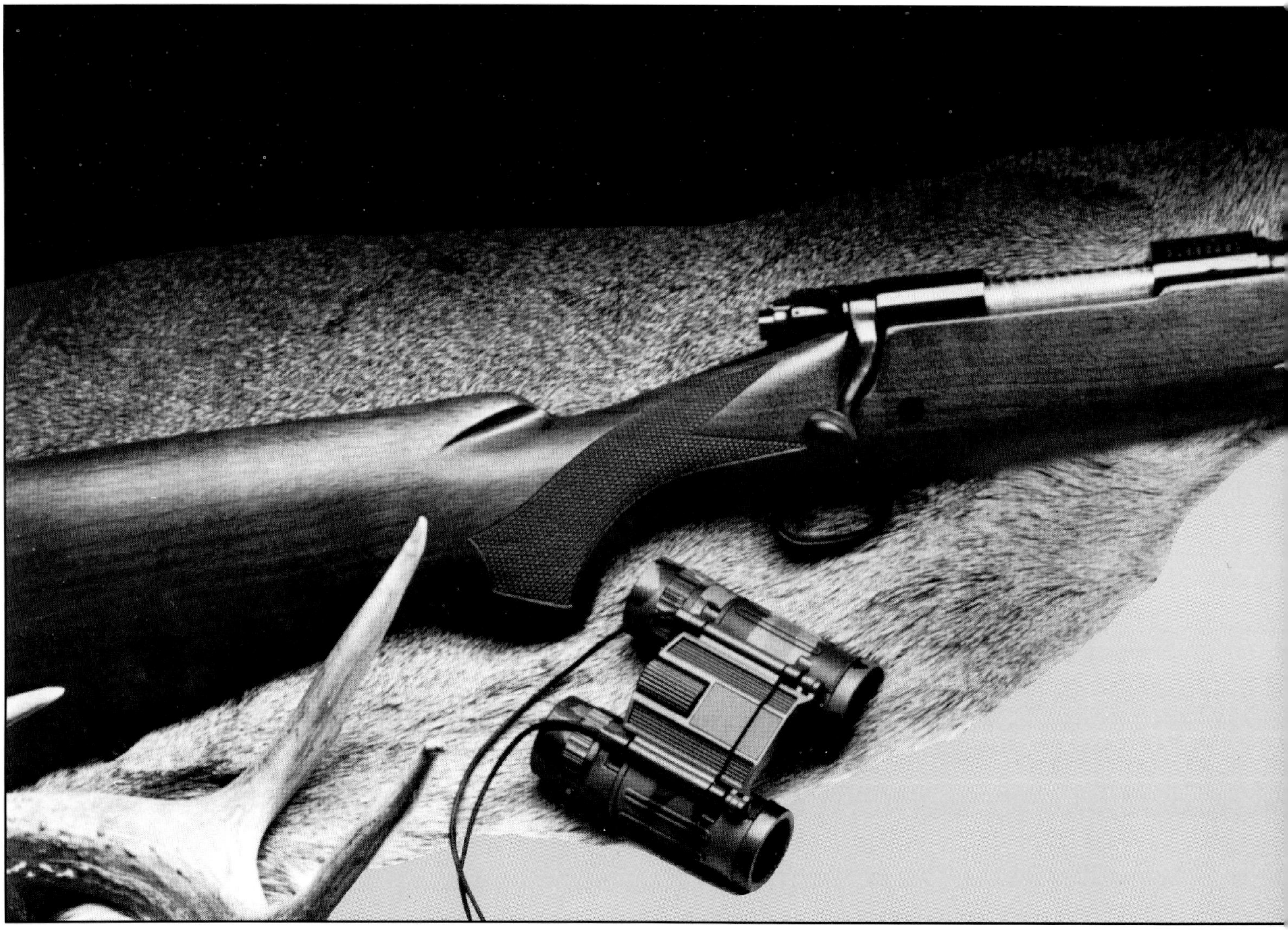

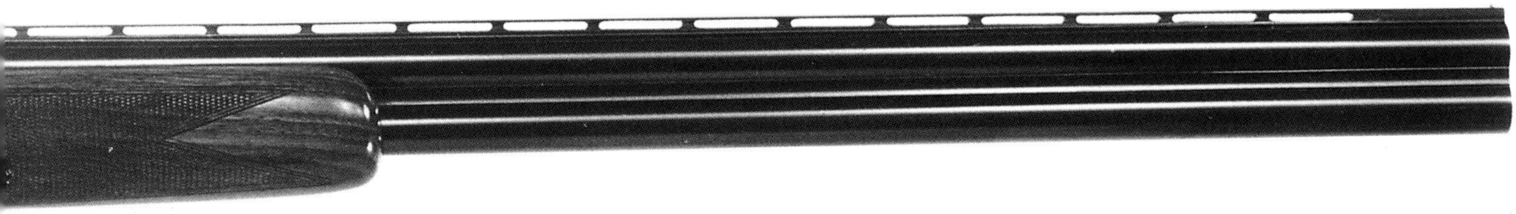

Winchester Model 25 Slide Action Repeating Shotgun. Manufactured from 1949 to 1955, the Model 25 is a hammerless, solid frame 12 gauge shotgun.

Winchester Model 50 Standard Grade Autoloader. Designed with a nonrecoiling barrel and independent chamber, the Model 50 is chambered for 12 or 20 gauge. Production for this model ran from 1954 to 1961.

Winchester Model 59 Autoloading Shotgun. The Model 59 has an alloy receiver and a 'Win Lite' steel and fiberglass barrel. Made from 1959 to 1965, this 12 gauge shotgun has a magazine that holds two shells.

Winchester Model 101 Over and Under Field Gun. The Model 101 is a box lock shotgun with an engraved receiver, automatic ejectors, single selective trigger and combination barrel selector and safety. This gun is chambered for 12 or 28 gauge and has been in production since 1963.

Winchester 'Xpert' Model 96 Over and Under Field Gun. The Model 96 has a box lock action similar to the Model 101. It has a plain receiver, automatic ejectors and a selective single trigger. Made in 12 and 20 gauge, it has been manufactured since 1976.

Winchester Model 1200 Slide Action Field Gun. The Model 1200 is a rotary bolt, takedown style shotgun in 12, 16 and 20 gauge with a four shot magazine. It has been manufactured from 1964 to date.

Winchester Model 1400 Automatic Field Gun. The Model 1400 is a gas operated, front-locking rotary bolt takedown style shotgun in 12, 16 or 20 gauge, with a two shot magazine. It was manufactured from 1964 to 1968.

Winchester Super X Model 1 Automatic Field Gun. Produced since 1974, this 12 gauge takedown shotgun is gas operated.

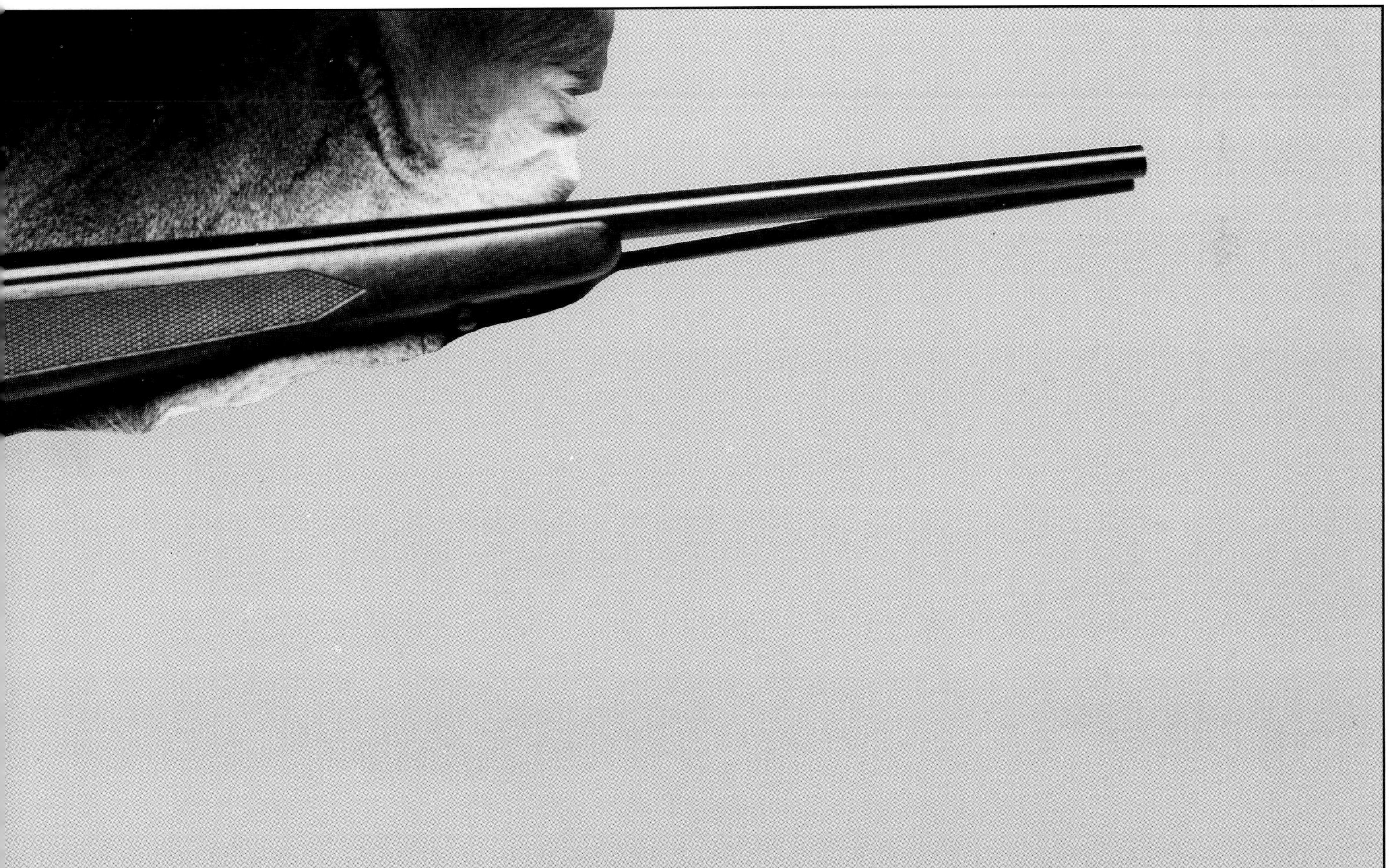

US Repeating Arms Rifles

The following rifles are produced under license from Olin Corporation.

Winchester Model 70 Bolt Action Center Fire Rifle. This bolt action, center fire rifle is avaialable with barrel lengths of 20 to 24 inches, weighs 5.75 to 8.5 pounds and has a magazine capacity of three to five rounds, depending on ammunition. It is available in a wide range of calibers, from .223 Remington to .458 Winchester Magnum.

As a result of having been in continuous production for close to 50 years, the Model 70 has partaken of many refinements and technological advancements. The Model 70 XTR Sporter Rifle series comes in various calibers. The Standard model has a Monte Carlo stock and cheekpiece, a hinged steel floorplate, jeweled bolt, detachable sling swivels, rifle sights, and a 24-inch barrel. The Magnum version has the same sporter features and 24-inch barrel. Available calibers are 7mm Remington Magnum and .264, .300 and .338 Winchester Magnum.

The Special Varmint model has a 24-inch, high strength Winchester steel barrel without sights. The Model XTR Super Express Rifle comes in two big game calibers—.375 H&H Magnum or .458 Winchester Magnum—and its sporter stock is reinforced with two steel crossbolts. In addition, this fine big game rifle comes equipped with a forward sling swivel and adjustable open rear and ramp front sights.

The Model 70 XTR is also available in a Featherweight version, which has a 22-inch barrel, weighs 6.75 pounds and has a receiver drilled and tapped for scope mounting. A special European version of the Featherweight combines the same features with 6.5 X 55 Swedish Mauser caliber chambering. A limited edition .270 Winchester Ultra Grade Featherweight with 24 karat gold hand engraving and custom hand fitting is also available, serial numbered 1 to 1000.

The Model 70 Lightweight Carbine is a light and fast handling utility and brush gun, weighing six pounds with a 20-inch barrel. The Ranger Bolt Action Rifle has a ramp bead front, adjustable rear sights and a one piece American hardwood stock. The Ranger Youth Bolt Action Carbine is size-scaled to fit younger or smaller shooters, weighs 5.75 pounds, has ramp bead front and semibuckhorn folding leaf rear sights and is complete with an American hardwood stock.

The Model 70 Winlite offers the Model 70 bolt action with a fiberglass stock for light weight, strength, accuracy and the ultimate stability for bedding of the barreled action. It is available in four calibers and in barrel lengths of 22 and 24 inches, and its stock has a contoured rubber recoil pad and sling swivel studs.

Above: **Designed for the smaller shooter—the Ranger Bolt Action Carbine.** ***Below:*** **Like the Model 70 Carbine on the previous page, the Model 70 XTR Featherweight Rifle is made for easy carrying in mountain terrain.**

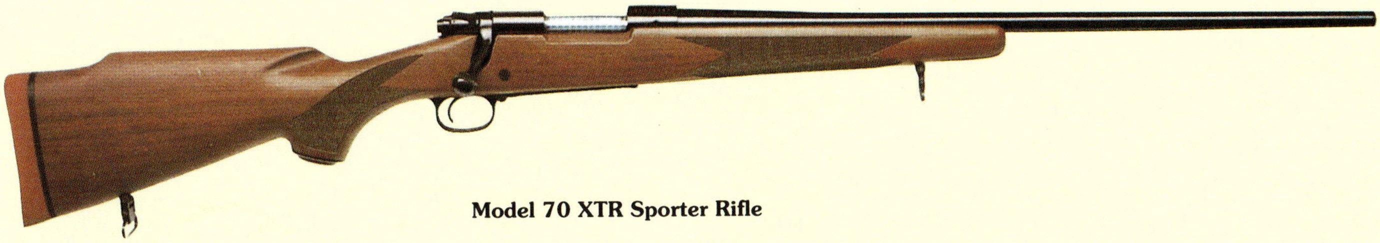

Model 70 XTR Sporter Rifle

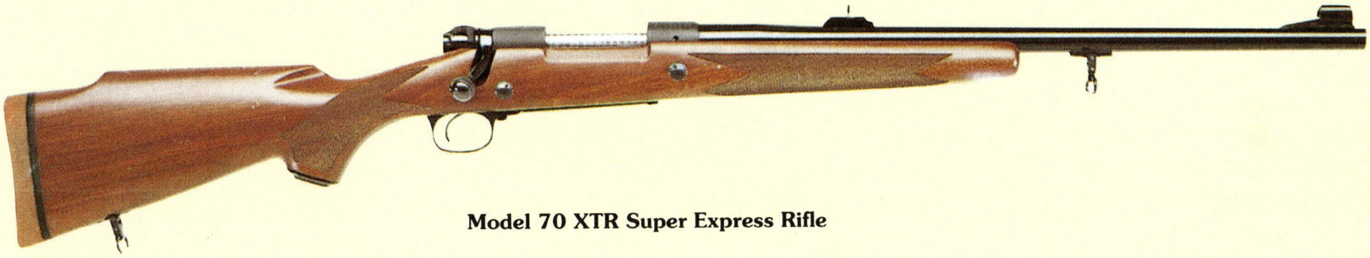

Model 70 XTR Super Express Rifle

Winchester Ranger Youth
Bolt Action Carbine

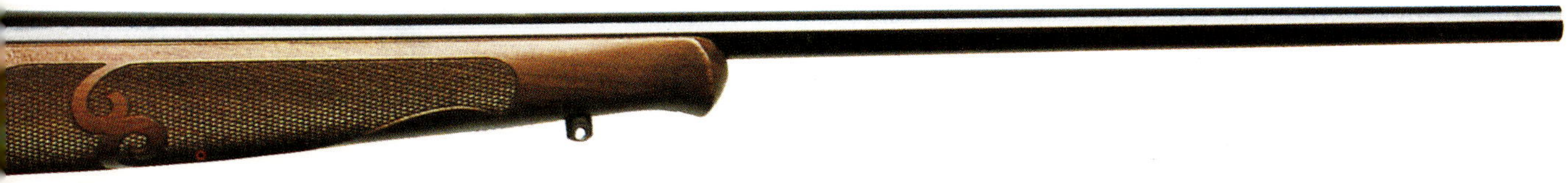

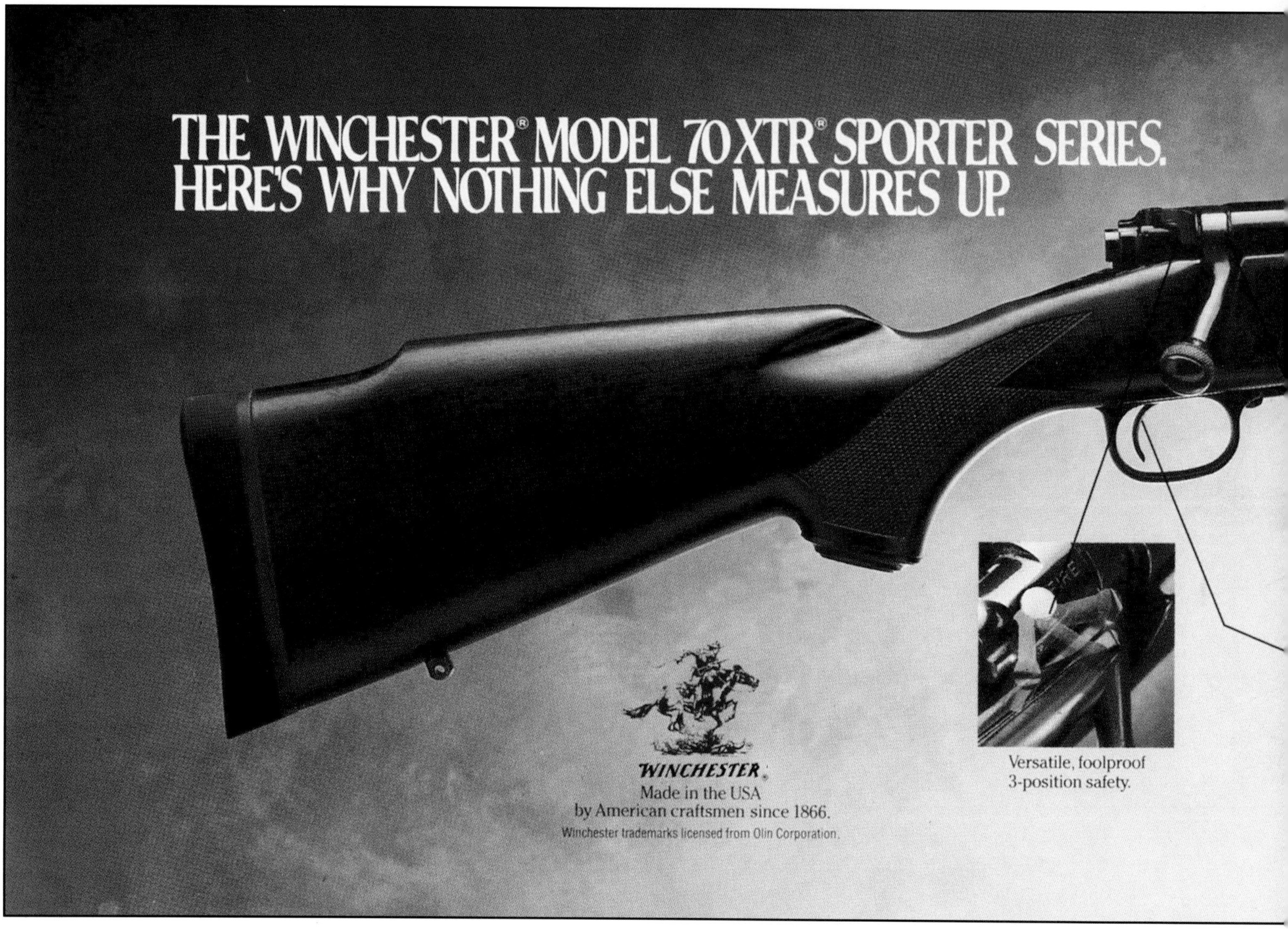

Winchester Model 94 Carbines. As a hunting rifle, the Model 94 has achieved legendary status—it is regarded by many as the symbol of the Wild West. The Model 94 is a lever action, center fire rifle with a magazine capacity of five to nine rounds, barrel lengths of 16 to 24 inches and weights of six to seven pounds, depending on the variant.

It is made with a forged steel receiver, designed for side ejection of spent cartridges and top mounting of scopes. Each carbine comes packaged with a thumb hammer extension that is reversible for right- or left-handed use with a scope.

The .30-30 caliber Model 94 XTR Carbine has a 20-inch barrel, dovetailed blade front, and semibuckhorn rear sights. It also has a six round capacity magazine, precise cut checkering and a butt plate. The XTR in 7-30 Waters, developed for higher muzzle velocity and flatter shooting accuracy, features a 24 inch barrel with a dovetailed blade front sight and seven cartridge capacity.

The Model 94 Standard Carbine is available in .30-30 Winchester with a six-shot magazine, 20-inch steel barrel, composition butt plate and dovetailed blade front, and adjustable rear, sights. The compact Trapper Carbine combines a 16-inch barrel with post front sight, and either a five shot magazine in .30-30 Winchester, or .45 Colt and .44 Remington Magnum calibers with nine-shot magazine capacity.

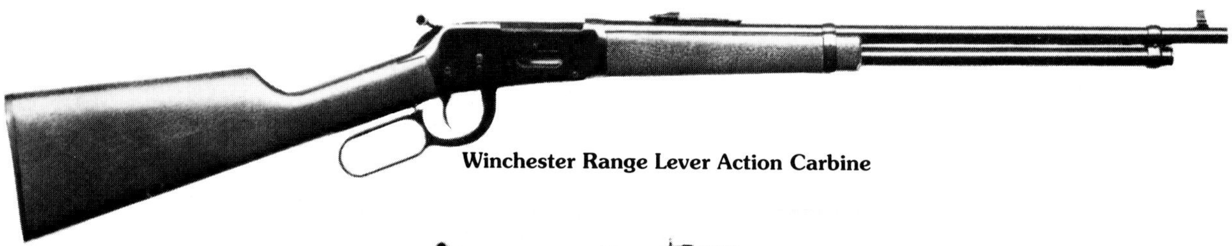

Winchester Range Lever Action Carbine

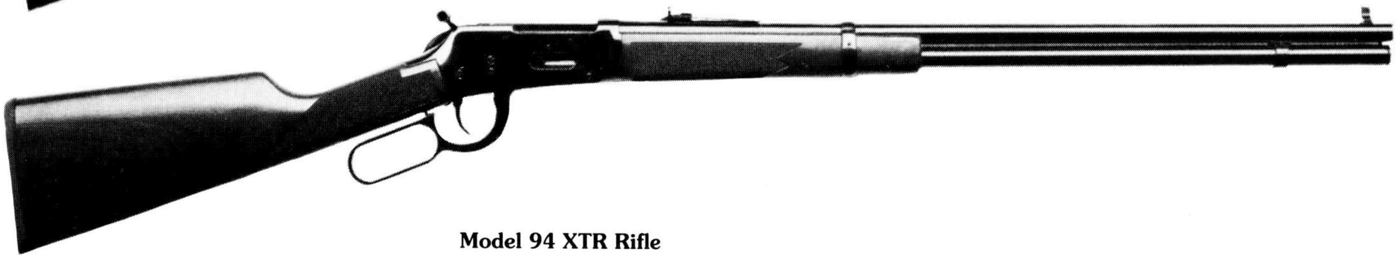

Model 94 XTR Rifle

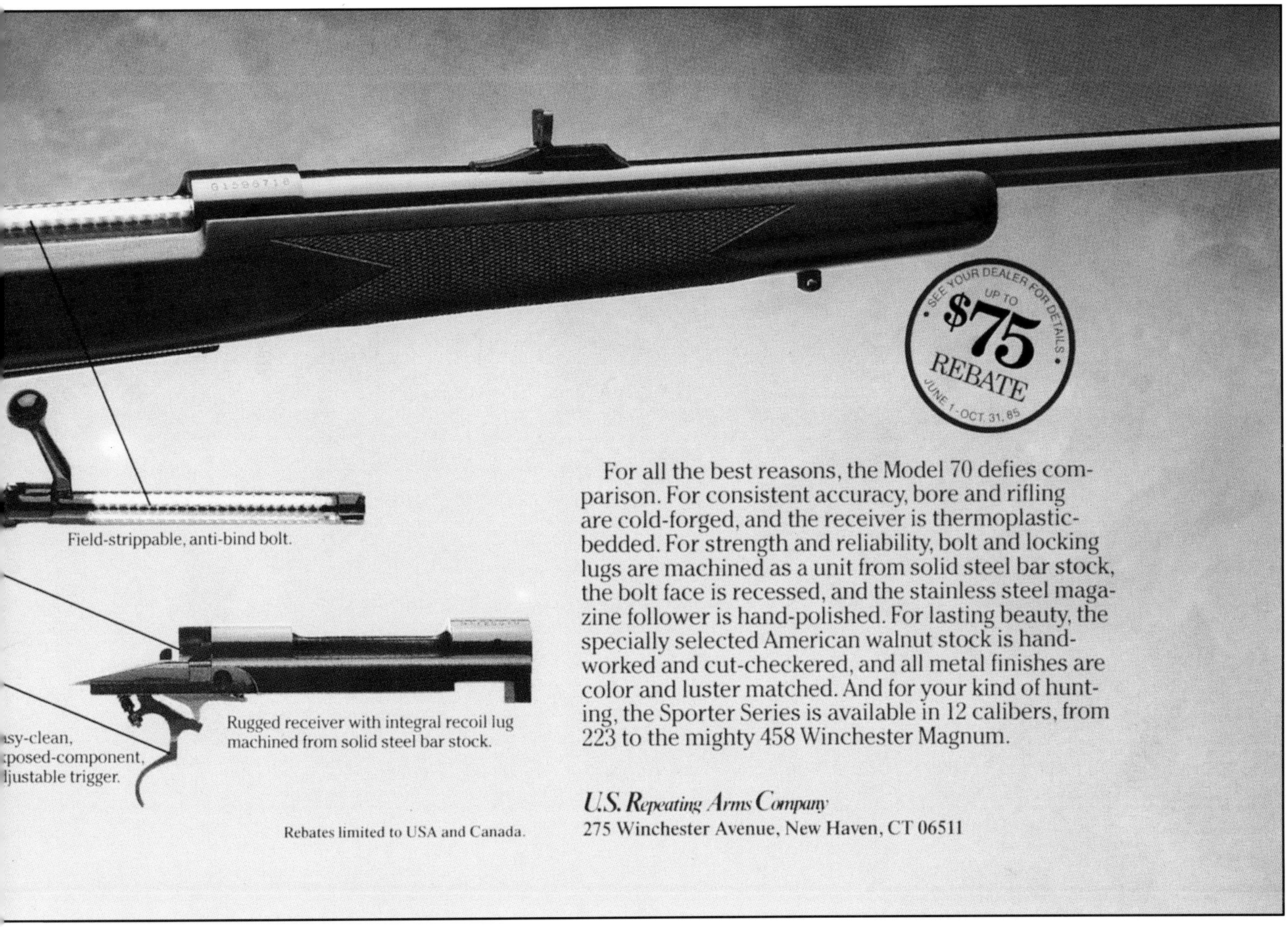

***Above:* The Model 70 XTR Sporter combines accuracy with the beauty of an American walnut stock. *Below:* The Model 94 Chief Crazy Horse Commemorative, complete with tribal decorations, honors the Sioux people.**

The Range Lever Action Carbine is a five shot .30-30 caliber with an American hardwood stock, a 20-inch barrel and blade front and semibuckhorn rear sights. For big game hunting the Model 94 Big Bore utilizes .375, .356 or .307 Winchester cartridges. This gun also features side ejection, Monte Carlo stocks of American walnut, sling swivels and a reversible thumb hammer extension. The receiver is forged steel with reinforced side panels, and has been drilled and tapped for top mounting of scopes.

To celebrate Winchester's 120th Anniversary, the company issued limited edition Model 94 carbines commemorating founder Oliver F Winchester, the horse-and-rider trademark, and Chief Crazy Horse. The Chief Crazy Horse Model 94 Winchester celebrates the great Sioux chief and his people, and is beautifully and symbolically engraved. This fine firearm is chambered for the classic .38-55 Winchester cartridge.

Winchester Model 9422 Rifles. This lever action, rimfire .22 caliber rifle has available barrel lengths of 20.5 inches and 22.2 inches, and weighs from 6.25 pounds to 6.5 pounds. The Model 9422 XTR, considered one of the world's finest production sporting arms, features positive lever action and bolt design for feeding and chambering from any shooting position.

The receiver, frame and finger lever are forged steel; receivers are designed for side ejection of spent cartridges and are grooved for top mounting of scopes. Each rifle has an adjustable thumb hammer extension with half-cock safety, ramped bead front and semibuckhorn rear sights.

The Standard Model 9422 XTR Rifle has a western saddle carbine profile with a straight stock and forearm with barrel band, traditional finger lever and composition butt plate. Model 9422 XTR Classic Rifle features include a satin finish walnut stock with fluted comb and crescent steel butt plate, curved finger lever and undercut pistol grip, and an extended forearm with barrel band and 22.5 inch barrel for long range accuracy.

The Commemorative Models are all limited edition firearms that feature the handsome Winchester engraving, which is designed around historical images and tastefully calligraphed lettering. The Model 9422 Boy Scouts of America Commemorative, complete with commemorative .22 Long ammunition, may well claim to be the the first such honor for that organization. A maximum 15,000 units were manufactured in the mid-1980s.

The .22 caliber, lever action, Annie Oakley Commemorative Model 9422 is the first US firearm to honor a historic American woman. Only 6000 units of the Annie Oakley Rifle were issued.

***Above:* The Wells Fargo Commemorative Carbine honors the 125th anniversary of Wells Fargo. *Below left:* The Bull Buffalo Skull with Blue Tails Gun Mount. *Right:* The Model 9422 Annie Oakley Commemorative—a tribute to sharpshooter Annie Oakley *(below)*, heroine of the Old West.**

WINCHESTER MODEL 9422
ANNIE OAKLEY™ COMMEMORATIVE

The First Commemorative Winchester® Rimfire Rifle to Honor an American Heroine.

The Annie Oakley Commemorative Model 9422 is a highly decorative 22-caliber rifle . . . a tribute to the sharpshooting woman who has become a central figure in American folklore.

Annie Oakley gained immense fame in Buffalo Bill's Wild West Show from 1885 to 1902. She created a sensation in America and Europe because of her uncanny accuracy with a rifle. Her highly-publicized use of Winchester firearms was an important factor in establishing the reputation of Winchester guns throughout the world.

It is fitting that this ultimate shooter be honored with the Model 9422, considered one of the world's finest production sporting arms. Its classic styling, accuracy, and feel are the results of superb craftsmanship. Finger lever, receiver, and barrel bands are antique gold-plated. The receiver is roll-engraved with her portrait and a scene from her show. The barrel is inscribed in gold "Annie Oakley Commemorative." The stock and forearm are select American walnut with a protective high-luster finish.

Functional features include a brass internal magazine tube, half-cock safety, hooded bead front sight and semi-buckhorn rear sight. Internal components are carefully finished for smoothness of action. Positive lever action and bolt design ensure feeding and chambering from any shooting position. Take-down for inspection or cleaning is greatly simplified with a single-screw construction.

In keeping with established traditions for Winchester commemorative rifles, the Annie Oakley 9422 is offered in a limited issue. Six thousand of these special rifles will be produced, bearing serial numbers AOK1 through AOK6000.

The Annie Oakley Commemorative Model 9422 is a decorative, distinctive tribute to a remarkable woman. It will be a treasured possession for collectors, sportsmen, and sportswomen.

WINCHESTER®

Winchester trademarks licensed from Olin Corporation.

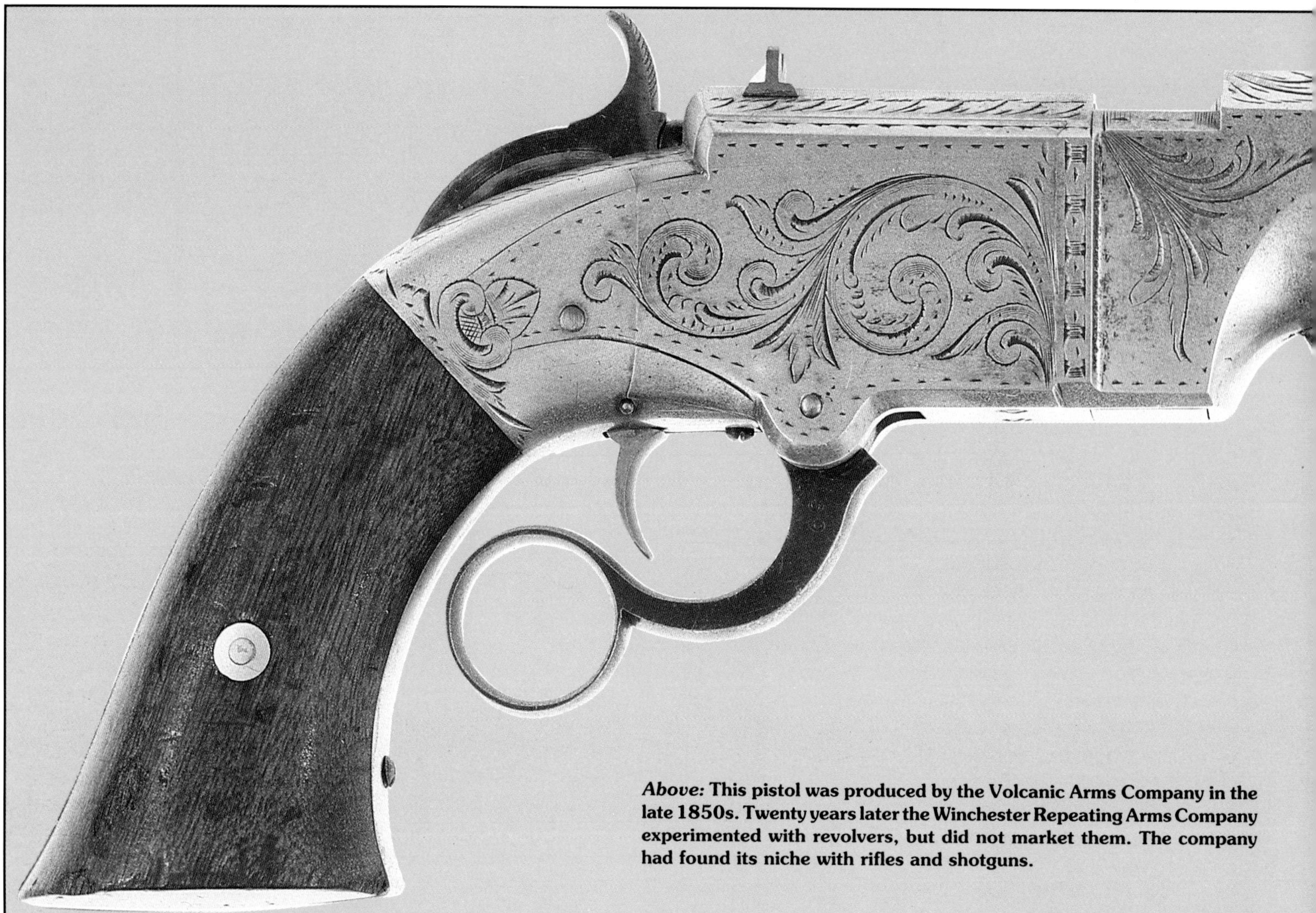

Above: **This pistol was produced by the Volcanic Arms Company in the late 1850s. Twenty years later the Winchester Repeating Arms Company experimented with revolvers, but did not market them. The company had found its niche with rifles and shotguns.**

Forerunners of the True Winchester

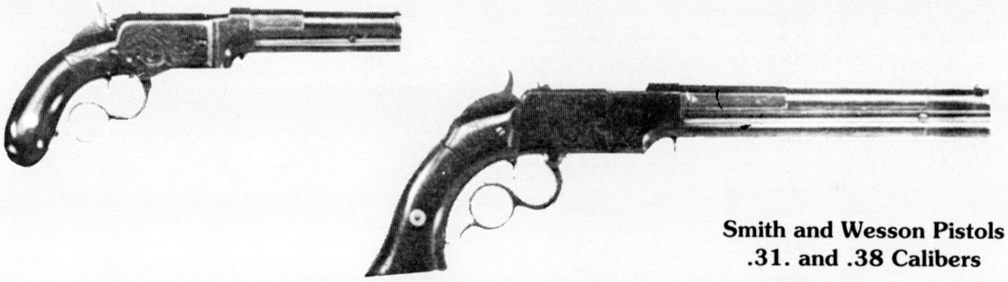

Smith and Wesson Pistols .31. and .38 Calibers

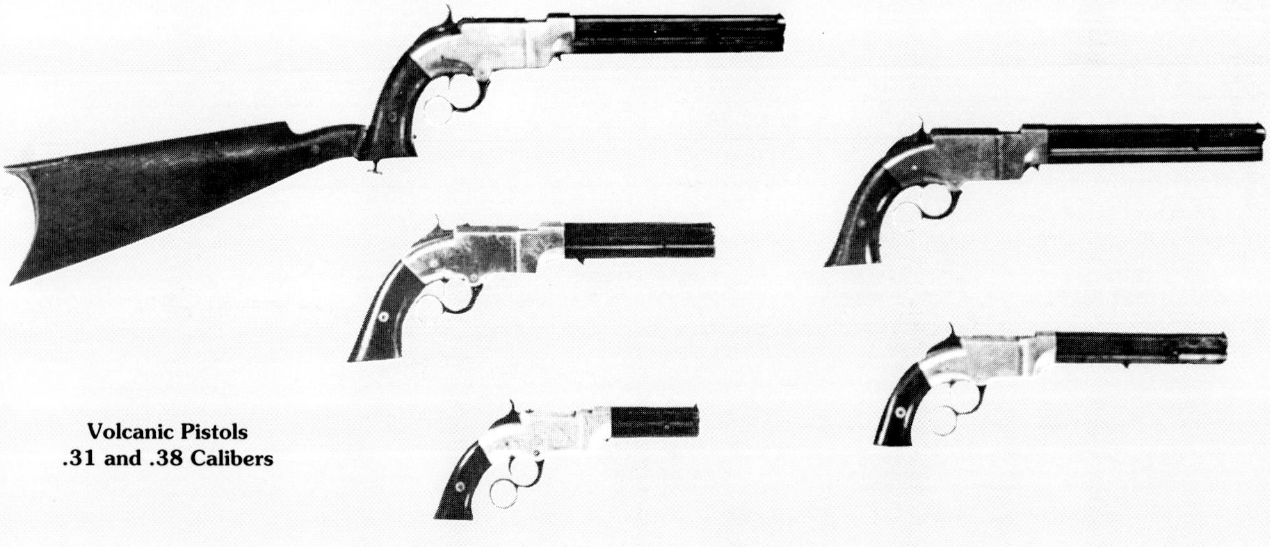

Volcanic Pistols .31 and .38 Calibers

Winchester Pistols

In a letter to Ed Martin dated 17 October 1862, Oliver F Winchester mentioned that 3000 revolvers were being produced by the New Haven Arms Company. Technically, these are the first Winchester pistols. They held six shots and retailed for about $15. Historians believe that John Walch, John Parker Lindsay and Cyrus Manville were all involved in the contracting and patenting of these first Winchester pistols.

These 'Walch Revolvers,' as they came to be known, were of two major types: the brass frame model and the iron frame model. The early Winchester Company produced these revolvers from 1860 until 1862. At the Centennial Celebration in Philadelphia in 1876, Winchester displayed models and drawings of a number of proposed pistols that were all built to the same design in three basic model classifications, all featuring solid frame construction.

Apparently Winchester's work on pistols was in the direction of developing a design that would have the solid frame of the unsuccessful Colt revolver and the rapid ejection capability of the Smith and Wesson pistols. All of the Winchester revolvers, of which there were very few, closely followed either their Colt or Smith and Wesson counterparts in exterior appearances. None of these revolvers played an important part in Winchester history, as they were all unsuccessful and were not produced commercially—except for extremely small quantities, usually for government contracts.

For example, Winchester had contracts with the US government for the US Ordnance Trials, and with Imperial Russia. Around the turn of the century, Winchester did produce a .22 Single Shot Bolt Action pistol in limited numbers, but it was never successfully marketed.

The War Department contracted with Winchester to manufacture the Colt Model 1911 .45 Automatic Pistol, but due to war contracts and other business at the time, Winchester subcontracted manufacture of these pistols to other firms. When the Armistice was signed in November of 1918, production ceased after only a few hundred of these automatics were made.

It is interesting to note that, as late as the 1960s, Winchester produced some experimental revolvers that were never marketed. Winchester had made its mark in history with repeating rifles, and wisely never ventured very far into the realm of pistols, which was already dominated by other patents and design innovations.

Winchester Experimental Pistols

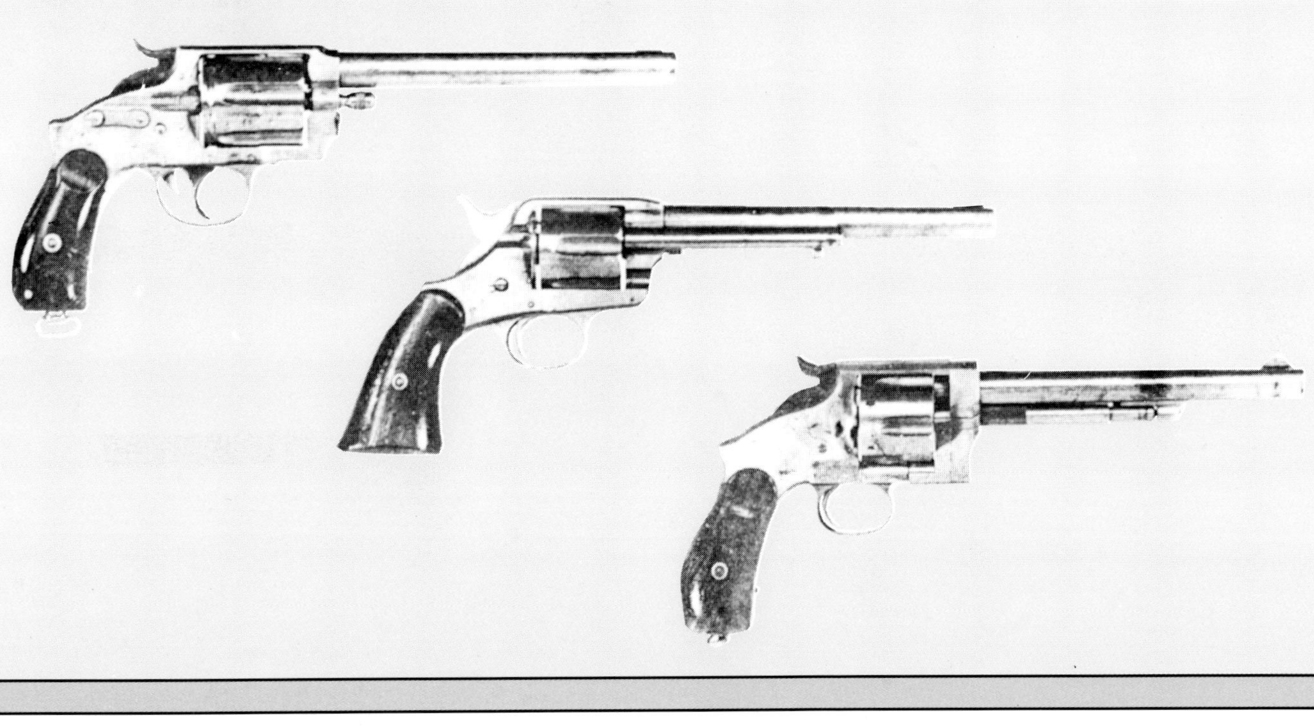

Fresh &

Great stir-frys

R&R

R&R PUBLICATIONS MARKETING PTY LTD

Published by:
R&R Publications Marketing Pty Ltd
ABN 78 348 105 138
PO Box 254, Carlton North, Victoria 3054 Australia
Phone (61 3) 9381 2199 Fax (61 3) 9381 2689
E-mail: info@randrpublications.com.au
Website: www.randrpublications.com.au
Australia-wide toll-free: 1800 063 296

Fresh & Tasty Great stir-fry

Publisher: Richard Carroll
Creative Director: Aisling Gallagher
Cover Designer: Lucy Adams
Typesetter: Elain Wei Voon Loh
Production Manager: Anthony Carroll
Food Photography: Steve Baxter, Phillip Wilkins, David Munns, Thomas Odulate, Christine Hanscomb and Frank Wieder
Home Economists: Sara Buenfeld, Emma Patmore, Nancy McDougall, Louise Pickford, Jane Stevenson, Oded Schwartz, Alison Austin and Jane Lawrie
Food Stylists: Helen Payne, Sue Russell, Sam Scott, Antonia Gaunt and Oded Schwartz
Recipe Development: Terry Farris, Jacqueline Bellefontaine, Becky Johnson, Valerie Barrett, Emma Patmore, Geri Richards, Pam Mallender and Jan Fullwood
Proofreader: Paul Hassing

Disclaimer: The nutritional information listed with each recipe does not include the nutrient content of garnishes or any accompaniments not listed in specific quantities in the ingredient list. The nutritional information for each recipe is an estimate only, and may vary depending on the brand of ingredients used, and due to natural biological variations in the composition of natural foods such as meat, fish, fruit and vegetables. The nutritional information was calculated by using the computer program Foodworks dietary analysis software (version 3.01, Xyris Software Pty Ltd. Queensland Australia), and is based on the Australian food composition tables and food manufacturers' data. Where not specified, ingredients are always analysed as average or medium, not small or large.
The analysis shown is for 100g of the recipe specified.

Includes Index
ISBN 978-1-74022-443-7

This edition printed February 2007
Computer Typeset in Futura

Printed in Singapore

Cover: Lamb Stir-fry with Noodles and Capsicums, page 47

Contents

Introduction

Stir-fry cooking should always be done at medium-high to high heat. This fast cooking method preserves the colour, texture and flavour of the ingredients, as well as the nutrient value. If any ingredients need marinating or soaking, this should be done in advance. It's important to have all the ingredients cut and ready, since the stir-fry process is so quick.

Organisation is essential. Once you start cooking a stir-fried dish, there's no time to cut up the ginger or carrots or run to the kitchen cabinet for the soy sauce. So cut, measure, marinate and assemble all the ingredients before you turn on the heat.

It's also a good idea to combine ingredients that will go into the cooker at the same time. Assemble all the tools you will need – spatula, ladle and serving plate – before beginning to cook.

Some stir-fry recipes call for cooking the meat first and then removing it while the vegetables cook. In others, the ingredients are simply added to the cooker according to their cooking times, so they all finish and are cooked at once. Your recipe should specify the appropriate technique.

There are four main steps to ensure successful stir-fry cooking.

1. Begin by adding the oil in a thin stream around the outside of your wok or skillet. Heat the oil until ripples form on the surface. Rotate the wok or skillet to distribute the oil evenly over the surface.
2. Add the first ingredient. Using a spatula or wooden spoon, briskly toss the food in the hot oil until it's well coated. This will preserve the colour and texture and help seal in the vitamins and minerals as the food cooks.
3. Add the next ingredients in the order given in the recipe when the first ingredient looks bright in colour (if vegetable) or slightly opaque (if seafood, chicken or lean meat).
4. If your wok or skillet has a long handle, tip the cooked food into the serving platter, scraping the sauce over it with the spatula. If it doesn't, scoop the food into a ladle with the spatula and transfer to a serving dish.

Instructions

1. Always have everything totally prepared, chopped, mixed and sliced, before you turn on the wok.
2. Heat the wok first, then add the oil and ingredients 'hot wok, cold oil, foods won't stick'. If using an electric stove rather than gas, leave the element on high and control the heat by moving the wok on and off the element.
3. Use fresh ingredients if possible.
4. Do not overcook the food.
5. Serve the dish the moment it's done, no matter what's going on at the table. An old Chinese proverb says, 'A man should wait for the dish. The dish should never wait for the man.'

Stir-Fry Tips

Stir-frying requires high heat and high speed. Here are a few tips to make the process go smoothly.

1 Add dense vegetables (carrots) first.

2 Tender vegetables (mushrooms) and leafy greens (spinach, bok choy) require less cooking time.

3 Meats can be stir-fried first, set aside, then reintroduced at the last minute. This prevents overcooking.

Vegetable Stir-Frys

The secret to success when creating vegetable stir-frys lies in crisp, fresh ingredients, advance preparation and speed! These delicious recipes are quick and easy to prepare, ideal for busy cooks, and have the added bonus of being great for your health.

Stir-Fry Bitter Melon

Preparation 8 mins + standing **Cooking** 10 mins **Calories** 54 **Fat** 0g

1 medium bitter melon (gourd), peeled, deseeded, cut into 1cm thick slices
2 tbsps salt
1 tsp vegetable oil
3 tbsps small dried prawns
6 French shallots, sliced
2 cloves garlic, sliced
2 stalks fresh lemongrass, finely sliced, or 1 tsp finely grated lemon rind
3 fresh green chillies, finely sliced
1 small red pawpaw, cut into 3cm cubes
125g snow peas, halved
1 tbsp tamarind concentrate

1. Rub each slice of bitter melon (gourd) with salt, place in a colander and set aside for 30 minutes. Rinse under cold water and drain thoroughly.
2. Heat the oil in a wok over a medium heat, add the dried prawns, French shallots, garlic and lemongrass or rind and stir-fry for 4 minutes or until the French shallots are golden.
3. Add the chillies and bitter melon (gourd) and stir-fry for 4 minutes or until the melon is tender. Add the pawpaw, snow peas and tamarind and stir-fry for 2 minutes or until the snow peas are tender.

Serves 4

Note: This dish is delicious served on a bed of cellophane noodles and topped with fried onions. Bitter melon (gourd) looks like a cucumber with a lumpy skin and, as the name suggests, has a bitter taste. It should always be degorged with salt before using.

Chilli Mushroom Stir-Fry with Noodles

Preparation 10 mins + 15 mins soaking **Cooking** 10 mins **Calories** 188 **Fat** 8g

15g dried porcini mushrooms
200g fresh Chinese noodles
2 tbsps sunflower oil
4 cloves garlic, sliced
1 red chilli, deseeded and chopped
2 tsps ready-made ginger purée or finely grated fresh ginger
500g fresh mushrooms, quartered or sliced
4 spring onions, sliced
4 tbsps rice wine or dry sherry
4 tbsps dark soy sauce
2 tbsps lemon juice
1 tbsp sugar, or to taste
2 tbsps chopped fresh coriander

1 Cover the dried mushrooms with 75mL of boiling water and soak for 15 minutes or until softened. Strain and reserve the liquid, then slice the mushrooms. Meanwhile, prepare the noodles according to the instructions on the packet, until tender but still firm to the the bite, then drain.

2 Heat the oil in a wok or large frying pan until smoking, then add the garlic, chilli and ginger and stir-fry for 15 seconds or until they release their flavours. Add all the mushrooms and stir-fry for 2 minutes or until softened.

3 Add the spring onions, sake or sherry, soy sauce, lemon juice, sugar, coriander, reserved soaking liquid from the mushrooms and the noodles, and heat for 1–2 minutes, until warmed through.

Serves 4

Note: The chilli adds extra bite to this oriental mushroom and ginger stir-fry.

Vegetable Stir-Fry with Noodles

Preparation 25 mins **Cooking** 15 mins **Calories** 474 **Fat** 22g

250g pack broad ribbon egg noodles
2 tbsps sunflower oil
1 garlic clove, sliced
2 carrots, thinly sliced diagonally
150g green beans, halved
150g broccoli florets
1 red capsicum, deseeded and cut into matchsticks
4 spring onions, thinly sliced diagonally
chopped fresh coriander, to garnish
lemon wedges, to serve

Sauce

4 tbsps smooth peanut butter
1 tbsp tomato purée
1 tbsp balsamic vinegar
sea salt and freshly ground black pepper

1 Cook the noodles according to the packet instructions, then drain well.

2 Heat the oil in a wok or large frying pan until very hot. Add the garlic, carrots and green beans and stir-fry for 2 minutes, until lightly coloured. Add the broccoli and stir-fry for 2–3 minutes or until softened. Add the red capsicum and spring onions, then cook for a further 1 minute.

3 Add the sauce, 125mL water and the drained noodles. Combine well and stir-fry for 4–5 minutes or until everything is hot. Garnish with the coriander and serve with the lemon wedges to squeeze over.

Sauce

1 Mix together the peanut butter, tomato purée, balsamic vinegar and seasoning, with about 4 tablespoons of cold water. Set aside.

Serves 4

Note: *This stir-fry has a secret ingredient; the peanut butter adds instant sweetness and depth of flavour. You can use whatever vegetables you happen to have in the refrigerator. Like most other nuts, peanuts are high in 'healthy' monounsaturated fats and low in 'unhealthy' saturated fats. They're also an extremely useful source of Vitamin E and zinc.*

Warm Spinach Salad with Walnuts

Preparation 5 mins **Cooking** 2 mins **Calories** 166 **Fat** 15g

2 tbsps walnut oil
5 sun-dried tomatoes in oil, drained and chopped
250g baby spinach
1 red onion, sliced into thin rings
2 tbsps walnut pieces
salt
3 tbsps chopped fresh coriander, to garnish

1 Heat the oil in a wok or large, heavy-based frying pan. Add the tomatoes, spinach, onion, walnut pieces and salt to taste. Cook for 1 minute or until the spinach begins to wilt, tossing to combine.

2 Transfer the vegetables to a large salad bowl and sprinkle with the coriander to garnish. Serve immediately.

Serves 4

Note: There's something seductive about warm salads – their flavours seem more intense. In this easy salad, walnuts, spinach and sun-dried tomatoes create a magical result.

Noodles with Broccoli and Carrots

Preparation 20 mins **Cooking** 40 mins **Calories** 293 **Fat** 9g

- 250g pack stir-fry noodles
- 3 tbsps vegetable oil
- $2\frac{1}{2}$cm piece fresh ginger, finely chopped
- 2 red chillies, deseeded and finely chopped
- 4 cloves garlic, finely sliced
- 2 onions, thinly sliced
- 2 tbsps clear honey
- 1 cup vegetable or chicken stock or white wine
- 3 tbsps white wine vinegar
- 600g broccoli, cut into florets
- 300g carrots, pared into ribbons with a vegetable peeler
- snipped fresh chives, to garnish

1 Prepare the noodles according to the packet instructions, then drain. Heat the oil in a large wok or heavy-based frying pan, then add the ginger and chillies and stir-fry for 1–2 minutes to soften.

2 Add the garlic and onions and fry for 5–6 minutes, until the onions have browned. Stir in the honey and cook for 6–8 minutes, until the honey starts to caramelise.

3 Add the stock or wine and vinegar to the onion mixture. Bring to the boil, then reduce the heat and simmer, uncovered, for 8 minutes or until the liquid has slightly reduced. Stir in the broccoli and carrots, cover, and simmer for 8–10 minutes or until the vegetables are cooked but still crunchy.

4 Stir in the noodles and mix well. Cook, stirring, for 2–3 minutes until the noodles are hot and most of the liquid has evaporated. Sprinkle the chives over the top just before serving.

Makes 6

Snow Peas and Carrots with Sesame Seeds

Preparation 10 mins **Cooking** 5 mins **Calories** 90 **Fat** 8g

$\frac{1}{2}$ cucumber
2 tbsps sesame seeds
1 tbsp sunflower oil
4 carrots, cut into matchsticks
250g snow peas
6 spring onions, chopped
1 tbsp lemon juice
black pepper

1. Peel the cucumber, cut it in half lengthways and scoop out the seeds. Slice into half moons.
2. Heat a non-stick wok or large frying pan. Add the sesame seeds and dry-fry for 1 minute or until toasted, tossing constantly. Remove and set aside. Add the oil, then the cucumber and carrots and stir-fry over a high heat for 2 minutes. Add the snow peas and spring onions and stir-fry for a further 2–3 minutes, until all the vegetables are cooked but still crisp.
3. Sprinkle over the lemon juice and sesame seeds, toss to mix and stir-fry for a few seconds to heat through. Season with pepper and serve.

Serves 4

Spinach with Sesame Seeds

Preparation 15 mins + 3 mins standing **Cooking** 5 mins **Calories** 89 **Fat** 7g

- 700g fresh spinach, stalks removed
- 1 tbsp peanut oil
- 1 tsp sesame oil
- 3 cloves garlic, chopped
- 2 tbsps sesame seeds
- juice of ½ lemon
- ¼ tsp finely grated lemon rind (optional)
- salt and black pepper

1. Place the spinach in a large bowl, cover with boiling water, then leave for 2–3 minutes. Drain, then refresh under cold running water. Squeeze out any excess water, then coarsely chop.
2. Heat the peanut and sesame oils in a wok or large, heavy-based frying pan. Add the garlic and the sesame seeds and fry for 1–2 minutes, until the garlic begins to brown and the seeds start to pop.
3. Stir in the spinach and fry for 1–2 minutes, until heated through. Add the lemon juice and rind, if using, then season and mix well.

Serves 6

Note: Lemony spinach adds a refreshing tang to roast meat and fish dishes. It can also make a substantial snack with poached eggs and bread.

Wilted Rocket Cheese Salad

Preparation 4 mins **Cooking** 10 mins **Calories** 310 **Fat** 7g

- 3 tbsps olive oil
- 4 slices white bread, crusts removed and cut into cubes
- 3 spring onions, sliced diagonally
- 2 cloves garlic, crushed
- 2 zucchini, cut lengthwise into thin strips
- 1 red capsicum, thinly sliced
- 1/2 cup raisins
- 250g rocket
- 125g blue cheese, crumbled
- 2 tbsps balsamic vinegar

1. Heat 2 tablespoons of oil in a wok over a medium heat, add the bread and stir-fry for 3 minutes or until golden. Drain on absorbent paper.
2. Heat the remaining oil in the wok, add the spring onions and garlic and stir-fry for 2 minutes. Add the zucchini, capsicum and raisins and stir-fry for 3 minutes or until the vegetables are just tender. Remove them from the wok and set aside.
3. Add the rocket to the wok and stir-fry for 2 minutes or until just wilts. Place the rocket on a serving platter or divide between individual bowls or plates, then top with the vegetable mixture and scatter with the croûtons and blue cheese. Drizzle with the balsamic vinegar and serve immediately.

Serves 4

Note: If rocket is unavailable this salad is also delicious made with English spinach or watercress.

Snow Pea and Mango Stir-Fry

Preparation 10 mins **Cooking** 10 mins **Calories** 146 **Fat** 8g

- 300g snow peas, trimmed
- 1 onion, cut into rings
- 1 clove garlic, chopped
- 1 tbsp peanut oil
- 2 tbsps chopped fresh ginger
- 440g can mangoes in juice
- 1/4 cup roasted peanuts, to garnish

1 Heat the oil in a wok or large frying pan. Stir-fry the onion, garlic and ginger until the onion is clear. Add the snow peas and stir for 2–3 minutes. Drain the mangoes, reserving 1/4 cup of juice.

3 Cut the mangoes into slices. Add the reserved juice and mangoes to the wok. Cover and cook for 3–5 minutes or until the snow peas are just tender. Garnish with the peanuts.

Serves 4

Green Vegetable Stir-Fry with Sesame Seeds

Preparation 10 mins **Cooking** 15 mins **Calories** 154 **Fat** 12g

- 2 tbsps sesame seeds
- 2 tbsps peanut oil
- 1 clove garlic, roughly chopped
- 2½cm piece fresh ginger, finely chopped
- 150g broccoli, cut into very small florets
- 2 zucchini, halved lengthways and finely sliced
- 170g snow peas
- 1 tbsp rice wine or medium-dry sherry
- 1 tbsp dark soy sauce
- 1 tbsp oyster sauce

1. Heat a wok. Add the sesame seeds and dry-fry for 2 minutes or until golden, shaking the pan frequently. Remove and set aside.
2. Add the oil to the wok, heat for 1 minute, then add the garlic and ginger and stir-fry over a medium heat for 1–2 minutes, until softened. Add the broccoli and stir-fry for a further 2–3 minutes.
3. Add the zucchini and snow peas and stir-fry for 3 minutes. Pour over the rice wine or sherry and sizzle for 1 minute. Add the soy and oyster sauces, mix well, then stir-fry for 2 minutes. Sprinkle over the fried sesame seeds just before serving.

Serves 4

Note: Dry-fry or toasted sesame seeds add a nutty taste to this quick and healthy Chinese dish. It's best to prepare all the vegetables before you start cooking.

Chicken and Poultry Stir-Frys

These fabulous stir-frys can take you on a gourmet adventure through many foreign lands. From the distinctly Chinese flavours of sweet and sour chicken to the Indian delights of samosas and rogan josh, and from Japanese pan-fried glazed chicken to Thai-spiced chicken with zucchini, there's something for everyone. Collected from around the world, they all have one thing in common – they taste sensational!

Hoisin Chicken

Preparation 15 mins **Cooking** 15 mins **Calories** 95 **Fat** 2g

- oil, for deep frying
- 350g chicken stir-fry
- 1/2 cup cornflour
- 1 slice ginger root
- 2 onions, sliced
- 1 capsicum, sliced
- 2 sticks celery, sliced
- 250g broccoli, cut into flowerets
- 125g mushrooms, sliced
- 2 tbsps hoisin sauce
- 2 tbsps dry sherry
- 1 tbsp soy sauce
- 2 tbsps vinegar
- 1 cup chicken stock
- 1/2 tsp sesame oil
- 1 1/2 tbsps cornflour, extra
- 85g packet 2 minute noodles, boiled or 2 cups cooked long grain rice

1. Place oil about 5cm deep in a wok or frying pan and heat. Dip the stir fry pieces in cornflour, a few at a time, and fry until golden. Drain on absorbent paper.
2. Pour some oil from wok, leaving about 3 tablespoons. Add the ginger and onions, cook for 1 minute, add the capsicum, celery and broccoli and stir fry for 2 minutes.
3. Add the mushrooms, hoisin sauce, sherry, soy sauce, vinegar and stock. Blend the sesame oil with extra cornflour and a little water. Add it to the wok and stir until the contents come to the boil and thicken. Return the chicken to the wok and stir to reheat.
4. Serve over boiled noodles or rice.

Serves 4

Sweet and Sour Chicken

Preparation 5 mins **Cooking** 7 mins **Calories** 227 **Fat** 2g

- 400g can pineapple pieces
- 1 red capsicum, deseeded
- 6 spring onions
- 2 tsps soy sauce
- 2 tbsps malt vinegar
- 2 tbsps brown sugar
- 1 tbsp lemon juice
- 1 tsp finely grated fresh ginger
- 2 tbsps tomato sauce
- 1 tbsp cornflour
- 2 tbsps water
- 500g chicken thigh fillets
- 3 tbsps oil

1. Drain the pineapple pieces and reserve the juice. Cut the capsicum into strips or squares. Cut the spring onions, including most of the green shoot, into 1cm diagonal pieces. Mix together the pineapple juice, soy sauce, vinegar, sugar, lemon juice, ginger and tomato sauce. Blend the water and cornflour and set aside. Cut each thigh fillet into 1cm wide strips.
2. Heat the wok, add 2 tablespoons of oil and, when hot, add a third of the chicken. Stir-fry over a high heat until cooked, about 1 minute. Remove and cook the remaining chicken in 2 batches, adding extra oil if needed. Drain the chicken well on absorbent paper. Drain all oil from the wok.
3. Pour the sauce mixture into the wok and add the blended cornflour. Cook, stirring, until the mixture boils and thickens. Stir in the capsicum, spring onions and pineapple pieces and cook for 1 minute. Add the chicken and heat through. Serve immediately with boiled rice.

Serves 6

Spring Rolls

Preparation 20 mins **Cooking** 10 mins **Calories** 56 **Fat** 1g

500g chicken stir-fry
1/4 Chinese cabbage, finely chopped
1/2 red capsicum, seeded and thinly sliced
4 mushrooms, thinly sliced
1 tbsp soy sauce
2 tbsps dipping sauce (see below)
2 tbsps olive oil
2 tsps finely chopped fresh ginger
1 small onion, finely chopped
2 tsps cornflour, blended with 1 tbsp water
1 packet frozen spring roll wrappers
vegetable oil for deep frying

Dipping Sauce

1/2 cup apricot jam
1 tbsp soy sauce
1 tbsp lemon juice
2 tbsps white vinegar
1 tbsp water

1. Chop the chicken stir-fry into smaller pieces, Prepare Chinese cabbage, capsicum and mushrooms, combine the soy sauce and 2 tablespoons dipping sauce. Heat the wok and add 2 tablespoons of olive oil. Add ginger and onion and stir-fry until onion is pale gold in colour. Add chicken and stir-fry until white all over about 2 minutes, toss in the vegetables and stir-fry one minute, mixing chicken through the vegetables.
2. Pour in the combined sauces, tossing to mix through. Push the mixture to one side and add blended cornflour to the juices in the base of the wok. As juices thicken, stir and toss through the vegetables. Spread mixture out onto a flat tray to cool. Wrap one heaped tablespoon chicken mixture in each wrapper according to packet directions.
3. Wipe out the wok, heat and add fresh oil to approximately 5cm deep. Heat oil but do not boil and fry rolls a few at a time until gold colour and crisp. Drain on paper towels. Serve hot with dipping sauce.

Dipping Sauce

1. Mix all ingredients together, heat gently while stirring.

Yields 65 rolls

Tip: Mini Spring Rolls are ideal finger food for a crowd. Cut spring roll wrappers in half and use 2 teaspoons of Spring Roll mixture. Place mixture on bottom end of strip and roll once. Fold in side and continue to roll. Seal end with a little egg white. Serve with hot dipping sauce.

Portuguese Chicken

Preparation 10 mins **Cooking** 40 mins **Calories** 125 **Fat** 8g

- 4 tbsps vegetable oil
- 8 chicken thighs, skinned and all visible fat removed
- 2 onions, diced
- 3 cloves garlic, crushed
- 440g canned tomatoes, drained and mashed
- 8 mushrooms, sliced
- ½ cup chicken stock
- 2 tbsps tomato paste
- freshly ground black pepper
- 2 tbsps chopped fresh parsley

1. Heat ½ the oil in a frying pan over a medium heat, add the chicken and cook for 2–3 minutes each side or until brown. Remove the chicken from the pan and set aside.
2. Heat the remaining oil in the pan, add the onions and cook, stirring, for 5 minutes or until golden. Add the garlic and cook for 1 minute longer.
3. Return the chicken to the pan, add the tomatoes, mushrooms, stock and tomato paste and bring to the boil. Reduce the heat, cover and simmer for 30 minutes or until chicken is cooked. Season to taste with black pepper and sprinkle with parsley.

Serves 4

Note: *For a complete meal, serve on a bed of boiled white or brown rice. The cooking time will vary according to the size of the chicken thighs.*

Samosas

Preparation 20 mins **Cooking** 45 mins **Calories** 92 **Fat** 1g each

1 tbsp vegetable oil
2 medium onions, finely chopped
1 clove garlic, crushed
2 tsps curry paste
$\frac{1}{2}$ tsp salt
1 tbsp white vinegar
250g chicken mince
$\frac{1}{2}$ cup water
2 tsps sweet chilli sauce
2 tbsps coriander, chopped
1 packet frozen spring roll wrappers
1 $\frac{1}{2}$ cups vegetable oil

1 Heat the wok, add the oil and fry the onions and garlic until the onions are soft. Add the curry paste and salt and fry a little (about 30 seconds). Stir in the vinegar. Add the chicken mince and stir-fry on high until the chicken changes colour. Break up any lumps. Reduce heat, add the water, cover and cook until most of the water is absorbed (about 6 minutes). Uncover, and add the chilli sauce and coriander. Stir until the water has evaporated and the chicken is dry. Remove to a plate to cool. Rinse the wok.

2 Cut 10 spring roll wrappers into 3 even pieces 7$\frac{1}{2}$ x 20cm. Place a teaspoon of filling at bottom end and fold over the pastry diagonally, forming a triangle. Fold again on the straight. Continue to make 3 more folds in same way. Moisten the inside edge of the last fold with water and press gently to seal.

3 Heat the clean wok. Add about 5cm of oil. Heat the oil but take care not to overheat. Add 3–4 samosas and fry until golden. Remove with a slotted spoon to a tray lined with absorbent paper. Repeat with the remainder. If the samosas become dark in colour, immediately remove them from the heat to drop the oil temperature.

Makes 30–36

Thigh Fillets with Fruity Mint Salsa

Preparation 10 mins **Cooking** 15 mins **Calories** 130 **Fat** 6g

500g chicken thighs
canola oil spray
salt, pepper to taste (optional)
½ tsp dried oregano
1 pear, peeled and diced
1 banana, peeled and diced
2 tbsps lemon juice
3 tbsps finely chopped mint
2 tsps sweet chilli sauce

1. Pound thigh fillets on both sides with a meat mallet to flatten. Sprinkle with salt (if using), pepper and oregano.
2. Heat a non-stick frying pan and lightly spray with oil, place in the thigh steaks and cook for 3 minutes on each side. Remove to a heated plate and keep hot. Add diced pear, banana, lemon juice, mint and chilli sauce to the pan. Scrape up pan juices and stir to heat fruit.
3. Pile hot fruit salsa on top of thigh steaks. Serve immediately with mashed potatoes or rice.

Serves 3–4

Chicken Rogan Josh

Preparation 15 mins **Cooking** 1 hr **Calories** 236 **Fat** 9g

- 8 skinless boneless chicken thighs
- 1 tbsp vegetable oil
- 1 small red and 1 small green capsicum, deseeded and thinly sliced
- 1 onion, thinly sliced
- 5cm piece of fresh ginger, finely chopped
- 2 cloves garlic, crushed
- 2 tbsps garam masala
- 1 tsp each paprika, turmeric and chilli powder
- 4 cardamom pods, crushed
- salt
- 200g Greek yoghurt
- 400g can chopped tomatoes
- fresh coriander, to garnish

1. Cut each thigh into 4 pieces. Heat the oil in a large heavy-based frying pan and add the capsicums, onion, ginger, garlic, spices and a good pinch of salt. Fry over a low heat for 5 minutes or until the capsicums and onion have softened.
2. Add the chicken to the pan, then add 2 tablespoons of the yoghurt. Increase the heat to medium and cook for 4 minutes or until the yoghurt is absorbed. Repeat the step above until all yoghurt is used.
3. Increase the heat to high, stir in the tomatoes and 200mL of water and bring to the boil. Reduce the heat, cover, and simmer for 30 minutes or until the chicken is tender, stirring occasionally and adding more water if the sauce becomes too dry.
4. Uncover the pan, increase the heat to high and cook, stirring constantly, for 5 minutes or until the sauce thickens. Garnish with coriander.

Serves 4

Fragrant Duck with Pineapple

Preparation 20 mins + 20 mins marinating **Cooking** 10 mins **Calories** 203 **Fat** 9g

- 2 boneless duck breasts, about 175g each, skinned and cut into strips
- 1 tsp five spice powder
- 2 tbsps soy sauce
- 2 tbsps rice wine or dry sherry
- 1 tsp sugar
- 1 tbsp peanut oil
- 1 orange or red capsicum, deseeded and cut into thin strips
- 5cm piece fresh ginger, cut into matchsticks
- 2 spring onions, white and green parts separated, thinly shredded
- 170g fresh pineapple, cut into bite-size pieces, plus juice
- salt

1. Place the duck, five spice powder, soy sauce, rice wine or sherry and sugar in a shallow non-metallic bowl. Cover and marinate for 20 minutes.
2. Heat the oil in a wok. Remove the duck from the marinade and reserve. Stir-fry the duck over a high heat for 2 minutes. Add the capsicum, ginger and the white spring onion parts and stir-fry for a further 3–4 minutes, until the capsicum starts to soften.
3. Add the pineapple and juice and the marinade. Stir-fry for 1–2 minutes. Season with salt if desired. Serve immediately, sprinkled with the green spring onion parts.

Serves 4

Note: Fresh pineapple cuts through the richness of tender duck breasts marinated in Chinese spices. Serve this dish with plain boiled noodles or some fragrant Thai rice.

Chicken Stir-Fry with Lemon and Mango

Preparation 15 mins + 3 mins standing **Cooking** 5 mins **Calories** 89 **Fat** 7g

1 ripe mango
2 tbsps sunflower oil
2 garlic cloves, crushed
2½cm piece fresh ginger, finely chopped
4 chicken breast fillets, cut into strips
150g snow peas, halved lengthways
2 celery sticks, thinly sliced
1 yellow capsicum, deseeded and cut into matchsticks
4 spring onions, thinly sliced
sea salt and freshly ground black pepper
juice of ½ lemon
2 tbsps white wine or apple juice
1 tbsp balsamic vinegar
1 tbsp clear honey
2 tbsps chopped fresh coriander

1. Slice the two fatter 'cheeks' of the mango from either side of the stone. Cut a criss-cross pattern across the flesh of each piece to separate it into small cubes, then push the skin upwards and slice off the cubes. Set aside.
2. Heat the oil in a wok or large frying pan until hot. Add the garlic, ginger and chicken and stir-fry for 3 minutes.
3. Add the snow peas, celery and capsicum and stir-fry for 3–4 minutes. Add the spring onions, mango and seasoning, then stir-fry for a further 2 minutes.
4. Combine the lemon juice with the white wine or apple juice, balsamic vinegar and honey in a small bowl. Add to the wok and continue to cook for 2 minutes. Add the coriander and serve.

Serves 6

Stir-Fry Lemongrass Chicken

Preparation 20 mins + 2 hrs marinating **Cooking** 10 mins **Calories** 281 **Fat** 18g

- 4 stalks lemongrass
- 500g skinless boneless chicken breasts, cut into 2½cm cubes
- 1 tsp sesame oil
- 2 tbsps vegetable oil
- ½ red capsicum, deseeded and chopped
- 2 tbsps roasted salted peanuts, roughly chopped
- 2 tbsps Thai fish sauce (nam pla)
- 1 tsp sugar
- salt
- 2 spring onions, chopped

1. Peel the outer layers from the lemongrass stalks and finely chop the lower white bulbous parts, discarding the fibrous tops. Put the chicken into a large bowl, add the lemongrass and sesame oil and stir to coat the chicken well. Cover and marinate in the refrigerator for 2 hours, or overnight.
2. Heat a wok or a large, heavy-based frying pan, then add the vegetable oil. Add the chicken with its marinade and stir-fry for 5 minutes or until the chicken has turned white.
3. Add the capsicum, peanuts, fish sauce, sugar and salt to taste. Stir-fry for another 5 minutes or until the chicken and capsicum are cooked. Sprinkle over the spring onions just before serving.

Serves 4

Note: Red capsicum and roasted peanuts add a crunchy texture to this chicken stir-fry dish from Vietnam. The simple marinade gives the meat a delicate citrus flavour.

Japanese Pan-Fry Glazed Chicken

Preparation 5 mins **Cooking** 15 mins **Calories** 125 **Fat** 5g

1 tbsp peanut oil
4 skinless boneless chicken breasts, sliced diagonally
spring onions, shredded, to garnish

Glaze

75mL Japanese or other dark soy sauce
75mL rice wine or medium-dry sherry
3 tbsps granulated sugar

1. Heat the oil in a large, heavy-based frying pan. Fry the chicken for 3–5 minutes, until lightly coloured. Pour over the glaze.
2. Fry for 5 minutes or until the glaze has nearly evaporated and the chicken pieces are coated and cooked through, turning them occasionally. Serve garnished with spring onions.

Glaze

1. Place the soy sauce, rice wine or sherry and the sugar into a small saucepan. Cook gently, stirring, for 3 minutes or until the sugar has dissolved.

Serves 4

Note: In Japan, this sweet glazed dish is known as teriyaki. The recipe works equally well with beef or pork and is traditionally served with rice.

Braised Chicken Wings

Preparation 10 mins **Cooking** 45 mins **Calories** 469 **Fat** 22g

- 1 kg chicken wings
- 2 tbsps peanut oil
- 4 tbsps soy sauce
- 2 tbsps honey
- grated rind of 1 lemon
- 2 tbsps dry sherry
- 1 clove garlic, chopped
- $2^1/2$cm piece of fresh root ginger, grated

1. Using a sharp knife, remove the wing tips from the chicken wings and cut each wing in half at the joint.
2. Heat a wok and pour in the oil. When the oil is very hot, add the wings and stir-fry for 3–4 minutes. Stir in the soy sauce, honey, lemon rind, sherry and garlic. Keep stirring until the liquid comes to the boil.
3. Cover the wok with a tight-fitting lid and reduce the heat. Simmer the wings over a gentle heat for 30 minutes or until tender. Stir occasionally to stop the sauce from sticking, especially towards the end of the cooking time.

Serves 4

Noodles with Chicken and Snow Peas

Preparation 20 mins **Cooking** 12 mins **Calories** 398 **Fat** 11g

- 250g pack dried thread egg noodles
- 2 tbsps peanut oil
- 1 red or yellow capsicum, deseeded and chopped
- 1cm piece fresh ginger, finely chopped
- 1 clove garlic, finely chopped
- 2 spring onions, cut into 2½cm lengths, white and green parts separated
- 2 skinless boneless chicken breasts, cut into strips
- 170g pack snow peas
- 2 tbsps dark soy sauce
- 1 tbsp oyster sauce

1. Cook the noodles according to the packet instructions. Drain and rinse.
2. Heat a wok, then add the oil. Stir-fry the capsicum, ginger, garlic and the white parts of the spring onions for 1 minute. Add the chicken and stir-fry for 5 minutes or until it has turned opaque.
3. Add the snow peas to the chicken and stir-fry for 1 minute. Add the noodles and the green parts of the spring onions, mixing well, then stir in the soy and oyster sauces. Stir-fry for 5 minutes or until the chicken is cooked through.

Serves 4

Chicken with Chilli Jam

Preparation 8 mins **Cooking** 12 mins **Calories** 287 **Fat** 2g

- 2 tsps vegetable oil
- 3 chicken breast fillets or 4 boneless thigh fillets, cut into thin strips
- 4 French shallots, chopped
- 185g broccoli, chopped
- 125g snow peas, halved
- 55g unsalted, roasted cashews
- 2 tbsps light soy sauce

Chilli Jam

- 2 tsps vegetable oil
- 4 fresh red chillies, sliced
- 1 tbsp shredded fresh ginger
- 1 tsp prawn paste
- $^1/_3$ cup sugar
- $^1/_3$ cup water
- 2 tbsps lime juice

1. To make the jam, heat the oil in a wok over a medium heat, add the chillies, ginger and prawn paste, and stir-fry for 1 minute or until golden. Stir in the sugar, water and lime juice and cook, stirring, for 3 minutes or until the mixture is thick. Remove the jam from the wok and set it aside.
2. Heat the oil in a clean wok over a high heat for 1 minute, add the chicken and French shallots and stir-fry for 3 minutes or until the chicken is lightly browned.
3. Add the broccoli, snow peas, cashews and soy sauce and stir-fry for 3 minutes longer or until the vegetables change colour and are cooked.
4. To serve, place the chicken on a serving plate and top with the chilli jam

Serves 4

Note: *Serve this tasty chicken dish with steamed jasmine rice. If you prefer, the chilli jam can be served separately so that each diner can season their serving according to taste.*

Thai-Spiced Chicken with Zucchini

Preparation 15 mins **Cooking** 10 mins **Calories** 172 **Fat** 6g

1 tbsp olive oil
1 clove garlic, finely chopped
2½cm piece fresh ginger, finely chopped
1 small fresh red chilli, deseeded and finely chopped
350g skinless boneless chicken breasts, cut into strips
1 tbsp Thai 7-spice seasoning
1 red and 1 yellow capsicum, deseeded and sliced
2 zucchini, thinly sliced
215g can bamboo shoots, drained
2 tbsps dry sherry or apple juice
1 tbsp light soy sauce
black pepper
2 tbsps chopped fresh coriander, plus extra to garnish

1. Heat the oil in a non-stick wok or large frying pan. Add the garlic, ginger and chilli and stir-fry for 30 seconds to release the flavours.
2. Add the chicken and Thai seasoning and stir-fry for 4 minutes or until the chicken has coloured. Add the capsicums and zucchini and stir-fry for 1–2 minutes, until slightly softened.
3. Stir in the bamboo shoots and stir-fry for another 2–3 minutes, until the chicken is cooked through and tender. Add the sherry or apple juice, soy sauce and black pepper and sizzle for 1–2 minutes. Remove from the heat and stir in the chopped coriander, then garnish with more coriander.

Serves 4

Note: This stir-fry is quick to make and tastes sensational. It helps if you prepare all the vegetables in advance and keep the wok really hot. Serve with rice or noodles.

Stir-Fry Duck with Greens

Preparation 10 mins **Cooking** 10 mins **Calories** 614 **Fat** 12g

- 1 kg Chinese barbecued or roasted duck
- 2 tsps vegetable oil
- 1 tbsp Thai red curry paste
- 1 tsp prawn paste
- 1 stalk fresh lemongrass, finely sliced, or 1/2 tsp dried lemongrass, soaked in hot water until soft
- 4 fresh red chillies
- 1 bunch Chinese broccoli or Swiss chard, chopped
- 1 tbsp palm or brown sugar
- 2 tbsps tamarind concentrate
- 1 tbsp Thai fish sauce (nam pla)

1. Slice the meat from the duck, leaving the skin on, and cut it into bite-size pieces. Reserve as many of the cavity juices as possible.
2. Heat the oil in a wok over a medium heat, add the curry paste, prawn paste, lemongrass and chillies and stir-fry for 3 minutes or until fragrant.
3. Add the duck and the reserved juices and stir-fry for 2 minutes or until coated in the spice mixture and heated. Add the broccoli or chard, sugar, tamarind and fish sauce and stir-fry for 3–4 minutes or until the broccoli is wilted.

Serves 4

Note: Chinese broccoli is a popular Asian vegetable. It has dark green leaves on firm stalks, often with small white flowers. The leaves, stalks and flowers are all used in cooking, however the stalks are considered the choicest part of the plant. To prepare, remove the leaves from the stalks and peel, then chop both the leaves and the stalks.

Green Banana Chicken Curry

Preparation 10 mins **Cooking** 40 mins **Calories** 165 **Fat** 6g

- 1 tsp salt
- 1 tsp ground turmeric
- 10 green bananas, peeled
- 2 tbsps vegetable oil
- 3 spring onions, chopped
- 1 tbsp finely grated fresh ginger
- 2 small fresh red chillies, deseeded and chopped
- 375mL coconut milk
- 1 cinnamon stick
- 45g sultanas
- 30g roasted cashews
- 6 chicken breast fillets, cut into thin strips

1. Combine the salt and turmeric and rub over the bananas.
2. Heat the oil in a wok over a medium heat, add the bananas and stir-fry for 5 minutes or until brown. Remove the bananas from the pan and drain on absorbent paper.
3. Add the spring onions, ginger and chillies to the pan and stir-fry for 2 minutes or until the mixture is soft. Stir in the coconut milk, cinnamon, sultanas, cashews and chicken and bring to simmering. Simmer, stirring occasionally, for 20 minutes.
4. Slice the bananas, return to the pan and simmer, stirring occasionally, for 10 minutes or until the chicken is tender. Remove the cinnamon stick before serving.

Serves 6

Meat Stir-Frys

These dishes are so delightfully easy, you'll be cooking with confidence in no time at all, regardless of your culinary ability. The simplicity of these recipes and the freshness of the ingredients combine to produce deliciously complex flavours that you'll want to come back to again and again.

Orange Pork Chops

Preparation 10 mins **Cooking** 30 mins **Calories** 130 **Fat** 6g

- 2 tsps ground coriander
- freshly ground black pepper
- 4 pork chops
- 1 tbsp oil
- 15g butter
- 250mL orange juice
- 2 tbsps orange marmalade
- 1 orange

1. Combine the coriander and black pepper and sprinkle over the chops. Heat the oil and butter in a frying pan and cook the chops over the high heat for 2–3 minutes each side.
2. Add the orange juice and marmalade and cook for 10–15 minutes longer, or until the chops are cooked through and the sauce thickens slightly.
3. Garnish with halved orange slice.

Serves 4

Pork Chop Suey

Preparation 15 mins **Cooking** 15 mins **Calories** 129 **Fat** 9g

500g diced pork
3 cups sliced mixed fresh vegetables
100g peeled green prawns
1 large onion, sliced
1cm fresh peeled ginger, finely chopped
3 tbsps olive oil
4 tsps freshly crushed garlic
fresh sliced green onions, to garnish

1. Bring water to a rapid boil in a frying pan.
2. Add the fresh vegetables and blanch, over a high heat, for 2 minutes. Drain, cool under cold water and drain again.
3. Heat the oil in a frying pan over a medium heat and cook the prawns until they just turn pink. Remove. Add the pork and sauté it with the onion, garlic and ginger until pork is cooked, about 5 minutes.
4. Add a little extra oil if necessary and toss through the blanched vegetables. Reduce the heat to low, add the combined sauce ingredients and stir until thickened.
5. Return the prawns to the frying pan and simmer for 1 minute. Garnish with green onions and serve with hot steamed rice.

Serves 4

Mongolian Lamb

Preparation 12 mins **Cooking** 12 mins **Calories** 232 **Fat** 3g

2 tsps vegetable oil
500g lamb fillet, cut into paper-thin slices
2 onions, cut into 8 wedges
4 spring onions, chopped
3 cloves garlic, crushed
2 small fresh red chillies, deseeded and chopped
1 tbsp chopped fresh coriander

Mongolian Sauce

2½ tsps cornflour
1½ tbsps light soy sauce
1 tbsp oyster sauce
½ cup chicken stock

1 To make the sauce, place the cornflour in a small bowl, then stir in the soy sauce, oyster sauce and stock. Set aside.

2 Heat the oil in a wok or frying pan over a medium heat, add the lamb and stir-fry for 3–4 minutes or until it just changes colour. Remove the lamb from the pan and set aside.

3 Add the onions to the pan and stir-fry for 2–3 minutes. Add the spring onions, garlic and chillies and stir-fry for 2 minutes.

4 Return the lamb to the pan, add the sauce and cook, stirring, for 2–3 minutes or until the mixture thickens slightly. Sprinkle with the coriander and serve immediately.

Serves 4

Note: When handling fresh chillies, don't put your hands near your eyes or let them touch your lips. To avoid discomfort, wear rubber gloves.

Beef and Vegetables with Black Bean Sauce

Preparation 10 mins **Cooking** 15 mins **Calories** 126 **Fat** 7g

1 tbsp vegetable oil
1 tsp minced garlic
1 tsp ground ginger
1 onion, finely sliced
375g lean rump steak, cut into strips
2 tsps sesame oil
½ red capsicum, sliced
100g bean sprouts
60g snow peas
1½ tbsps black bean sauce
1 tbsp soy sauce
3 tbsps beef stock
1 tsp sugar
1 tsp cornflour blended with 1 tbsp water

1 Heat the vegetable oil in a wok or frying pan and cook the garlic and ginger over a medium heat for 1 minute. Add onion and beef and stir-fry for 3 minutes or until beef is browned. Remove from pan and set aside.

2 Heat the sesame oil in the pan; add the capsicum, bean sprouts and snow peas and stir-fry for 1 minute. Add the black bean, soy sauce, stock, sugar and cornflour mixture and cook, stirring, until the mixture thickens slightly. Return the beef and onions to the pan and cook for 2–3 minutes or until heated through. Serve with rice.

Serves 4

Stir-Fry Chilli Prawns

Preparation 10 mins **Cooking** 10 mins **Calories** 100 **Fat** 2g

1 tsp vegetable oil
1 tsp sesame oil
3 cloves garlic, crushed
3 fresh red chillies, chopped
1 kg uncooked medium prawns, shelled and deveined
1 tbsp brown sugar
90mL tomato juice
1 tbsp soy sauce

1 Heat the vegetable and sesame oils together in a wok over a medium heat, add the garlic and chillies and stir-fry for 1 minute. Add the prawns and stir-fry for 2 minutes or until they change colour.

2 Stir in the sugar, tomato juice and soy sauce and stir-fry for 3 minutes or until the sauce is heated through.

Serves 4

Note: For a complete meal, serve prawns with boiled rice or noodles of your choice and stir-fried vegetables.

Lamb Stir-fry with Noodles and Capsicums

Preparation 15 mins **Cooking** 12 mins **Calories** 619 **Fat** 26g

- 225g pack medium egg noodles
- 2 tbsps vegetable oil
- 455g lamb shoulder fillet, sliced into 1cm pieces
- 2 carrots, cut into matchsticks
- 1 red capsicum and 1 yellow capsicum, deseeded and cut into matchsticks
- 200g pak choi, sliced or whole baby spinach leaves
- 200g bean sprouts
- 4 spring onions, cut into thin strips
- 4 tbsps oyster sauce
- 1 tbsp dark soy sauce
- 2 tbsps clear honey
- finely grated zest and juice of ½ lemon
- freshly ground black pepper

1. Prepare the noodles according to the packet instructions, then drain well. Meanwhile, heat the oil in a wok or large frying pan until very hot. Add the lamb and stir-fry for 5 minutes, until seared on all sides.
2. Add the carrots and capsicums and stir-fry for 4 minutes or until softened. Add the pak choi or spinach, bean sprouts and spring onions, then cook for a further 1 minute.
3. Reduce the heat, then add the drained noodles, oyster sauce, soy sauce, honey, lemon zest and juice and black pepper. Combine well and stir-fry for 2 minutes or until everything is hot and the lamb is cooked through.

Serves 6

Note: *It takes a little time to chop everything for a stir-fry, but the cooking time is minimal. This recipe uses the sweet and sour combination of honey and lemon - the result is superb!*

Korean Marinated Beef Strips

Preparation 20 mins + 4 hrs marinating **Cooking** 10 mins **Calories** 315 **Fat** 15g

500g lean beef fillet, sliced into 5mm thick strips
2 spring onions, chopped, plus extra to garnish
vegetable oil, for brushing
chilli sauce, to serve

Marinade

2 tbsps sesame seeds
2 cloves garlic, finely chopped
2 1/2cm piece fresh ginger, finely chopped
2 tbsps sugar
3 tbsps light soy sauce
3 tbsps dark soy sauce
1 tbsp sesame oil

1 To make the marinade, heat a frying pan, then add the sesame seeds and dry-fry for 5 minutes or until golden, stirring constantly. Grind finely, using a mortar and pestle or a coffee grinder. Add the garlic, ginger, sugar, light and dark soy sauces and sesame oil to the sesame seeds and grind or blend to a paste, using the mortar and pestle or a food processor.

2 Mix together the beef, spring onions and marinade in a non-metallic bowl, turning to coat the beef well. Cover and marinate in the refrigerator for 4 hours.

3 Brush a ridged, cast-iron grill pan or large, heavy-based frying pan with the oil and heat until very hot. Add the beef strips in a single layer (you may have to cook them in batches) and cook for 1–2 minutes, turning once, until browned. Serve with chilli sauce, garnished with spring onions.

Serves 4

Pad Thai with Pork and Prawns

Preparation 20 mins **Cooking** 15 mins **Calories** 522 **Fat** 23g

250g pack rice noodles
4 tbsps peanut oil
2 cloves garlic, chopped
1 french shallot, chopped
125g pork fillet, cut into 5mm thick strips
1 tbsp Thai fish sauce (nam pla)
1 tsp sugar
juice of $^1/_2$ lime
1 tbsp light soy sauce
1 tbsp tomato sauce
200g pack fresh bean sprouts
125g cooked peeled prawns, defrosted if frozen
black pepper
55g roasted salted peanuts, chopped
1 tbsp chopped fresh coriander
1 lime, quartered, to serve

1. Prepare the noodles according to the packet instructions. Drain and rinse them. Heat a wok, then add the oil. Stir-fry the garlic, French shallot and pork for 3 minutes or until the pork turns opaque. Stir in the noodles and mix thoroughly.
2. Mix together the fish sauce, sugar, lime juice, soy sauce and tomato sauce, then add to the noodle mixture, stirring well. Stir-fry for 5 minutes. Mix in the bean sprouts and prawn and stir-fry for a further 5 minutes or until the bean sprouts are tender. Season with black pepper.
3. Transfer the mixture to a serving dish. Sprinkle the peanuts and coriander over the top and serve with the lime wedges.

Serves 4

Note: *Who can resist this mixture of sizzling pork, lime and seafood? In Thailand, you can smell the aromas from this dish wafting from the food stalls that line the streets.*

Keema Curry

Preparation 20 mins **Cooking** 40 mins **Calories** 135 **Fat** 10g

- 1 tbsp vegetable oil
- 1 onion, finely chopped
- $2^1/2$cm piece fresh ginger, grated
- 2 cloves garlic, crushed
- 500g lean minced lamb
- 2 tsps ground turmeric
- 1 tsp chilli powder
- 1 tbsp garam masala
- 3 tbsps tomato purée
- 2 cups lamb stock
- 125g frozen peas
- 2 tbsps chopped fresh coriander, plus extra leaves to garnish
- salt and black pepper

1 Heat the oil in a large heavy-based frying pan. Add the onion and ginger and cook over a low heat for 5 minutes or until softened. Add the garlic and minced lamb, breaking the meat into little pieces by pressing it with the back of a wooden spoon. Cook for 10 minutes or until the lamb browns.

2 Pour off any excess fat from the pan. Add the turmeric, chilli, garam masala and tomato purée, then stir-fry for 1–2 minutes. Add the stock and bring to the boil, stirring, then reduce the heat and simmer, uncovered, for 10 minutes or until slightly reduced.

3 Add the peas, then simmer for 5–10 minutes longer. Remove from the heat, stir in the coriander and season. Garnish with the extra coriander.

Serves 4

Note: This is a really easy way to turn minced lamb into a delicious spicy curry. It's best served the traditional way – with basmati rice, cucumber raita and mango chutney.

Nasi Goreng

Preparation 15 mins + 1 hr cooling **Cooking** 30 mins **Calories** 439 **Fat** 13g

- 250g long-grain rice
- 1 tsp ground turmeric
- 3 tbsps vegetable oil
- 1 bunch of spring onions, thinly sliced
- $2\frac{1}{2}$cm piece fresh ginger, finely chopped
- 1–2 fresh red chillies, deseeded and thinly sliced
- 250g pork fillet, trimmed of any excess fat and thinly sliced
- 2 cloves garlic, crushed
- 3 tbsps soy sauce, or to taste
- 200g cooked peeled prawns, defrosted if frozen and thoroughly dried
- juice of $\frac{1}{2}$ lemon
- fresh coriander, to garnish

1. Cook the rice with the turmeric, according to the instructions on the packet. Drain, then spread on a large plate. Leave to cool for 1 hour or until completely cold, fluffing up occasionally with a fork.
2. Heat 2 tablespoons of the oil in a wok or heavy-based frying pan. Add half the spring onions, the ginger and the chillies and stir-fry over a low heat for 2–3 minutes, until softened. Add the remaining oil, increase the heat to high, then add the pork and garlic and stir-fry for 3 minutes.
3. Add the rice in 3 batches, stirring after each addition to mix well with the other ingredients. Add the soy sauce and prawns and stir-fry for 2–3 minutes, until hot. Transfer to a bowl and mix in the lemon juice. Sprinkle with the remaining spring onions and garnish with coriander.

Serves 4

Note: Succulent pork and prawns combine with rice and aromatic spices to make this simple Indonesian dish. Serve with prawn crackers and plenty of dark soy sauce.

Sizzling Beef

Preparation 15 mins **Cooking** 20 mins **Calories** 328 **Fat** 14g

- 500g rump steak, trimmed of any excess fat and cut into thin strips
- 2 tbsps soy sauce
- 2 tbsps rice wine or sherry
- 1 1/2 tbsp cornflour
- 1 tsp sugar
- 3 tbsps peanut oil
- 145g broccoli, cut into bite-size pieces
- 1 large red capsicum, deseeded and cut into thin strips
- 2 cloves garlic, crushed
- 3 tbsps oyster sauce
- 200g pack fresh bean sprouts
- salt and black pepper

1. Put the steak, soy sauce, rice wine or sherry, cornflour and sugar into a non-metallic bowl and mix thoroughly.
2. Heat 1 tablespoon of the oil in a wok or large heavy-based frying pan, add a third of the beef mixture and stir-fry over a high heat for 2–3 minutes, until browned. Remove and cook the remaining beef in 2 more batches, adding a little more oil if necessary.
3. Heat the remaining oil in the wok, then add the broccoli and 6 tablespoons of water. Stir-fry for 5 minutes, then add the capsicum and garlic and stir-fry for a further 2–3 minutes, until the broccoli is tender but still firm to the bite.
4. Stir in the oyster sauce, return the beef to the wok and add the bean sprouts. Toss over a high heat for 2 minutes or until the beef is piping hot and the bean sprouts have softened slightly, then season.

Serves 4

Note: Before you start cooking this colourful stir-fry, make sure all your ingredients are cut into pieces of roughly the same shape and size so they cook evenly.

Beef with Peppercorns

Preparation 10 mins **Cooking** 7 mins **Calories** 207 **Fat** 5g

2 tsps vegetable oil
2 cloves garlic, crushed
1 fresh green chilli, chopped
500g topside or round steak, sliced
1 tbsp green peppercorns in brine, drained and lightly crushed
1 green capsicum, chopped
3 tbsps fresh coriander leaves
$^{1}/_{3}$ cup coconut milk
2 tsps Thai fish sauce (nam pla)

1 Heat oil in a wok over a high heat. Add the garlic and chilli and cook for 1 minute. Add the beef and peppercorns and stir-fry for 3 minutes or until the beef is browned.

2 Stir in the capsicum, coriander, coconut milk and fish sauce and cook for 2 minutes longer.

Serves 4

Note: Black peppercorns are a traditional Thai ingredient. Before the introduction of chillies by the Portuguese, they were used to add heat to dishes. This spicy stir-fry teams milder green peppercorns with chilli to make the most of two favourite ingredients.

Pork and Mango Curry

Preparation 15 mins **Cooking** 35 mins **Calories** 120 **Fat** 4g

1 large onion, chopped
4 cloves garlic, chopped
2 small fresh red chillies, chopped
2 tbsps curry powder
1 tbsp sesame oil
1 tbsp vegetable oil
1 kg pork fillets, cut into 2cm wide strips
2 stalks fresh lemongrass, finely chopped or 1 tsp dried lemongrass, soaked in hot water until soft
1 tbsp Thai fish sauce (nam pla)
2 tbsps lemon juice
2 mangoes, stoned, peeled and flesh sliced
3 tbsps mango chutney

1. Place the onion, garlic, chillies and curry powder into a food processor or blender and process to make a smooth paste.
2. Heat the sesame and vegetable oils together in a wok over a medium heat, add the paste and stir-fry for 5 minutes or until all the liquid evaporates.
3. Add the pork and stir-fry for 10 minutes or until the pork is brown. Add the lemongrass, fish sauce and lemon juice and cook over a low heat, stirring frequently, for 15 minutes or until all the liquid is absorbed. Stir in the mangoes and chutney and cook for 2–3 minutes longer or until heated through.

Serves 6

Pork with Pumpkin Stir-Fry

Preparation 10 mins **Cooking** 16 mins **Calories** 550 **Fat** 28g

- 2 tbsps Thai red curry paste
- 2 onions, cut into thin wedges, layers separated
- 2 tsps vegetable oil
- 500g lean pork strips
- 500g peeled butternut pumpkin, cut into 2cm cubes
- 4 kaffir lime leaves, shredded
- 1 tbsp palm or brown sugar
- 2 cups coconut milk
- 1 tbsp Thai fish sauce (nam pla)

1. Place the curry paste in wok and cook, stirring, over a high heat for 2 minutes or until fragrant. Add the onions and cook for 2 minutes longer or until the onions are soft. Remove from the wok and set aside.
2. Heat the oil in the wok, add the pork and stir-fry for 3 minutes or until brown. Remove the pork from the wok and set aside.
3. Add the pumpkin, lime leaves, sugar, coconut milk and fish sauce to the wok, bring to simmering and simmer for 2 minutes. Stir in the curry paste mixture and simmer for 5 minutes longer. Return the pork to the wok and cook for 2 minutes or until heated through.

Serves 4

Seafood Stir-Frys

The time it takes to chop up the ingredients for a stir-fry is more than made up for by the minimal cooking time. These delicious seafood stir-frys are full of seductive flavours that are guaranteed to have anyone who loves good food coming back for more.

South-East Asian Pan-Fry Prawns

Preparation 15 mins **Cooking** 10 mins **Calories** 225 **Fat** 2g

500g whole raw shell-on prawns, defrosted if frozen
3 small red chillies, deseeded and chopped
2 cloves garlic, chopped
$2^1/2$cm piece fresh ginger, chopped
1 French shallot, chopped
2 tbsps peanut oil
1 onion, chopped
2 tomatoes, quartered
1 tsp sugar
salt

1. Shell the prawns, leaving the tails attached. Cut a slit along the back of each prawn with a sharp knife and remove the vein. Rinse well, then refrigerate until needed.
2. Blend the chillies, garlic, ginger and French shallot to a paste in a food processor or with a mortar and pestle. Heat the oil in a wok or large, heavy-based frying pan over a high heat, then fry the onion for 2 minutes to soften it slightly. Add the paste and stir-fry for 1 minute to release the flavours.
3. Add the prawns and tomatoes, mixing thoroughly, then sprinkle over the sugar and salt to taste. Fry for 3–5 minutes, until the prawns turn pink and are cooked through, stirring often.

Serves 4

Note: It's well worth splashing out on large raw prawns for this spicy dish. But ready-cooked prawns are still tasty and take only a minute to warm through. Serve with rice.

Cashew and Prawn Egg-Fried Rice

Preparation 15 mins + 30 mins cooling **Cooking** 25 mins **Calories** 581 **Fat** 21g

370g long-grain rice
¼ tsp salt
2 tbsps peanut oil
1 clove garlic, finely chopped
1cm piece fresh ginger, finely chopped
2 spring onions, sliced diagonally, white and green parts separated
55g roasted salted cashew nuts, chopped
85g baby corn, cut into 1cm lengths
200g cooked peeled medium prawns
2 tbsps medium-dry sherry
3 tbsps light soy sauce
2 tsps sesame oil
1 large egg, beaten
black pepper to taste

1. Rinse the rice, then place it in a large saucepan with salt and 2 cups of water. Bring to the boil, reduce the heat, then cover and simmer for 15 minutes or until tender. Drain, then spread the rice on a plate and leave to cool for 20–30 minutes, fluffing it up occasionally with a fork.
2. Heat a wok or large frying pan, then add the oil. Add the garlic, ginger and the white parts of the spring onions and stir-fry for 1–2 minutes. Mix in the rice and stir-fry for 2 minutes.
3. Add the cashew nuts and corn and stir-fry for 2 minutes. Add the prawns and sherry and stir-fry for 1 minute. Pour over the soy sauce and sesame oil and cook for a further 2 minutes, stirring.
4. Add the egg and stir-fry for 2–3 minutes, until cooked through. Season with black pepper, then sprinkle the green parts of the spring onions over the top.

Serves 4

Note: The nutty taste of the sesame oil really brings out the flavour of the cashews. Juicy tiger prawns are always a favourite and baby corn adds extra crunch.

Fragrant Salmon Stir-Fry

Preparation 10 mins + 2 hrs marinating **Cooking** 10 mins **Calories** 444 **Fat** 30g

250g skinless salmon fillets, cut into strips 2½cm wide and 7½cm long
1½ tbsp peanut or sunflower oil
1 tbsp chilled butter, cubed

Marinade

1 stalk lemongrass, or 1 tsp finely grated lemon rind
1 tbsp soy sauce
125mL orange juice
1 tbsp chopped fresh dill
1 tbsp chopped fresh basil
1 tsp grated fresh ginger
1 clove garlic, crushed
salt and black pepper

1. Heat the oil in a large, heavy-based frying pan over a medium to high heat. Transfer the salmon to the pan, reserving the marinade. Cook for 2 minutes, then turn the salmon and cook for a further 1–2 minutes, until cooked through.
2. Arrange the salmon on serving plates. Pour the marinade into the frying pan, bring to the boil, then simmer for 2 minutes. Whisk in the butter and season. Spoon the sauce over the salmon and sprinkle the remaining dill and basil over the top.

Marinade

1. Peel the outer layer from the lemongrass stalk (if using), then chop the lower white bulbous part, discarding the top. Mix the lemongrass or lemon rind with the soy sauce, orange juice, half the dill, half the basil, the ginger and the garlic, then season. Arrange the salmon strips in a shallow non-metallic dish and pour the marinade over, turning to coat the salmon well. Cover and refrigerate for 2 hours.

Serves 2

Note: A lovely lemon-scented marinade with a hint of ginger caramelises slightly in the pan to make a good thick sauce for fillets of succulent salmon.

Goan-Style Fish and Coconut Curry

Preparation 25 mins **Cooking** 25 mins **Calories** 430 **Fat** 30g

- 2 tomatoes
- 2 cardamom pods, husks discarded and seeds reserved
- 1 tsp each of ground coriander, cumin, cinnamon and hot chilli powder
- ½ tsp ground turmeric
- 2 tbsps vegetable oil
- 1 onion, finely chopped
- 1 clove garlic, finely chopped
- 2½cm piece fresh ginger, finely chopped
- 400mL can coconut milk
- 750g skinless white fish fillet, such as haddock or cod, cut into 2½cm chunks
- salt
- fresh coriander, to garnish

1. Place the tomatoes in a bowl, cover with boiling water and leave to stand for 30 seconds. Peel, then finely dice the flesh.
2. Crush the cardamom seeds using a mortar and pestle. Add the coriander, cumin, cinnamon, chilli powder, turmeric and 2 tablespoons of water and mix to a paste. Set aside.
3. Heat the oil in a large, heavy-based saucepan. Fry the onion, garlic and ginger for 3 minutes or until softened. Add the spice paste, mix well and fry for 1 minute, stirring constantly.
4. Pour in the coconut milk and bring to the boil, stirring. Reduce the heat and simmer for 10 minutes or until the liquid has reduced slightly. Add the fish, tomatoes and salt to taste. Partly cover the pan and simmer, stirring occasionally for a further 10 minutes or until the fish turns opaque and is cooked through, stirring occasionally. Garnish with coriander to serve.

Serves 2

Prawn, Snow Pea and Mango Stir-Fry

Preparation 10 mins **Cooking** 40 mins **Calories** 274 **Fat** 14g

- 1 kg raw peeled medium prawns, defrosted if frozen, rinsed and dried
- 2 tbsps vegetable oil
- 1 1/2 tbsps finely grated fresh ginger
- 300g snow peas
- bunch of spring onions, sliced
- 1 large ripe mango, peeled and thinly sliced
- 2 tbsps light soy sauce

1. Cut a slit along the back of each prawn with a sharp knife and remove any thin black vein.
2. Heat the oil in a wok, add the ginger and prawns and stir-fry for 2 minutes or until the prawns are just turning pink. Add the snow peas and spring onions and stir-fry for a further minute to soften slightly. Stir in the mango and soy sauce and stir-fry for 1 minute to heat through.

Serves 4

Note: Succulent prawns, crunchy snow peas and juicy mango are flavoured with soy sauce and fresh ginger. Best of all, you can get this dish on the table in 20 minutes. Serve with rice.

Scallops with Zucchini in Apple Butter

Preparation 10 mins **Cooking** 5 mins **Calories** 327 **Fat** 18g

2 zucchini, cut into $2\frac{1}{2}$cm thick slices
8 large scallops with their corals
1 tbsp olive oil
salt and black pepper
75mL apple juice
30g butter
fresh flat-leaf parsley, to garnish

1 Turn the zucchini and scallops gently in the oil and season with salt and black pepper.

2 Heat a large heavy-based frying pan until hot, add the zucchini and cook for 2 minutes on 1 side. Turn over the zucchini and add the scallops to the pan. Cook for 1 minute, then turn over the scallops. Cook both the scallops and zucchini for a further minute, until the scallops are golden and the zucchini are browned.

3 Remove the scallops and zucchini from the pan and keep warm. Pour the apple juice into the pan, add the butter and cook until reduced to a syrupy sauce. Spoon the sauce over the scallops and zucchini and garnish with parsley.

Serves 2

Note: Scallops are expensive but delicious, so save this dish for a special treat for two. Make sure you sear them over a high heat; that way they'll be sealed and really tender.

Mussels with Coconut Vinegar

Preparation 5 mins **Cooking** 15 mins **Calories** 636 **Fat** 29g

1 1/2 kg mussels in their shells
6 whole coriander plants, washed and roughly chopped
3 stalks fresh lemongrass, bruised, or 1 1/2 tsp dried lemongrass, soaked in hot water until soft
5cm piece fresh ginger, shredded
1/2 cup water
1 tbsp vegetable oil
1 red onion, halved and sliced
2 fresh red chillies, sliced
2 tbsps coconut vinegar
fresh coriander leaves

1. Place the mussels, coriander, lemongrass, ginger and water in a wok over a high heat. Cover and cook for 5 minutes or until the mussels open. Discard any mussels that do not open after 5 minutes' cooking. Remove the mussels from the wok and discard coriander, lemon grass and ginger. Strain the cooking liquid and reserve.
2. Heat the oil in a wok over a medium heat, add the onion and chillies and stir-fry for 3 minutes or until the onion is soft. Add the mussels, reserved cooking liquid and coconut vinegar and stir-fry for 2 minutes or until the mussels are heated. Scatter with coriander leaves and serve.

Serves 4

Note: This dish is delicious served with boiled egg noodles and topped with coriander leaves and wok juices. Coconut vinegar is made from the sap of the coconut palm. It's available from oriental food shops. If unavailable, any mild vinegar can be used instead.

Stir-Fry Tamarind Prawns

Preparation 20 mins **Cooking** 50 mins **Calories** 543 **Fat** 20g

- 2 tbsps tamarind pulp
- ½ cup water
- 2 tsps vegetable oil
- 3 stalks fresh lemongrass, chopped, or 2 tsps finely grated lemon rind
- 2 fresh red chillies, chopped
- 500g medium uncooked prawns, shelled and deveined, tails intact
- 2 green (unripe) mangoes, peeled and thinly sliced
- 3 tbsps chopped fresh coriander leaves
- 2 tbsps brown sugar
- 2 tbsps lime juice

1 Place the tamarind pulp and water in a bowl and stand for 20 minutes. Strain, reserve the liquid and set aside. Discard the solids.

2 Heat the oil in a wok or frying pan over a high heat, add the lemongrass or lemon rind and the chillies and stir-fry for 1 minute. Add the prawns and stir-fry for 2 minutes or until they change colour.

3 Add the mangoes, coriander, sugar, lime juice and tamarind liquid and stir-fry for 5 minutes or until the prawns are cooked.

Serves 4

Note: *Tamarind is the large pod of the tamarind or Indian date tree. After picking, it's deseeded and peeled, then pressed into a dark brown pulp. It's also available as a concentrate. Tamarind pulp or concentrate can be purchased from Indian food stores. In oriental cooking it's used as a souring agent. If unavailable, a mixture of lime or lemon juice and treacle can be used instead.*

Pasta Stir-Frys

These recipes are sure to become firm family favourites. Simple, quick and full of fabulous ingredients, they're both delicious and nutritious. Add to this the appetite-quenching properties of pasta and you have the perfect solution to any mealtime dilemma. What more could a busy cook ask for?

Spaghettini and Scallops with Breadcrumbs

Preparation 20 mins **Cooking** 10 mins **Calories** 717 **Fat** 32g

12 fresh scallops with their corals
½ cup extra virgin olive oil
55g dried white breadcrumbs
4 tbsps chopped fresh flat-leaf parsley
2 cloves garlic, finely chopped
1 tsp crushed dried chillies
350g dried spaghettini
salt
4 tbsps dry white wine

1. Detach the corals from the scallops and set aside. Slice each white part into 3–4 pieces. Heat 2 tablespoons of oil in a frying pan, then add the breadcrumbs and fry, stirring, for 3 minutes or until golden. Remove from the pan and set aside.
2. Heat 5 tablespoons of oil in the pan, then add half the parsley, the garlic and the chillies and fry for 2 minutes or until the flavours are released. Meanwhile, cook the pasta in plenty of boiling salted water, until tender but still firm to the bite. Drain, return to the saucepan and toss with the remaining oil.
3. Stir the white parts of the scallops into the frying pan and fry for 30 seconds or until they start to turn opaque. Add the wine and the reserved scallop corals, cook for 30 seconds, then add the spaghettini and cook for 1 minute, tossing to combine. Sprinkle with the breadcrumbs and remaining parsley.

Serves 4

Fish in Lemon Dill Mayonnaise

Preparation 15 mins **Cooking** 12 mins **Calories** 609 **Fat** 42g

2 tbsps oil
2 tsps grated lemon rind
2 tbsps lemon juice
½ tsp minced garlic
2 tbsps white wine
freshly ground black pepper
4 white fish cutlets
60g butter

Dill Mayonnaise

1 tbsp lemon juice
1 tbsp grated lime rind
125g mayonnaise
3 tbsps sour cream
1 tbsp chopped fresh dill

1. Place the oil, lemon rind, lemon juice, garlic, wine and black pepper to taste in a small bowl and mix to combine. Brush the cutlets with lemon mixture.
2. Melt the butter in a large frying pan and cook the cutlets over a medium heat for 2–3 minutes each side or until the fish flakes when tested with a fork. Baste regularly with remaining lemon mixture during cooking.
3. To make the dill mayonnaise, combine the lemon juice, lime rind, mayonnaise, sour cream and dill in a small bowl and mix well. Spoon the mayonnaise over the cutlets and serve immediately with crusty bread rolls, carrots and broccoli.

Serves 4

Conchiglie with Broccoli and Sultanas

Preparation 10 mins + 15 mins soaking **Cooking** 15 mins **Calories** 703 **Fat** 29g

- 3 tbsps sultanas
- 2 tbsps pine nut kernels
- 500g broccoli, cut into florets, thick stem discarded
- salt
- 4 tbsps extra virgin olive oil
- 1 small onion, thinly sliced
- 4 anchovy fillets, drained and chopped
- black pepper
- 400g dried pasta shells (conchiglie)
- 30g butter
- 55g Parmesan cheese, freshly grated

1. Place the sultanas in a bowl, cover with hot water and leave to soak for 15 minutes or until they plump up. Drain well. Heat a large heavy-based frying pan over a high heat, then add the pine nut kernels and dry-fry for 2–3 minutes, until golden. Remove from the pan and set aside. Cook the broccoli in boiling salted water for 3 minutes, then drain well.
2. Heat the oil in the frying pan, then gently fry the onion for 5 minutes or until softened. Add the anchovies and mash well with a fork, then stir in the broccoli, sultanas and pine nut kernels and cook, stirring, for 5 minutes. Season to taste.
3. Cook the pasta in plenty of boiling salted water, until tender but still firm to the bite. Drain, return to the pan, then toss with the butter, Parmesan cheese and half the broccoli mixture. Transfer to a bowl and top with the remaining broccoli mixture.

Serves 4

Note: Plump sultanas give this dish from Puglia a wonderful sweetness which helps bring out the flavours of the broccoli and pine nut kernels.

Fusilli with Capsicum and Sun-Dried Tomatoes

Preparation 20 mins + 10 mins cooling **Cooking** 50 mins **Calories** 626 **Fat** 32g

- 1 large yellow and 1 large red capsicum
- 5 tbsps extra virgin olive oil
- 2 French shallots, very finely chopped
- 1 clove garlic, very finely chopped
- 1 tsp crushed dried chillies
- 125mL vegetable stock
- 125g sun-dried tomatoes in oil, drained and chopped
- 2 tbsps capers, rinsed and dried
- 2 tbsps balsamic vinegar
- 340g dried tricolour pasta twists (fusilli)
- salt
- 2 tbsps chopped fresh oregano, to garnish

1. Preheat the oven. Place the capsicums in an ovenproof dish and cook for 30 minutes or until soft. Leave to cool for 10 minutes, then remove the skins, deseed and chop.
2. Heat half the oil in a heavy-based saucepan, then add the French shallots and cook for 5 minutes or until softened. Add the garlic, chillies and 2 tablespoons of the stock and cook for 5 minutes, then add the capsicums and sun-dried tomatoes and cook for a further 10 minutes, adding a little more stock if the sauce starts to dry out. Mix in the capers and vinegar and cook for 1 minute.
3. Cook the pasta in plenty of boiling salted water, until tender but still firm to the bite. Drain, then toss with the remaining oil. Spoon over the sauce, toss again, then serve at room temperature, garnished with the oregano.

Serves 4

Note: This brightly coloured pasta is great warm, hot or cold. On a summer's day, it makes a fabulous pasta salad. If you haven't got fresh oregano, use basil instead.

Oven temperature 230°C, 450°F, Gas 8

Tagliatelle with Asparagus and Prosciutto

Preparation 10 mins **Cooking** 15 mins **Calories** 692 **Fat** 40g

500g asparagus spears
55g unsalted butter
2 tbsps olive oil
1 spring onion, white part only, sliced
55g proscuitto, cut into thin strips
145mL double cream
salt and black pepper
500g fresh tagliatelle
freshly grated Parmesan cheese, to serve

1. Cut the asparagus spears into 1 cm pieces, leaving the tips whole. Heat the butter and oil in a large heavy-based frying pan, add the spring onion and cook for 2 minutes to soften.
2. Mix in the proscuitto, fry for 2 minutes, then add the asparagus and cook for 5 minutes or until softened, turning occasionally. Pour in the cream and bring to the boil, then season to taste.
3. Meanwhile, cook the pasta in plenty of boiling salted water, until tender but still firm to the bite. Drain, reserving some of the cooking water. Transfer a third of the pasta to a warmed bowl and toss with some of the sauce. Repeat, then spoon the remaining sauce over the top. If the pasta looks a little dry, add 1–2 tablespoons of the reserved cooking water. Serve with the Parmesan cheese.

Serves 4

Sautéed Calamari and Vegetables

Preparation 15 mins **Cooking** 10 mins **Calories** 75 **Fat** 2g

- 2 large calamari tubes
- 2 tsps sesame oil
- 1 small red capsicum, cut into 2cm cubes
- 2 zucchini, sliced
- 2 spring onions, chopped
- 2 tsps ground ginger
- ½ tsp minced garlic
- 3 tbsps white wine
- 1 tbsp lemon juice
- 2 tbsps plum sauce
- 1 tsp grated lemon rind
- 1 tsp cornflour blended with 125mL chicken stock
- sprigs of Italian parsley

1. Open out the calamari tubes. Score the inside of each tube lightly in a diamond pattern, making cuts 1cm apart. Slice the tube into 3cm squares.
2. Heat the sesame oil in a frying pan and cook the calamari over a moderate heat for 1 minute or until it just starts to curl.
3. Add the capsicum, zucchini, spring onions, ginger and garlic and cook for 2 minutes longer. Remove all ingredients from the pan and set aside to keep warm.
4. Pour the wine and lemon juice into the pan and cook for 15 seconds. Add the plum sauce, lemon rind and cornflour mixture and cook, stirring constantly, until the sauce thickens. Return the calamari mixture to the pan and toss to coat.
5. Garnish with a few sprigs of Italian parsley.

Serves 4

Rigatoni with Turkey and Sage Ragu

Preparation 15 mins **Cooking** 35 mins **Calories** 506 **Fat** 12g

- 2 tbsps olive oil
- 1 onion, finely chopped
- 1 small red chilli, deseeded and finely chopped
- 1 green capsicum, deseeded and diced
- 500g minced turkey
- 200g can chopped tomatoes
- 1 tbsp tomato purée
- salt and black pepper
- 55g pitted black olives, sliced
- 2 tbsps chopped fresh sage or 2 tsps dried sage
- 500g fresh pasta tubes (rigatoni)

1. Heat the oil in a large saucepan and gently fry the onion, chilli and capsicum, stirring, for 5 minutes or until softened but not browned.
2. Add the turkey mince, breaking it up with the back of a wooden spoon, and stir over a fairly high heat for 5 minutes or until lightly browned. Add the tomatoes, tomato purée and seasoning. Cover and simmer for 20 minutes. Stir the olives into the pan with half the sage. Simmer for 2–3 minutes.
3. Meanwhile, cook the pasta according to the packet instructions, until firm to the bite. Drain well, then add to the sauce and toss gently. Serve sprinkled with the remaining sage.

Serves 4

Note: A tomato, sage and chilli sauce livens up turkey for a quick and healthy mid-week treat. If you're in the mood, make it really fiery by adding an extra chilli.

Penne with Mushrooms and Blue Cheese

Preparation 10 mins **Cooking** 15 mins **Calories** 839 **Fat** 38g

2 tbsps olive oil
1 small leek, thinly sliced
8 strips smoked streaky bacon, thinly sliced
250g closed-cup mushrooms, quartered
6 tbsps dry white wine or stock
500g pack fresh pasta quills (penne)
200g blue cheese, chopped
salt and black pepper
flat-leaf parsley, to garnish

1. Heat the oil in a large frying pan. Fry the leek for 3–4 minutes, until softened. Add the bacon and fry, stirring, for a further 3–4 minutes, until golden.
2. Add the mushrooms to the pan and cook for 3–4 minutes, stirring occasionally. Stir in the wine or stock, and simmer for 2–3 minutes, until most of the liquid has evaporated.
3. Meanwhile, cook the pasta according to the packet instructions, until firm to the bite. Drain well, then add it to the mushroom mixture along with the cheese. Stir gently for 1–2 minutes, until the cheese has melted. Season and garnish with parsley.

Serves 4

Note: *Smoked bacon, creamy cheese, leeks and mushrooms make this pasta dish completely addictive. Serve it with a fresh green salad. Wild mushrooms can also be used.*

Glossary

Acidulated water: water with added acid, such as lemon juice or vinegar, which prevents discolouration of ingredients, particularly fruit or vegetables. The proportion of acid to water is 1 teaspoon per 300mL.

Al dente: Italian cooking term for ingredients that are cooked until tender but still firm to the bite; usually applied to pasta.

Américaine: method of serving seafood, usually lobster and monkfish, in a sauce flavoured with olive oil, aromatic herbs, tomatoes, white wine, fish stock, brandy and tarragon.

Anglaise: cooking style for simple cooked dishes such as boiled vegetables. Assiette anglaise is a plate of cold cooked meats.

Antipasto: Italian for 'before the meal', it denotes an assortment of cold meats, vegetables and cheeses, often marinated, served as an hors d'oeuvre. A typical antipasto might include salami, prosciutto, marinated artichoke hearts, anchovy fillets, olives, tuna fish and provolone cheese.

Au gratin: food sprinkled with breadcrumbs, often covered with cheese sauce and browned until a crisp coating forms.

Bain marie: a saucepan standing in a large pan which is filled with boiling water to keep liquids at simmering point. A double boiler will do the same job.

Balsamic vinegar: a mild, extremely fragrant, wine-based vinegar made in northern Italy. Traditionally, the vinegar is aged for at least seven years in a series of casks made of various woods.

Baste: to moisten food while it is cooking by spooning or brushing on liquid or fat.

Beat: to stir thoroughly and vigorously.

Beurre manie: equal quantities of butter and flour kneaded together and added, a little at a time, to thicken a stew or casserole.

bird: see *paupiette*.

Blanc: a cooking liquid made by adding flour and lemon juice to water in order to keep certain vegetables from discolouring as they cook.

Blanch: to plunge into boiling water and then, in some cases, into cold water. Fruits and nuts are blanched to remove skin easily.

Blanquette: a white stew of lamb, veal or chicken, bound with egg yolks and cream and accompanied by onion and mushrooms.

blend: to mix thoroughly.

Bonne femme: dishes cooked in the traditional French 'housewife' style. Chicken and pork *bonne femme* are garnished with bacon, potatoes and baby onion; fish *bonne femme* with mushrooms in a white-wine sauce.

Bouquet garni: a bunch of herbs, usually consisting of sprigs of parsley, thyme, marjoram, rosemary, a bay leaf, peppercorns and cloves, tied in muslin and used to flavour stews and casseroles.

Braise: to cook whole or large pieces of poultry, game, fish, meat or vegetables in a small amount of wine, stock or other liquid in a closed pot. Often the main ingredient is first browned in fat and then cooked in a low oven or very slowly on top of the stove. Braising suits tough meats and older birds and produces a mellow, rich sauce.

Broil: the American term for grilling food.

Brown: cook in a small amount of fat until brown.

Burghul (also bulgur): a type of cracked wheat, where the kernels are steamed and dried before being crushed.

Buttered: to spread with softened or melted butter.

Butterfly: to slit a piece of food in half horizontally, cutting it almost through so that when opened it resembles butterfly wings. Chops, large prawns and thick fish fillets are often butterflied so that they cook more quickly.

Buttermilk: a tangy, low-fat cultured milk product; its slight acidity makes it an ideal marinade base for poultry.

Calzone: a semicircular pocket of pizza dough, stuffed with meat or vegetables, sealed and baked.

Caramelise: to melt sugar until it is a golden-brown syrup.

Champignons: small mushrooms, usually canned.

Chasseur: French for 'hunter'; a French cooking style in which meat and chicken dishes are cooked with mushrooms, spring onions, white wine and often tomato.

Clarify: to melt butter and drain the oil off the sediment.

Coat: to cover with a thin layer of flour, sugar, nuts, crumbs, poppy or sesame seeds, cinnamon sugar or a few of the ground spices.

Concasser: to chop coarsely, usually tomatoes.

Confit: from the French verb *confire*, meaning to preserve, food that is made into a preserve by cooking very slowly and thoroughly until tender. In the case of meat, such as duck or goose, it is cooked in its own fat, and covered with the fat so that the meat does not come into contact with the air. Vegetables such as onions are good in confit.

Consommé: a clear soup usually made from beef.

Coulis: a thin purée, usually of fresh or cooked fruit or vegetables, which is soft enough to pour (in French *couler* means 'to run'). A coulis may be rough-textured or very smooth.

Court bouillon: the liquid in which fish, poultry or meat is cooked. It usually consists of water with bay leaf, onion, carrots and salt and freshly ground black pepper to taste. Other additives may include wine, vinegar, stock, garlic or spring (green) onions.

Couscous: cereal processed from semolina into pellets, traditionally steamed and served with meat and vegetables in the classic North African stew of the same name.

Cream: to make soft, smooth and creamy by rubbing with the back of a spoon or by beating with a mixer. Usually applied to fat and sugar.

Croutons: small toasted or fried cubes of bread.

Cruciferous vegetables: certain members of the mustard, cabbage and turnip families with cross-shaped flowers and strong aromas and flavours.

Crudités: raw vegetables, cut in slices or sticks to nibble plain or with a dipping sauce, or shredded vegetables tossed as salad with a simple dressing.

Cube: to cut into small pieces with six equal sides.

Curdle: to cause milk or sauce to separate into solid and liquid. Example, overcooked egg mixtures.

Daikon radish (also called mooli): a long white Japanese radish.

Dark sesame oil (also called Oriental sesame oil): dark polyunsaturated oil with a low burning point, used for seasoning. Do not replace with lighter sesame oil.

Deglaze: to dissolve congealed cooking juices or glaze on the bottom of a pan by adding a liquid, then scraping and stirring vigorously whilst bringing the liquid to the boil. Juices may be used to make gravy or to add to sauce.

Degrease: to skim grease from the surface of liquid. If possible the liquid should be chilled so the fat solidifies. If not, skim off most of the fat with a large metal spoon, then trail strips of paper towel on the surface of the liquid to remove any remaining globules.

Devilled: a dish or sauce that is highly seasoned with a hot ingredient such as mustard, Worcestershire sauce or cayenne pepper.

Dice: to cut into small cubes.

Dietary fibre: a plant-cell material that is undigested or only partially digested in the human body, but which promotes healthy digestion of other food matter.

Dissolve: mix a dry ingredient with liquid until absorbed.

Dredge: to coat with a dry ingredient, such as flour or sugar.

Drizzle: to pour in a fine thread-like stream over a surface.

Dust: to sprinkle or coat lightly with flour or icing sugar.

Dutch oven: a heavy casserole with a lid usually made from cast iron or pottery.

Emulsion: a mixture of two liquids that are not mutually soluble; for example, oil and water.

Entrée: in Europe, the 'entry' or hors d'oeuvre; in North America entree means the main course.

Fenugreek: a small, slender annual herb of the pea family. The seeds are spice. Ground fenugreek has a strong maple sweetness, spicy but bitter flavour and an aroma of burnt sugar.

Fillet: special cut of beef, lamb, pork or veal; breast of poultry and game; fish cut off the bone lengthwise.

Flake: to break into small pieces with a fork.

Flame: to ignite warmed alcohol over food.

Fold in: a gentle, careful combining of a light or delicate mixture with a heavier mixture, using a metal spoon.

Frenched: when fat and gristle is scraped and cut from meat on a bone, leaving the meaty part virtually fat free.

Fricassé: a dish in which poultry, fish or vegetables are bound together with a white or velouté sauce. In Britain and the United States, the name applies to an old-fashioned dish of chicken in a creamy sauce.

Galangal: A member of the ginger family, commonly known as Laos or Siamese ginger. It has a peppery taste with overtones of ginger.

Galette: sweet or savoury mixture shaped as a flat round.

Ganache: a filling or glaze made of full cream, chocolate, and/or other flavourings, often used to sandwich the layers of gourmet chocolate cakes

Garnish: to decorate food, usually with something edible.

Gastrique: caramelised sugar deglazed with vinegar and used in fruit-flavoured savoury sauces, in such dishes as duck with orange.

Ghee: butter, clarified by boiling. Commonly used in Indian cooking.

Glaze: a thin coating of beaten egg, syrup or aspic which is brushed over pastry, fruits or cooked meats.

Gluten: a protein in flour that is developed when dough is kneaded, making the dough elastic.

Gratin: a dish cooked in the oven or under the grill so that it develops a brown crust. Breadcrumbs or cheese may be sprinkled on top first. Shallow gratin dishes ensure a maximum area of crust.

Grease: to rub or brush lightly with oil or fat.

Infuse: to immerse herbs, spices or other flavourings in hot liquid to flavour it. Infusion takes 2–5 minutes depending on the flavouring. The liquid should be very hot but not boiling.

Jardinière: a garnish of garden vegetables, typically carrots, pickling onions, French beans and turnips.

Joint: to cut poultry, game or small animals into serving pieces by dividing at the joint.

Julienne: to cut food into match-like strips.

Lights: lungs of an animal, used in various meat preparations such as pates and faggots.

Line: to cover the inside of a container with paper, to protect or aid in removing mixture.

Knead: to work dough using heel of hand with a pressing motion, while stretching and folding the dough.

Macerate: to soak food in liquid to soften.

Marinade: a seasoned liquid, usually an oil and acid mixture, in which meats or other foods are soaked to soften and give more flavour.

Marinara: Italian 'sailor's style' cooking that does not apply to any particular combination of ingredients. Marinara tomato sauce for pasta is the most familiar.

Marinate: to let food stand in a marinade to season and tenderise.

Mask: to cover cooked food with sauce.

Melt: to heat until liquified.

Mince: to grind into very small pieces.

Mix: to combine ingredients by stirring.

Monounsaturated fats: one of three types of fats found in foods. It is believed these fats do not raise the level of cholesterol in the blood.

Naan: a slightly leavened bread used in Indian cooking.

Niçoise: a garnish of tomatoes, garlic and black olives; a salad with anchovy, tuna and French beans is typical.

Noisette: small 'nut' of lamb cut from boned loin or rack that is rolled, tied and cut in neat slices. Noisette also means flavoured with hazelnuts, or butter cooked to a nut brown colour.

Non-reactive pan: a cooking pan whose surface does not chemically react with food. Materials used include stainless steel, enamel, glass and some alloys.

Normande: a cooking style for fish, with a garnish of prawn, mussels and mushrooms in a white-wine cream sauce; for poultry and meat, a sauce with cream, calvados and apple.

Olive oil: various grades of oil extracted from olives. Extra virgin olive oil has a full, fruity flavour and the lowest acidity. Virgin olive oil is slightly higher in acidity and lighter in flavour. Pure olive oil is a processed blend of olive oils and has the highest acidity and lightest taste.

Panade: a mixture for binding stuffings and dumplings, notably quenelles (fish rissoles), often of choux pastry or simply breadcrumbs. A panade may also be made of frangipane, puréed potatoes or rice.

Papillote: to cook food in oiled or buttered greasepoof paper or aluminum foil. Also a decorative frill to cover bone ends of chops and poultry drumsticks.

Parboil: to boil or simmer until part cooked (i.e. cooked further than when blanching).

Pare: to cut away outside covering.

Pâté: a paste of meat or seafood used as a spread for toast or crackers.

Paupiette: a thin slice of meat, poultry or fish spread with a savoury stuffing and rolled. In the United States this is also called 'bird' and in Britain an 'olive'.

Peel: to strip away outside covering.

Plump: to soak in liquid or moisten thoroughly until full and round.

Poach: to simmer gently in enough hot liquid to cover, using care to retain shape of food.

Polyunsaturated fat: one of the three types of fats found in food. These exist in large quantities in such vegetable oils as safflower, sunflower, corn and soya bean. These fats lower the level of cholesterol in the blood.

Purée: a smooth paste, usually of vegetables or fruits, made by putting foods through a sieve, food mill or liquefying in a blender or food processor.

Ragout: traditionally a well-seasoned, rich stew containing meat, vegetables and wine. Nowadays, a term applied to any stewed mixture.

Ramekins: small oval or round individual baking dishes.

Reconstitute: to put moisture back into dehydrated foods by soaking in liquid.

Reduce: to cook over a very high heat, uncovered, until the liquid is reduced by evaporation.

Refresh: to cool hot food quickly, either under running water or by plunging it into iced water, to stop it cooking. Particularly for vegetables and occasionally for shellfish.

Rice vinegar: mild, fragrant vinegar that is less sweet than cider vinegar and not as harsh as distilled malt vinegar. Japanese rice vinegar is milder than the Chinese variety.

Roulade: a piece of meat, usually pork or veal, that is spread with stuffing, rolled and often braised or poached. A roulade may also be a sweet or savoury mixture that is baked in a Swiss-roll tin or paper case, filled with a contrasting filling, and rolled.

Roux: A binding for sauces, made with flour and butter or another fatty substance, to which a hot liquid is added. A roux-based sauce may be white, blond or brown, depending on how the butter has been cooked.

Rubbing-in: a method of incorporating fat into flour, by use of fingertips only. Also incorporates air into mixture.

Safflower oil: the vegetable oil that contains the highest proportion of polyunsaturated fats.

Salsa: a juice derived from the main ingredient being cooked, or a sauce added to a dish to enhance its flavour. In Italy the term is often used for pasta sauces; in Mexico the name usually applies to uncooked sauces served as an accompaniment, especially to corn chips.

Saturated fats: one of the three types of fats found in foods. These exist in large quantities in animal products, coconut and palm oils; they raise the level of cholesterol in the blood. As high cholesterol levels may cause heart disease, saturated-fat consumption is recommended to be less than 15 percent of calories provided by the daily diet.

Sauté: to cook or brown in small amount of hot fat.

Scald: to bring just to boiling point, usually for milk. Also to rinse with boiling water.

School prawns: delicious eaten just on their own. Smaller prawn than bay, tiger or king. They have a mild flavour, low oiliness and high moisture content, they make excellent cocktails.

Score: to mark food with cuts, notches or lines to prevent curling or to make food more attractive.

Sear: to brown surface quickly over high heat in hot dish.

Seasoned flour: flour with salt and pepper added.

Sift: to shake a dry, powdered substance through a sieve or sifter to remove any lumps and give lightness.

Simmer: to cook food gently in liquid that bubbles steadily just below boiling point so that the food cooks in even heat without breaking up.

Singe: to quickly flame poultry to remove all traces of feathers after plucking.

Skim: to remove a surface layer (often of impurities and scum) from a liquid with a metal spoon or small ladle.

Slivered: sliced in long, thin pieces, usually refers to nuts, especially almonds.

Souse: to cover food, particularly fish, in wine vinegar and spices and cook slowly; the food is cooled in the same liquid. Sousing gives food a pickled flavour.

Steep: to soak in warm or cold liquid in order to soften food and draw out strong flavours or impurities.

Stir-fry: to cook thin slices of meat and vegetable over a high heat in a small amount of oil, stirring constantly to even cooking in a short time. Traditionally cooked in a wok; however, a heavy-based frying pan may be used.

Stock: the liquid that results from cooking meat, bones and/or vegetables in water to make a base for soups and other recipes. You can substitute stock cubes for fresh bouillon, but those on a reduced sodium diet will need to take note of the salt content on the packet.

Stud: to adorn with; for example, baked ham studded with whole cloves.

Sugo: an Italian sauce made from the liquid or juice extracted from fruit or meat during cooking.

Sweat: to cook sliced or chopped food, usually vegetables, in a little fat and no liquid over very low heat. Foil is pressed on top so that the food steams in its own juices, usually before being added to other dishes.

Thicken: to make a liquid thicker by mixing together arrowroot, cornflour or flour with an equal amount of cold water and pouring it into hot liquid, cooking and stirring until thickened.

Timbale: a creamy mixture of vegetables or meat baked in a mould. French for 'kettledrum'; also denotes a drum-shaped baking dish.

Toss: to gently mix ingredients with two forks or fork and spoon.

Total fat: the individual daily intake of all three fats previously described in this glossary. Nutritionists recommend that fats provide no more than 35 percent of the energy in the diet.

Vine leaves: tender, lightly flavoured leaves of the grapevine, used in ethnic cuisine as wrappers for savoury mixtures. As the leaves are usually packed in brine, they should be well rinsed before use.

Whip: to beat rapidly, incorporate air and produce expansion.

Zest: thin outer layer of citrus fruits containing the aromatic citrus oil. It is usually thinly pared with a vegetable peeler, or grated with a zester or grater to separate it from the bitter white pith underneath.

Weights and Measures

Cooking is not an exact science. You do not require finely calibrated scales, pipettes and scientific equipment to cook, yet the variety of measures in countries have confused many a good cook.

Although different in the recipes weights are given for ingredients such as meats, fish, poultry and some vegetables, in normal cooking a few ounces or grams one way or another will not affect the success of your dish.

Although recipes have been tested using the Australian Standard 250mL cup, 20mL tablespoon (tbsp) and 5mL teaspoon (tsp), they will work just as well with the US and Canadian 8fl oz cup, or the UK 300mL cup. We have used graduated cup measures in preference to tablespoon measures so that proportions are always the same. Where tablespoon measures have been given, they are not crucial measures, so using the smaller tablespoon of the US or UK will not affect the recipe's success. At least all three countries agree on the teaspoon size.

For breads, cakes and pastries, the only area which might cause concern is where eggs are used, as proportions will then vary. If working with a 250mL or 300mL cup, use large eggs (65g/2¼oz), adding a little more liquid to the recipe for 300mL cup measures if it seems necessary. Use medium-sized eggs (55g/2oz) with an 8fl oz cup measure. A graduated set of measuring cups and spoons is recommended for measuring dry ingredients. Remember to level the ingredients in the measure to ensure an accurate quantity.

English Measures

English measurements are all similar to Australian with two exceptions: the English cup measures 300mL/10½ fl oz, whereas the American and Australian cup measures 250mL/8¾fl oz. The English tablespoon (the Australian dessertspoon) measures 14.8mL / ½ fl oz against Australian tablespoon of 20mL/¾fl oz. The Imperial measurement is 20fl oz to the pint, 40fl oz a quart and 160fl oz one gallon.

American Measures

The American reputed pint is 16fl oz, a quart is equal to 32fl oz and the American gallon equals 128fl oz. The American tablespoon is equal to 14.8mL/½ fl oz, while the teaspoon is 5mL/⅙ fl oz. The cup measure is 250 mL/8¾ fl oz.

Dry Measures

All the measures are level, so when you have filled a cup or spoon, level it off with the edge of a knife. The scale below is the 'cook's equivalent'; it is not an exact conversion of metric to imperial measurement. To calculate the exact metric equivalent yourself, multiply ounces by 28.349523 to obtain grams, or divide grams by 28.349523 to obtain ounces.

Metric grams (g), kilograms (kg)	**Imperial** ounces (oz), pound (lb)
15g	½oz
20g	⅓oz
30g	1oz
55g	2oz
85g	3oz
115g	4oz/¼lb
125g	4½oz
140/145g	5oz
170g	6oz
200g	7oz
225g	8oz/½lb
315g	11oz
340g	12oz/¾lb
370g	13oz
400g	14oz
425g	15oz
455g	16oz/1lb
1,000g/1 kg	35.3oz/2.2lb
1.5kg	3.33lb

Oven Temperatures

The Celsius temperatures given here are not exact; they have been rounded off and are given as a guide only. Follow the manufacturer's oven guide, relating it to the temperature description given in the recipe. Remember gas ovens are hottest at the top, electric ovens at the bottom and convection-fan forced ovens are usually even throughout. We have included Regulo numbers for gas cookers which may assist. To convert °C to °F multiply °C by 9 and divide by 5 then add 32.

	C°	F°	Gas mark
Very slow	120	250	1
Slow	150	300	2
Moderately slow	160	325	3
Moderate	180	350	4
Moderately hot	190–200	370–400	5–6
Hot	210–220	410–440	6–7
Very hot	230	450	8
Super hot	250–290	475–500	9–10

Cup Measurements

One Australian cup (250mL) is equal to the following weights.

	Metric	Imperial
Almonds, flaked	85g	3oz
Almonds, kernel	155g	5½oz
Almonds, slivered, ground	125g	4½oz
Apples, dried, chopped	125g	4½oz
Apricots, dried, chopped	190g	6¾oz
Breadcrumbs, packet	125g	4½oz
Breadcrumbs, soft	55g	2oz
Cheese, grated	115g	4oz
Chocbits	155½g	5oz
Coconut, desiccated	90g	3oz
Cornflakes	30g	1oz
Currants	155½g	5oz
Flour	115g	4oz
Fruit, dried (mixed, sultanas etc)	170g	6 oz
Ginger, crystallised, glace	250g	8oz
Honey, treacle, golden syrup	315g	11oz
Mixed peel	225g	8oz
Nuts, chopped	115g	4oz
Prunes, chopped	225g	8oz
Rice, cooked	155g	5½oz
Rice, uncooked	225g	8oz
Rolled oats	90g	3oz
Sesame seeds	115g	4oz
Shortening (butter, margarine)	225g	8oz
Sugar, brown	155g	5½oz
Sugar, granulated or caster	225g	8oz
Sugar, sifted icing	155g	5½oz
Wheatgerm	60g	2oz

Length

Some of us have trouble converting imperial length to metric. In this scale, measures have been rounded off to the easiest figures. To convert inches to centimetres exactly, multiply inches by 2.54. One inch equals 25.4 millimetres and 1 millimetre equals 0.03937 inches.

Cake Dish Sizes

Metric	15cm	18cm	20cm	23cm
Imperial	6in	7in	8in	9in

Loaf Dish Sizes

Metric	23 x 12cm	25 x 8cm	28 x 18cm
Imperial	9 x 5in	10 x 3in	11 x 7in

Liquid Measures

Metric millilitres (mL)	Imperial fluid ounce (fl oz)	Cup and Spoon
5mL	⅙fl oz	1 teaspoon
20mL	⅔fl oz	1 tablespoon
30mL	1fl oz	1 tbsp + 2 tsp
55mL	2fl oz	
63mL	2¼fl oz	¼ cup
85mL	3fl oz	
115mL	4fl oz	
125mL	4½fl oz	½ cup
150mL	5¼fl oz	
188mL	6⅔fl oz	¾ cup
225mL	8fl oz	
250mL	8¾fl oz	1 cup
300mL	10½fl oz	
370mL	13fl oz	
400mL	14fl oz	
438mL	15½fl oz	1¾ cups
455mL	16fl oz	
500mL	17½fl oz	2 cups
570mL	20fl oz	
1 litre	35.3fl oz	4 cups

Length Measures

Metric millimetres (mm), centimetres (cm)	Imperial inches (in), feet (ft)
5mm, 0.5cm	¼in
10mm, 1.0cm	½in
20mm, 2.0cm	¾in
2.5cm	1in
5cm	2in
7½cm	3in
10cm	4in
12½cm	5in
15cm	6in
18cm	7in
20cm	8in
23cm	9in
25cm	10in
28cm	11in
30cm	12in, 1 foot

Index